Attitudes, Chaos and the Connectionist Mind

JB

Attitudes, Chaos and the Connectionist Mind

J. Richard Eiser

BLACKWELL
Oxford UK & Cambridge USA

First published 1994

Blackwell Publishers
108 Cowley Road
Oxford   OX4 1JF
UK

238 Main Street
Cambridge, Massachusetts 02142
USA

British Library Cataloguing in Publication Data

A CIP catalogue record for this book is available from
the British Library.

Library of Congress Cataloging-in-Publication Data

Eiser, J. Richard.
Attitudes, chaos, and the connectionist mind / J. Richard Eiser.
p.   cm.
Includes bibliographical references and indexes.
ISBN 0–631–19129–1 (alk. paper). — ISBN 0–631–19131–3 (pbk. :
alk. paper)
1. Attitude (Psychology)   2. Attitude change.   3. Philosophy of
mind.   4. Psychology and philosophy.   I. Title.
BF327.E364   1994
153—dc20   93–23963
                                                  CIP

Typeset in 10 on 12 pt Melior
by Graphicraft Typesetters Ltd, Hong Kong
Printed in Great Britain by
Hartnolls Ltd, Bodmin, Cornwall

This book is printed on acid-free paper

For Chris, David and Ben

Contents

List of Figures

Preface

Thoughts have no meaning in isolation. It is only by our relating different thoughts to one another that we come to understand the world and our own place within it. In just the same way, no intellectual (or practical) activity can survive in good health for very long if it isolates itself from every other. This is despite the feelings of security that such isolation can provide. Isolation permits specialization and specialization can be efficient. You can get on with your work without having to justify everything from first principles, something which is always time-consuming and usually difficult. But such efficiency carries its dangers, the most common of which is a loss, from time to time, of a sense of purpose and direction, without which it is difficult to explain how one has come to be looking at a particular set of problems or indeed what advantage a solution to such problems might bring. At such times, the way forward is to take a step back, to look around, to experiment with different perspectives, and to try to see the wood for the trees.

My own specialism is that of social psychology, and many of the issues I shall be considering stem from, or at least relate to, social psychological research. This, however, is not a 'specialist' book, nor even, in the conventional sense, a social psychological one. Social psychology, after all, is just one way of studying human social behaviour and the feelings we have about one another. Its distinctiveness lies in the approaches it adopts to the study of such topics, not in the topics themselves. I hope to communicate something of the flavour of these approaches, but certainly do not intend to remain consistently within them. Instead, I plan to embark on a premeditated act of trespass, crossing over some conventional boundaries between different disciplines and, as importantly, between what counts as academic research on the one hand and everyday experience on the other. If I pick some of the fruit from neighbouring fields, it will be more from admiration than from greed and I hope excusable by a general welcome to anyone to pay a similar visit in return. I will be bringing some provisions with me, so that fair exchange need be no robbery. If sometimes I seem to tarry on my way, it will be because the surroundings are so congenial that anyone can feel at home.

I have a mixture of motives for embarking on this journey. At a personal level, nostalgia is a large part of the story. My first degree was jointly in psychology and philosophy, but when I was a student, the encouragement to bring these two forms of thought together was little more than tepid. Afterwards I moved into social psychology for my postgraduate work and subsequent career, with little time to pick up again the philosophical questions which had engrossed me for too short a time. For myself, yet I hope not merely from self-indulgence, I feel a need to join these intellectual halves together again.

A less personal set of motives stems from mild misgivings about the state of my own (official) discipline as currently and narrowly conceived. I need not dwell on these, but they boil down to the sense that social psychology, for all its practical success at predicting behaviour under defined conditions, undersells itself in terms of its potential relevance to a broader understanding of the essential quality of human experience. For the most part, social psychologists are a fairly pragmatic crowd, more concerned with finding research techniques that seem to work than with asking how it is that these, *or indeed any*, techniques can provide objective evidence about people's inner thoughts and feelings. Yet it is a remarkable fact that we *can* make objective statements about thoughts and feelings, and this fact – indeed, this achievement – should not be passed over without reflection.

Far more important, though, is a sense that (some of) the traditional relationships between different disciplines may be about to undergo a radical change, and that the focus of this change may be a convergence, from fields as diverse as physics, philosophy and computer science, on problems that are the proper, though not proprietary, concern of psychology. This convergence will be my central theme. I see in philosophy a new willingness to unite conceptual analysis with what we can learn from science about the actual world and universe which we inhabit. I see in the physical sciences a new willingness to consider the implications of fundamental theories for an understanding of the workings of the human mind. I see computer science becoming less concerned with

computing as such, and more with the simulation of cognitive processes, so that what is known about the brain is used as a model for
what computers might become. There are signs of a matching open-
ness within my own discipline, but these are still rather few and far
between. I hope this book will help to open a few doors; I feel sure
that most will need only a little push.

Writing this book has consumed much of my attention over the
past two to three years, though with many more interruptions than
those of my own choosing. I therefore owe a special debt of grati-
tude to the Faculty of Social Sciences, Carleton University, Ottawa,
where I was fortunate to spend two terms' sabbatical in 1991, mostly
simply reading and writing, safe in the realization that it was generally either too cold or too hot outside to contemplate doing anything else for very long. This has also been a solitary business, like
all writing, and since it has taken me at times far from my home
base, I have more than ever needed advice and encouragement from
those with whom I have discussed my half-formed ideas along the
way. Within this category I should mention particularly Noel
Sharkey, Bibb Latané, Andrzej Nowak, Robin Vallacher, Peter Killeen
and Michael Lockwood. If I fail to reach my journey's end, blame
them for not telling me to turn back sooner! I shall not mention the
others who, no doubt with the best intentions, clearly regard the
expedition as completely crazy. If events prove them right and I fall
over the world's edge, they will doubtless make themselves known
soon enough.

None the less, I am well aware that, by my own (perhaps cau-
tious) standards, this is a risky undertaking. Quite apart from committing the cardinal sin of describing the work of other disciplines,
I have presented my own as simpler than it really is. The academic
convention is to suffix every generalization or conclusion with multiple citations of anyone who has said something similar before,
perhaps so as to convey the message that nothing new or subversive
could really be afoot. I have deliberately avoided this style. Instead,
I have confined my references to a limited number of key authors
– those I specifically wish to discuss and those whose own writings
have helped me. I have reproduced some illustrations from other
publications, and am grateful to the various publishers for the relevant copyright permission. Likewise, I acknowledge with special
thanks the permission granted by Academic Press Inc. for allowing
me to adapt and reuse, mainly in chapters 8 and 9, some material
from a chapter entitled 'Toward a dynamic conception of attitude
consistency and change' contributed by myself to *Dynamical Systems*

in Social Psychology, edited by R. R. Vallacher and A. Nowak, published in 1993. Otherwise, I have included only a small selection of more conventional citations of *examples* of empirical work consistent with the broader statements I am making. When describing previous empirical work, moreover, I have contented myself with broader statements – ones, for sure, which I believe to be fair and accurate in general, but not ones which I regard as admitting no exceptions. Take these statements, please, only as I offer them, as broad guides to what you may find on closer inspection. Although there are empirical findings which support the generalizations I shall draw, this is not a textbook. If you want detailed descriptions of these findings, you will need to look elsewhere.

As I leave the territorial waters of social psychology, I am acutely conscious of the precariousness of my own interpretations. I am sure there must be many crucial details I have overlooked and others I have misunderstood, but I hope I have not made too many errors that seriously undercut my argument. Had I confined myself, in many chapters, to remarks I could make with absolute certainty, I would have had little to say. So of course much of my argument is speculative. Yet I am not offering it as an ornament. I believe the interconnections I shall attempt to draw are really there. If I am right, my conclusions may hint at the beginnings of a paradigm, within which others may see the opportunities for new research.

Interconnections – between thoughts and between modes of thought – are a persistent theme of this book. Nature weaves the most complex patterns from the simplest elements, and so does the human mind. Thoughts, self-awareness, personal identity, attitudes – these all are *patterns* which emerge from our ability to associate mental events with one another. Yet we can find such patterns in our own experience only because *what* we experience is also patterned. Cognitive structures reflect natural structures. Between the theories which account for these different structures, therefore, we may find a surprising similarity. I hope that this book contains a few surprises, but I would be even more gratified to feel that I had taken familiar aspects of both everyday and academic knowledge and convinced you of some of the links between them. Theories are not just summaries of knowledge, but the relating of different kinds of knowledge to one another. To build new theories, we need to find new connections. So let's start the search.

J. Richard Eiser
Exeter

1

A Brief History of Attitude Research

The concept of attitude

Much of this book will be concerned with attitudes – with what they are, how they are formed, how they change and how they relate to behaviour. This does not cover, by any means, the whole field of social psychology, but it offers a representative, and proportionately far from negligible, sample of what social psychological theory and research is generally about. Indeed, the concept of attitude was once described (by Allport, 1935) as 'probably the most distinctive and indispensable' in social psychology. Indispensable it certainly is. Even those who feel that the exclusive concerns of social psychologists should be with collective as opposed to individual behaviour cannot avoid using some version of the concept entirely, so as to account for the relationships existing between members of groups and the ways different groups relate to one another. Its distinctiveness is harder to argue for. In one sense, there is nothing else quite like it. On the other hand, there can seem to be so many different uses to which the concept is put that one might well want to argue that it is little more than an umbrella term for a variety of processes that ought strictly to be distinguished.

Even so, the term 'attitude' shows little prospect of disappearing either from more technical or more everyday vocabularies. The reason for this is very simple. Broadly speaking, we all feel we know what it is to have an attitude towards something or somebody. We may not be able to say how we come to have such a feeling, or whether this feeling has much influence on our behaviour. We may often find it difficult to put such a feeling into words, but we are none the less conscious of (or in?) having such a feeling, and if we did not call it an attitude, we would have to call it by another name that meant the same thing.

At this level, there is nothing mysterious about the concept of attitude, and I, for my part, am not proposing any abandonment of the common-sense use of the term. The mysteries appear (and they appear quite quickly) at a deeper level, once we start probing below the surface to see what we need to assume in order for such common-sense usage to be intelligible. It is common sense (and true) that we acquire attitudes through learning and interaction with our environment: but how does such learning coalesce to produce the feeling we call an attitude? It is common sense (and true) that we can discuss our attitudes with other people: but how can we understand the private events of other minds? It is common sense (and true) that our attitudes are *about* things that happen in the real world: but how can things that happen 'out there' produce (and be represented in) feelings 'in here'? It is common sense (and true) that our attitudes have a great deal to do with how we choose to behave: but how exactly should this relationship be regarded? It is common sense (and true) that we need a brain in order to have attitudes: but what is it about the brain that allows us to have *our* kinds of attitudes (or any attitudes at all)? More controversially, perhaps, it is common sense that a computer cannot have an attitude. But, if so, what does this tell us about the essence of consciousness and the minds of living creatures? And if common sense is correct in this respect, does this merely reflect our present relative lack of technical sophistication? If we can design artificial systems (as we already can) which can categorize, select, generalize and *learn*, what more is needed for them to have attitudes too?

These and other such questions are for later chapters. For the moment, let me give a brief outline of how attitude research has developed within social psychology, so that particular issues can be looked at from a more general perspective.

Attitudes can be measured

Social psychologists have often adopted methods and conceptual frameworks that have proved successful, or have simply been fashionable, in other areas of psychology. By the end of the nineteenth century, there had already been some quite remarkable achievements in the experimental psychology of perception (especially in

Germany). Of these, the most influential for attitude research were those in the specialty known as *psychophysics*. The focus of this work was on the measurement of different kinds of sensation and on the discovery of quantitative laws relating differences in the perceived intensity or magnitude of a set of stimuli (how heavy, bright or loud they appeared) to differences in their objective, physical attributes (weight in grams, etc.). The most famous of these psychophysical laws, the 'Weber-Fechner law', predicts that, in order to produce an increase in the apparent intensity of one stimulus over another by a constant amount, one needs to increase the *physical* magnitude between successive stimuli by ever *larger* intervals as one goes higher up the scale.

This led to a long debate over the precise mathematical form of the relationship (e.g. Stevens, 1975), but this need not concern us here. More important is the fact that quantitative calculations are possible at all when applied to something supposedly as 'subjective' as perceptual sensation. Our feelings about physical things can be measured, and very precise predictions can be made about such measurements. In crossing over from the 'external' world of things to the 'internal' world of feelings we have *not* passed through some door beyond which empirical methods and the rules of mathematics have no sway. Perhaps it is misleading even to think of there being any door at all, but this is a question to which we must return later. For the moment, the significance of work on psychophysics is that it invites the question: if we can do all this with perceptual sensations, can we not do it with attitudes as well? Someone who declared emphatically that we can was Thurstone (1928). His work, based on the methods and theories of the psychophysicists, provided the foundation for modern techniques of attitude measurement:

> It will be conceded at the outset that an attitude is a complex affair which cannot be wholly described by any single numerical index. For the problem of measurement this statement is analogous to the observation that an ordinary table is a complex affair which cannot be wholly described by any single numerical index. Nevertheless, we do not hesitate to say that we measure the table. The context usually implies what it is about the table that we propose to measure. We say without hesitation that we measure a man when we take some anthropometric measurements of him. The context may well imply without explicit declaration what aspect of the man we are measuring, his cephalic index, his height or weight or what not. Just in the same sense we shall say here that we are measuring attitudes. We shall state or imply by the context the aspect of people's attitudes

that we are measuring. The point is that it is just as legitimate to say that we are measuring attitudes as it is to say that we are measuring tables or men (Thurstone, 1928, p. 530).

Thus, attitudes may be complex, but they are not necessarily more complex, or less measurable by virtue of their complexity, than many other *physical* things. Measurement of anything, however, requires a selection of contexts and perspectives. Measures are informative in so far as they provide answers to *particular* questions. The principal question which Thurstone himself addressed was that of how *favourable or unfavourable* an individual or group of people could be said to be towards a given issue. He was not especially concerned with a person's reasons for holding a given position, but simply with locating that position on an 'attitude continuum' ranging from extreme unfavourability (anti) to extreme favourability (pro). The assumption of continuity here is very important. It leads us to thinking in terms of *degrees* of favourability, rather than looking for dividing points between different 'sides'.

With the techniques that Thurstone and others developed (the details of which need not detain us here), we can derive (interval) scores to specify *quantitatively* the extent to which, say, a sample of fundamentalist Christians are more opposed to abortion than a sample of atheists, or the amount by which an audience's approval for a politician is increased or decreased following a televised speech. Attitude favourability is regarded as something you can have more or less of, much like money in the bank, or feelings of hunger before a meal. So long as we are prepared to suspend our interest in the complexity of people's underlying motives or whatever – so long, that is, that we are happy to work with this concept of a single continuum of opposition/support or disapproval/approval for the one issue – we can end up with a definition of a person's attitude as a single numerical score. This is not just simple. It is very, very useful. But (as Thurstone's own words should warn us) there may be contexts in which it hides more difficult but deeper truths.

Attitudes have meaning

Not all attitude measurement restricts itself to Thurstone's single continuum of opposition/support. Other techniques have been developed to try and take more account of the 'complex affair' which Thurstone acknowledged people's attitudes to be. These techniques attempt to get at the meaning implied in any statement of attitude, over and above the bare bones of a good or bad evaluation. These techniques are particularly useful when you want to measure people's attitudes towards a variety of issues at the same time. Often, you suspect that some of these issues will be regarded as more or less the same as one other, while others will be regarded as quite distinct. Statistical software packages now offer a choice of techniques for summarizing the relationships between many variables at the same time. Such techniques are termed 'multidimensional' in that they involve measurements on many different scales or dimensions.

A good starting-point for an understanding of simpler multidimensional approaches – good, that is, because the discussion is primarily psychological rather than statistical – is *The Measurement of Meaning* by Osgood, Suci and Tannenbaum (1957). In this monograph, Osgood *et al.* present the background to what was then a novel measurement technique, the *semantic differential*. The essence of this technique is very simple: the researcher presents a list of adjective-pairs and the subject has to say (conventionally in terms of seven categories from –3 to +3) which adjective in each pair is the more applicable (and how definitely so) to each of the concepts presented for judgement. So one might have a list of adjective-pairs such as beautiful–ugly, happy–sad, strong–weak, successful–unsuccessful, hard–soft, kind–cruel, clean–dirty and a list of (possibly quite heterogeneous) concepts such as Margaret Thatcher, coal-fired power stations, cigarette smoking, nuclear missiles. Let us leave aside the question of why anyone would want to ask for exactly these particular ratings rather than any others, since, within the Osgood *et al.* framework, it doesn't matter. What matters is the procedure of asking for multiple descriptive ratings of multiple objects, something which is now quite familiar in many different kinds of questionnaire research.

What can we get out of these kinds of ratings? Well, a first thing we can look for is whether different concepts (objects) are rated similarly to each other on particular scales. We might find, for instance, that both coal-fired power stations and cigarette smoking are rated by most of our subjects as 'dirty', whereas both Margaret Thatcher and nuclear missiles are rated as 'strong'. We might find many individual differences: by some Margaret Thatcher might be seen as 'beautiful', 'strong' and 'successful', by others as 'hard' and 'cruel'. The real pay-off, however, comes from looking at such judged differences between objects in combination with relationships between different adjectives. If something is 'sad' is it more or less likely to be 'soft'? If something is 'successful', is it more or less likely to be 'strong'? Osgood *et al.* submitted their data to the statistical technique known as *factor analysis*. This technique infers the presence of a limited number of common, underlying dimensions, with which particular adjective rating-scales correlate to greater or lesser extents. (Factor analysis, for instance, is used when constructing measures of ability or intelligence to identify particular underlying skills, e.g. verbal reasoning, which can be assessed by a variety of different tests or tasks.)

The surprising assertion made by Osgood *et al.* was that, despite the many thousands of adjectives to be found in any dictionary, factor analysis could identify a very limited number of factors, or underlying dimensions, which could account for a great deal of the variability in the way in which any particular adjectives were used. What is more, this set of identified dimensions proved to be remarkably stable across different groups of subjects and across different national and linguistic groups. To any but the most dubious sceptic, the data could be taken to imply that the connotative meaning of words in any language could be represented in terms of a highly stable – if not universal – 'semantic space'. Of the dimensions defining this space, the three most important are *evaluation* (e.g. good–bad) *potency* (e.g. strong–weak) and *activity* (e.g. active–passive). Osgood *et al.* equated their dimension of evaluation with the favourability dimension of conventional attitude measurement, considering that potency, activity and other minor dimensions captured other aspects of 'meaning'.

Any given adjective may 'load on' (be correlated with) one or more of these dimensions to a greater or lesser extent. The loadings of specific adjectives may vary somewhat between samples and contexts. For example, a word like 'strong', though typically high in 'potency', may sometimes also be seen as evaluatively positive. Connotations of particular words can also change over time. (A possible example is 'aggressive', which seems (intuitively) to have shifted from being a close synonym of 'hostile' to something much closer to 'energetic'. So now political commentators can coin abominations such as 'an agressive peace offensive'.) There can also be some difference in the relative importance of the different dimensions. But the general picture of a 'semantic space' structured in terms of dimensions of evaluation, potency and activity, is one which recurs recognizably in a wide variety of situations.

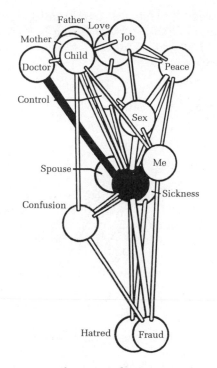

Figure 1.1 Semantic space for Eve White
Source: C. E. Osgood *et al.* (1957) *The Measurement of Meaning*, University of Illinois Press

Despite this emphasis on generality, the semantic differential can be extremely sensitive to differences between, and even within, individuals. A celebrated study by Osgood and Luria (1954) examined rating data obtained from a woman with a triple personality. This woman was tested on two occasions (earlier and later in therapy) within each of her three 'personalities' (referred to as 'Eve White', 'Eve Black' and 'Jane'). The data provided consisted of ratings of fifteen concepts (e.g. love, child, doctor, me) in terms of ten semantic differential scales (e.g. valuable–worthless, clean–dirty). Osgood and Luria were not the therapists and they analysed the data 'blind' without access to the woman's history. The data were factor-analysed separately for each 'personality' and comparable three-dimensional structures were obtained (each with a strong evaluative factor). What is striking, however, is the manner in which different concepts took up different locations in the three-dimensional space, depending on the woman's current state of mind. Figures 1.1 to 1.3

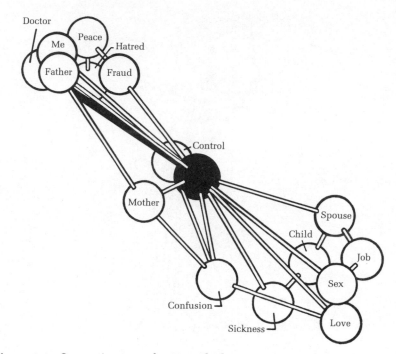

Figure 1.2 Semantic space for Eve Black
Source: C. E. Osgood *et al.* (1957) *The Measurement of Meaning*, University of Illinois Press

illustrate this. These 'maps' are drawn with the vertical axis representing evaluation (good is up); the axis at right-angles to the page represents potency (strong is to the back) and the horizontal axis represents activity (active is to the left). Concepts further from the origin – i.e. further out – are said to be more 'meaningful' in that their position is more definite or extreme.

As regards Eve White (figure 1.1), Osgood and Luria highlight the following: 'ME (the self-concept) is considered a little bad, a little passive, and definitely weak. Substantiating evidence is the weakness of her child and the essential meaninglessness to her of her spouse and sex.' This compares with the description in the original case history (Thigpen and Cleckley, 1954): 'Eve White . . . was an ordinary case with commonplace symptoms and a relatively complex but familiar constellation of marital conflicts and personal frustration'.

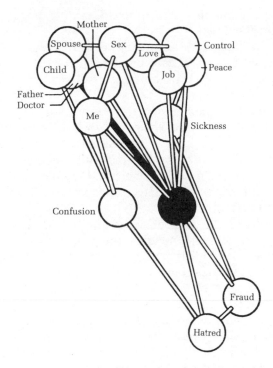

Figure 1.3   Semantic space for Jane (after therapy)
Source: C. E. Osgood *et al.* (1957) *The Measurement of Meaning*, University of Illinois
Press

Moving to Eve Black (figure 1.2) we find, according to Osgood and Luria:

> ... a violent kind of adjustment in which she perceives herself as
> literally perfect, but, to accomplish this break, her way of perceiving
> 'the world' becomes completely disoriented from the norm ... she
> also has to accept hatred and fraud as positive values, since (we
> assume) she has strong hatred, and is socially fraudulent. What are
> positive values for most people – child, spouse, job, love, and sex –
> are completely rejected as bad and passive, and all of these except
> child are also weak.

Thigpen and Cleckley similarly describe Eve Black as: 'free from the
habitual signs of care, seriousness, and underlying distress, so long
familiar in her predecessor [Eve White] ... She herself freely tells

of episodes when she emerged [in childhood] to engage in acts of mischief or disobedience.'

Finally, Jane (figure 1.3), according to Osgood and Luria, is the 'healthiest' in that: '. . . she accepts the usual evaluations of concepts by her society yet still maintains a satisfactory evaluation of herself . . . The self-concept, me, while still not strong (but not weak, either) is nearer the good and active directions of the semantic space. Her attitude toward her husband, spouse, is for the first time meaningful (unlike Eve White) and tending toward the good, strong, active directions.' Likewise, for Thigpen and Cleckley: 'It is easy to sense in her (Jane) a capacity for accomplishment and fulfillment . . . In her are indications of initiative and powerful resources never shown by the other [Eve White].'

The extraordinary nature of this case should not distract us from a more general message. We judge the world in different ways. Events and objects carry different meanings for us, depending on our judgements. Your judgements will not be altogether the same as mine, and for most of us, our judgements will vary somewhat from one situation to another. What is remarkable about this case is the abruptness and extremity of such variation within a single individual. What is important about the data is that such variation in judgement, that is, in attitude, goes together meaningfully with differences in emotional state and social behaviour.

Attitudes can be changed

If we can measure something, we can see if it changes. In the research just described, dramatic shifts in the personality of a single individual were reflected in changes in how she evaluated and decribed a limited set of concepts. What we say about things can reflect how we feel and behave more generally. External influences can be brought to bear on our thoughts and feelings, and on the judgements which we make. There are many different kinds of influence, including therapy (in the above example) and many forms of mass communication, advertising and persuasive information. Once we can measure attitudes, we can also perform experiments to test if they change more in response to some influences than others. We can test theories about the direction and extent of change we may predict under certain conditions. The development of attitude measurement techniques thus offered opportunities for experimental research on attitude change. These opportunities were exploited with special enthusiasm during the fifties and early sixties, most influentially in America with a large research programme at Yale University (e.g. Hovland, Janis and Kelley, 1953).

There are a number of reasons for needing to see the Yale studies in their academic and historical context. Academically, American psychology in the first half of the twentieth century was a success story for applications of experimental methods to the study of behaviour. To a very large extent, this work had used non-human animals as subjects. *Behaviourism*, associated particularly with the names of Watson and then Skinner, was the most extreme expression of this approach in asserting the irrelevance of mental states and events for an understanding of behaviour. I shall have more to say about behaviourism later (in chapter 4). Not all behavioural experimentation, however, was or is behaviour*ist*. By behaviour*al*, I mean simply concerned with the prediction of observable behavioural responses under different controlled and/or observable conditions. It is an open question (though one in which behaviourists profess no sympathetic interest) what kinds of mental events accompany such observable responses.

The Yale researchers were not behaviourists, but they were happy to think of attitudes as *responses* (measurable through verbal and possibly other forms of behaviour) which could be 'shaped' (i.e. modified) by particular kinds of stimulus presentations, associations and reinforcements (i.e. rewards and punishments). If asked, they would have willingly asserted that attitudes were learned, but, like many learning researchers, they tended to fight shy of looking for the effects on learning of factors not easily submitted to experimental control (including some that might lead us to acquire a particular kind of attitude in the first place). Instead, they applied the techniques of behavioural analysis in order to specify classes of factors which, if compared or manipulated under controlled experimental conditions, can lead people to *change* their attitude on an issue, in a particular direction and to a greater or lesser extent.

But why this concern with change rather than acquisition? At least part of the reason is to be found in an historical context in which powers of 'mass persuasion' were greatly feared and poorly understood. It was only recently that Hitler had 'hypnotized' his public into unquestioning obedience, with the Nazi 'propaganda machine' overthrowing Germany's fragile democracry and leading the world to war. It was even more recently that American prisoners of war, captured by North Koreans, had been 're-educated' or, as the new word expressed it, 'brainwashed' with communist ideology. Could these veterans recover their previous personalities when they returned home, or would they remain the unwitting servants of their new masters? Less paranoiacally, what was to be made of the influence of films, the mass media and television? Quite what protection did any of us have against the 'hidden persuaders' of commercial advertising?

I am not suggesting that the Yale researchers themselves were constrained in their investigations by any direct political pressure. On the contrary, their experiments are models of propriety in the 'fundamental research' tradition. But social psychological questions, even so-called 'fundamental' ones, do not arise from thin air. By no means all, but certainly some, of the wider contemporary concerns could have led to a view of persuasion as somewhat sinister, and as possibly in more urgent need of explanation than the acquisition or even existence of attitudes in the first place.

The paradigm adopted in the Yale studies was to look at attitude change as a function of three sets of (potentially interacting) factors relating to a communication context: attributes of the communicator, attributes of the message, and attributes of the audience. The important feature of this paradigm is that the communication of the message is typically seen (and manipulated) as a discrete event, with a distinct 'before' and 'after'. This is not the place to go to for an understanding of the effects of a constant 'drip-feed' of some ever-present advertising campaign, or for the indirect dissemination of information through secondary sources. The standard communications considered are of the one-off, up-front, didactic 'I'm here to tell you' variety.

Some of the results of these studies are more memorable than others. It was confirmed, for instance, that credible communicators are more persuasive than those low in credibility, with information from unreliable sources tending to be discounted. Well-liked or attractive communicators, on the other hand, do not necessarily have a general advantage. Another reported finding relates to the amount of fear (e.g. of some dire health consequence) that is aroused by a given way of conveying a message. The claim is that very high levels of fear (e.g. those generated by lurid films of cancerous lungs) *inhibit* attitude change as compared with more moderate appeals (Janis and Feshbach, 1953). This claim has shaped a great deal of thinking in the field of health education, but is actually incorrect (Sutton, 1982). The problem with some 'high fear' messages may not be that they are frightening, but that they may contain overstatements that undermine the perception that the information applies to you personally. Research on attributes of the audience (or recipients of the message) failed to identify any general attribute of persuasibility (or link this reliably to being female!). More positively, there is a general finding that people committed to more extreme opinions are less easily persuaded than those with more neutral positions.

How can one characterize this programme of research from the hindsight of some thirty to forty years? Certainly it was thorough, within its own terms of reference. If you stay within those terms of reference, looking at attitude change as a result of one-off communications, it is difficult to point to many obvious gaps. Hovland, Janis, Kelley and their colleagues could, not unfairly and from their perspective perhaps not altogether unflatteringly, be said to have worked their questions into the ground. Indeed, they did such a comprehensive job that there seemed little or nothing left to do after they had finished. Research on attitude change in most of the sixties and early seventies, where it existed at all, was not concerned with persuasion as such but with the effects of 'cognitive dissonance' (of which more shortly) on people's reappraisals of their previous viewpoints.

It is only during the last ten to fifteen years that interest in persuasion has begun to recover (see e.g. Eagly and Chaiken, 1993). One sign of this recovery is a move to look at persuasion as a means of producing changes not simply in expressed attitudes, but in actual behaviour. This has applications in fields as diverse as health behaviour, marketing, and cognitive therapy. Another sign is a revisiting of some of the issues of message content from two radically different persectives: in relation to more recent theories of cognitive information-processing, bringing in discussion of the ease with which particular messages can be understood and recalled (e.g. Cialdini, Petty and Cacioppo, 1981); and in relation to the broader (not exclusively psychological) literature on rhetoric and persuasive argumentation (Billig, 1987).

There are, however, respects in which the Yale tradition was severely constrained. Persuasion was seen simply as producing a change in *response* along a unitary dimension. We learn something about some of the factors that can produce such changes, but – despite the researchers' professed reliance on concepts drawn from the psychology of learning and motivation – the choice of such factors selected for study can seem atheoretical. Although the later emphasis on cognitive processes is foreshadowed, it is not fully developed. We are too often left with a sense of incompleteness when we look for explanations of *why* some factors facilitate persuasion and others do not. We are told too little about the thoughts and emotions that having an attitude can involve, or about what it may feel like to be persuaded. These shortcomings are not unconnected.

Attitudes can be organized

Around the same time as the research just described, another tradition was beginning to have an impact on attitude theory. *Gestalt* psychology had achieved prominence in Europe during the first part of the century. Its central theme was that thoughts and perceptions were organized into coherent wholes (*Gestalten*), and that the meaning of any such whole or pattern was greater than the sum of its parts. In the field of visual perception, organizing principles such as symmetry and completeness (*Prägnanz*) reveal themselves in the ease with which we recognize shapes such as circles or other regular patterns, and in our ability to infer a whole shape when part of it is hidden from view.

Fritz Heider, a European émigré like many of the influential figures of American post-war science, was committed to the view that our attitudes, and more generally our interpretations of our social environment, form consistent patterns or *Gestalten*. His approach went under the name of the theory of 'cognitive balance'. Later variants and developments of this approach are referred to more generally as 'cognitive consistency theories'. The basic idea of all these theories is that people have a disposition or motivation to see the world as consistent and hence predictable (perhaps to a greater extent than it 'really' is). For social psychology, the most important manifestations of this drive for consistency are in the way we tend to *evaluate* other people and events. Attitudes, according to this approach, are a form of *evaluation*. Crucially, though, we are supposed to organize patterns among these evaluations so that they may be grouped together into higher-order structures.

One sign of balance is a disposition to believe good things about people we like and bad things about people we dislike. Why? Because there would be a kind of 'psychological' inconsistency in thinking that someone we liked (regarded positively) would have bad attributes, or do bad things, since these would imply that he or she should be regarded negatively. Another sign of balance is a disposition to share (what we believe to be) our friends' opinions. Why? Because there would be a similar kind of 'psychological' inconsistency between liking our friends and believing that they held 'bad' opinions (or evaluated our own opinions negatively).

This kind of consistency has nothing necessarily to do with logical entailment. Of course we can like people who disagree with us. There is no *logical* contradiction here. The word 'friend' does not *mean* 'someone who agrees with me'. Part of what Heider is saying, though, is that disagreements with our friends are less stable than are agreements with our friends or disagreements with our enemies. 'Less stable' implies easier to change. Such change may be initiated through new information, another's attempt at persuasion, or through self-initiated restructuring of our thoughts so as to resolve the inconsistency. More stable or 'balanced' structures, on the other hand, are regarded as resistant to change, more predictable, simpler to understand, easier to recall from memory, and (here the *Gestalt* tradition especially declares itself) more aesthetically pleasing and emotionally comfortable.

This last assumption is particularly important, in that it introduces a *motivational* principle or bias. Whatever the 'true' state of affairs, (the theory claims) we don't *like* contradiction, complication or ambivalence. We prefer to be able to think of some things as good and some as bad and to leave it at that. We don't *like* having our evaluative judgements challenged or muddled up. Give us a set of values, an outlook on the world (*Weltanschauung*) in which good and bad are nicely and simply separated, and we shall eagerly accept it and defend it. This way lies not the rule of reason, but intolerance and 'solutions' based on the elimination of mixture and opposition. The very blandness of the theory's superficial reasonableness disguises the warning it implies. Yet this warning has rarely been recognized, or commented upon even by authors working directly within this tradition. On the contrary, our ability to achieve and sustain consistency in our attitudes and in our impressions of one another is often portrayed as something of which we should be rather proud – as indeed it may be, but only if we can develop a more critical conception of consistency.

How should consistency be reconceptualized? Hopefully, some kind of answer will emerge from later pages, but perhaps the following thoughts may offer some signposts to my later argument. First, consistency in Heider's sense can only be achieved through a *selective* definition of one's context or frame of reference. Such consistency is relative, not absolute: it depends on what we choose to try to relate to what (that is, how we define the context). However, it is far from clear how we can make such a choice (or any choice, perhaps). Faced with multi-attribute objects in a multi-dimensional world, how do we choose what to relate to what? (In many experiments, the researcher defines the choice for us, but that is trivial). Do we merely home in on *any* consistent patterns that we can distinguish from the surrounding randomness, or do we look for markers to point us towards one interpretation, one possible form of consistency, rather than towards other conceivable alternatives which we can somehow simultaneously bear in mind? And if the latter, what lies behind this 'somehow', and how can it be that we are capable, not only of making up our minds, but of sustaining alternative options in suspension? There is a joke that the only truly consistent people are dead ones. But it is more than a joke. If we consider how live people differ from dead ones, we cannot avoid the fact of thought and its creative potentialities.

But this is to let things run ahead of themselves. The theory of cognitive balance appears to propose a principle that we strive for logical reasoning and coherence (as we may well do in some circumstances). What it really proposes is that we are *biased* towards resisting or reducing ambivalence in our evaluations. Comfortingly perhaps in view of the above considerations, it turns out that the empirical evidence in favour of this proposal is far from universally overwhelming. A bias in favour of 'balanced' relationships can be demonstrated. So much the experimental data allow us to conclude. But often balance appears as just one of a number of biases, and incapable by itself of accounting for the broader pattern of people's preferences. (There is strong evidence, for instance, that people prefer to construe relationships as evaluatively positive, even where there is disagreement within such relationships, entailing a lack of 'balance'.)

There are also demonstrable individual differences, with some people being more tolerant of inconsistency (or positively attracted to novel, unexpected experiences) than are others. For instance, Newcomb (1981) found that, whereas some groups of college students were more inclined to have friends whose outlooks were similar to their own, in other groups mutual liking was more predictable from *differences* in attitude. (The first group, incidentally, were predominantly engineers, whereas the latter were mainly liberal arts students.) The attraction of the similar and the attraction of the opposite may well coexist as potential principles of friendship choice for everyone, with something tipping the scales in one direction for some people (in some contexts) and in another direction for others.

Attitudes can be reappraised

A straightforward implication of the cognitive consistency approach is that we should evaluate things more positively if we see them as leading to (or associated with) good rather than bad consequences. This principle has had a widespread appeal. It is very influential in the field of economic decision-making (in the shape of expectancy-value or subjective expected utility theories). As we shall see, it also successfully accounts for many phenomena in the psychology of learning (with animals no less than with humans). The Yale studies invoked a similar principle: communications should be more persuasive (more accepted) if they had positive rather than negative associations.

There are nevertheless important exceptions to this principle. Festinger's (1957) Theory of Cognitive Dissonance can be regarded as a maverick version of the cognitive consistency approach. Like Heider and others, Festinger assumed that we are motivated to make (or see) our thoughts, feelings and decisions as consistent. He assumed too that the subjective experience of inconsistency (or dissonance, in his terms) is distressing and unpleasant. His innovation was to introduce a time dimension into his analysis of consistency processes. Heider regarded consistency or inconsistency as a matter of the pattern of relations between different thoughts or perceptions. Festinger was more concerned with the interaction of such thoughts with behaviour and hence paid more regard to questions of temporal sequence. Most notably, he argued that *if* one is induced to act in a manner that is inconsistent with some prior attitude, *then* the thought that one acted that way will be inconsistent with the thought that one held that attitude. This inconsistency will be experienced as a state of negative arousal (dissonance), which will *then* motivate attempts at cognitive restructuring to resolve the inconsistency. This restructuring *may* take the form of a reappraisal of one's initial attitude along the lines of 'I couldn't have really held that attitude, or I'd never have acted that way'. In other words, under certain conditions *we may change our attitudes to bring them into line with our prior behaviour.*

The prediction that we may reappraise our attitudes in this way is interesting but not extraordinary. What struck many researchers as counter-intuitive was the further prediction that such reappraisals are more likely to occur when we receive *smaller* rather than larger rewards for behaving in a manner contrary to our initial opinions. This prediction appeared directly contrary to the implications of any reinforcement or expectancy-value principle, yet it was clearly supported in a number of experimental studies.

Why should this effect occur? Festinger's own view was that receiving a large reward eliminates the negative arousal engendered by the counter-attitudinal behaviour and thereby removes the motivation for attitude reappraisal. Others, notably Aronson (1972), have interpreted such data as reflecting a general tendency for self-justification. This fits with evidence that Festinger's prediction only works if people feel they have made a *free choice*; if they feel they were *forced* to behave inconsistently with their prior attitudes, they show more attitude change (in the direction of increased consistency with their behaviour) if offered *larger* rewards (Linder *et al.*, 1967). The argument runs that, if you are forced to act in a given way, you do not need to justify your behaviour as being something in which you personally believe.

For a while, one of the strongest assaults on cognitive dissonance was mounted from a radical behaviourist perspective. Bem (1967) argued that there was no need to assume any motivational state of negative arousal resulting from counter-attitudinal behaviour. Furthermore, our self-reports of our attitudes should be regarded as nothing more than a particular kind of description of *behaviour*. He suggested that such self-reports are essentially equivalent to the descriptions that could be offered by a (suitably informed) independent observer and hence that we do *not* have any special authority in making statements purportedly about our own mental states. Someone who observed us acting under duress would not talk about our behaviour as though it corresponded to our attitudes. Someone who observed us acting apparently freely for no great reward would describe our behaviour in terms that could imply that we believed in what we were doing.

Bem's analysis fails in a number of crucial respects. As with all behaviourist accounts, there is the problem of why we should *want* to describe our behaviour in mentalistic (that is, attitudinal) terms if purely behavioural descriptions were as informative and less confusing. Granted, we cannot assume that mentalistic accounts are necessarily *true*, just because we have a language in which we can express them. But the fact that we have such an expressive language is something which, despite valiant attempts, behaviourism cannot adequately explain. This problem does not arise (although others do) if we take self-reports of attitudes as reports of thoughts and feelings. There are empirical shortcomings too. Sometimes people describe their attitudes in ways which cannot be second-guessed accurately by outside observers of their behaviour.

There is also now more direct evidence (from physiological measures and manipulations) that attitude change may be mediated by arousal (e.g. Cooper *et al.*, 1978). Interestingly, though, the same evidence that supports an arousal-based or motivational interpretation suggests that the negative feelings produced by dissonance manipulations have little to do with inconsistency as such (Cooper and Fazio, 1984). In other words, just knowing that you have done something that could seem inconsistent with your prior attitude need not make you feel uncomfortable or lead you to change your opinion: what would make you reappraise your attitude is if your freely chosen behaviour produced *bad consequences* (or created a risk of such consequences) which you now regret. This requires a view of attitudes in which people can reflect *evaluatively* upon their own thoughts, emotions and behavioural decisions. To understand the nature of this reflective process, however, we need to go well beyond the framework of consistency or dissonance theories.

Attitudes (sometimes) predict behaviour

In the early days of attitude research, it was taken for granted that attitudes predict many aspects of our social behaviour. This fitted in with a conception of attitude as some kind of motive or drive-state: our attitudes *make*, or at least predispose, us to act the way we do. It also fitted in with research findings in the area of attitude measurement. If you devise a new measuring instrument, say a scale to measure attitudes towards religious observance, you need to check that it actually measures what it is intended to measure. This process of checking is termed validation. A form of validation frequently used by Thurstone and his colleagues was to give the scale to contrasting groups of people who, according to any reasonable expectation, would differ in terms of the attitude being measured. For instance, one might compare a group of regular church-goers with a group of atheists. If the church-goers scored more positively than the group of atheists in terms of favourability towards religious observance, this would help confirm the validity of the scale. Conversely, if one failed to find a difference in the groups' scores, one would have doubts that the scale was measuring what it was intended to measure.

Validation is not just important from the point of view of measurement. What it shows is that the answers people give to questionnaires can be predictive of aspects of their social behaviour. Both the attitudes and behaviours in question tend to be defined quite broadly in these studies, but there is still a definite correspondence between the different criteria: on the whole, people who do more religious things also express more religious attitudes. And there the matter might have rested, had it not been for a series of studies in which researchers attempted to use indicators of general attitudes to predict rather more specific kinds of actions. Many of these concerned attitudes towards particular ethnic groups (especially black people in America). The typical finding was that many participants who might be identified as racially prejudiced from their verbal statements none the less behaved positively or at least politely towards individual members of another ethnic group in situations recorded by the researchers. In a review of these studies, Wicker (1969) concluded that there was typically only a weak relationship between verbally expressed attitudes and overt behaviour.

Faced with such findings, a good many social psychologists experienced a general disenchantment with the concept of attitude. If you couldn't predict anything from attitudes, why study them in the first place? At the other extreme, a few purists took the line that attitudes were interesting to study in their own right. In between, a number of people attempted new conceptual and methodological approaches to account both for our common-sense presumption of a close relationship between attitude and behaviour and for the demonstrated contradictions of this idea. In an influential statement, Rosenberg and Hovland (1960) proposed that attitude should be regarded, not as a simple unitary concept, but as a complex of three classes of 'components'. These they term 'affect' (e.g. feelings, emotions), 'cognition' (e.g. beliefs) and 'behaviour' (e.g. overt actions). Their 'three-component' model is shown in figure 1.4. It preserves the Yale assumption of attitudes as responses to stimuli, but introduces the idea of different psychological subsystems intervening between these stimuli and measurable output or 'dependent variables'. Because these subsystems are distinct, it is likely that they will sometimes cohere with each other and sometimes not. So

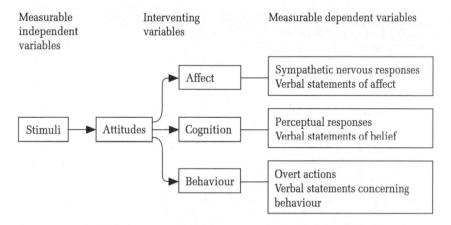

Figure 1.4 The three-component model of attitude organization
Source: Adapted from C. I. Hovland and M. J. Rosenberg (eds) (1960) *Attitude Organization and Change*, Yale University Press

far, so good. It is not unreasonable to talk of subsystems and to consider how they might interact (indeed, this is precisely the kind of issue being addressed by much contemporary work in the field of social cognition). But the model is far too vaguely specified. We are told little or nothing about the processes which the diagram supposedly represents (what exactly do those arrows mean?) and, most crucially, we are given little or nothing to go on in terms of predicting *when*, say, 'affect' and 'behaviour' will relate closely to one another and when they will appear independent of each other.

A more succesful solution was proposed by Fishbein and Ajzen (1975) and developed further by Ajzen and Fishbein (1980). There are a number of elements to their approach. First, they argue that the effect of attitude on behaviour is mediated by 'intention'. In simple terms, we shouldn't expect attitudes to predicted behaviour if the behaviour is unintended. It is therefore intention, rather than behaviour as such, which we should try and predict. Next, intention is supposedly influenced not just by attitude, but by what they call 'subjective norm'. This refers to the extent to which you believe that your acting in a given way will earn the approval or disapproval of other people whose opinions you value. Thus you may choose (or intend) to do something you would not personally 'want' to do because you wish to please or obey someone else. This would be an example of your subjective norm pulling you strongly in one

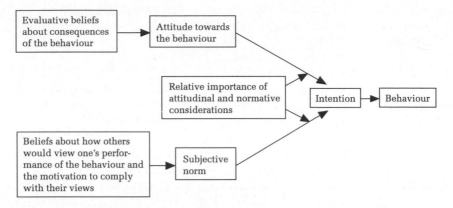

Figure 1.5 The theory of reasoned action
Source: Adapted from I. Ajzen and M. Fishbein (1980) *Understanding Attitudes and Predicting Social Behavior*, Prentice-Hall

direction and your attitude pulling you (more weakly) in the other. What you 'want' is specified by your attitude. This is because attitude is defined in expectancy-value terms. More specifically, your attitude is supposed to be *derived from* your beliefs (expectancies) about whether certain consequences are more or less likely to follow from your behaviour, weighted by your evaluations of how good or bad these consequences would be. The model in fact specifies that your attitude can be predicted according to a formula whereby the likelihood of each effect is multiplied by its value, and the products are added together.

The model (see figure 1.5) thus makes quite strong assumptions about the *causal* dependence of different kinds of thoughts (intentions, attitudes, norms, specific expectancies and values) on one another. Attitude–behaviour relationships are interpreted very much within the context of a view of behaviour as the product of a rational will. This is declared explicitly in their (1980) naming of the model as the Theory of Reasoned Action. More recently, Ajzen (1991) has amended the name to the Theory of Planned Behaviour. The extra element in the later version is the perceived controllability of the effects – essentially a recognition of the fact that we are less likely to (intend to) undertake actions where we have little confidence of success (see Eiser and Sutton, 1977, and Eiser *et al.*, 1985, for evidence of the importance of confidence in relation to decisions to give up smoking). How is this 'rational will' supposed to go about its business? According to the model, by building up global attitudes and norms from more *specific* beliefs concerning personal and social consequences.

I shall outline some criticisms of this causal analysis shortly, but first let us consider the undeniably positive contribution of Fishbein and Ajzen to the debate on attitude–behaviour relations. Because their model incorporates notions of specific beliefs, these beliefs have to be measured. Furthermore, the beliefs that matter are not just any kind of value judgement but *your* beliefs about the *consequences* of *you yourself* performing a specific *act* within a specific *situation* and probably towards a specific *target person*. In other words, what a test of the model requires is not just a measure of attitude *in general*, but of attitude towards a *behaviour*, performed by oneself in a specified time and place, to or in the presence of specified other people. These requirements clearly are not met in most of the studies that suggest a lack of relationship between attitudes and behaviour. In most cases, the behaviour observed is highly specific (e.g. being photographed next to a black student), and not precisely referred to in the measures of attitudes, which are typically highly general. In other words, the low correlations between attitudes and behaviour are often the result of measuring attitudes and behaviour at different levels of generality or specificity. Ajzen and Fishbein (1977) show that suitably constructed measures of attitude can be highly correlated with measures of behaviour when both are defined to relate to the same specific class of act and situation. Similarly, general classes of behaviour are predictable from general measures of attitude, as implied by the early studies on validation of attitude scales. For instance, people with more favourable attitudes to religious observance will be more religiously observant in general, but not necessarily all in the same specific ways.

Well and good. Ajzen and Fishbein give us some decent correlations. But is their causal interpretation convincing? There are some important respects in which, I would suggest, it is not. One of the gaps in the theory is any proper account of how the system is supposed to develop itself and sustain itself over *time*. True, the model (see figure 1.5) allows for the effects of behaviour to provide feedback to modify beliefs, but this is as far as it goes. What we really have is a model suited to the prediction of *discrete* decisions, isolated in time and space. Empirical difficulties arise when trying to apply the model to the prediction of *habitual* behaviour. Here we can find that the best predictor of your future behaviour is how you have behaved in similar contexts in the past, more or less irrespective of the attitudes and norms you now express (Bentler and Speckart, 1979). Ajzen and Fishbein might counter that their theory does not apply to such cases (of behaviour which is, in their terms, 'beyond volitional control'). But there is a danger of circularity here if such cases cannot be identified in advance. Besides, our behaviour and our attitudes in such cases still require some kind of explanation. Nor should we forget the lesson of cognitive dissonance research – attitudes can be readjusted to bring them into line with how we have *already* behaved.

Another drawback is that we are told that global attitudes depend on antecedent, molecular beliefs about specific effects or attributes. But where do these specific beliefs come from? From interaction with the environment. Fair enough, but why should it be just *these* beliefs, rather than any others that are conceivably relevant? Fishbein and Ajzen (1975) address this problem through introducing the notion of 'salient beliefs'. Beliefs are 'salient' if they are regarded as particularly important by the individual. Because of the limitations of our capacity for holding different pieces of information simultaneously in short-term memory, we are unlikely to consider more than about seven such 'salient' beliefs at any one time in arriving at a global evaluation of an object or behaviour.

But the question still remains – why *these* beliefs? Might other people base their attitudes on other beliefs? The answer we are effectively given would run something like this:

> Well, yes, they might, but, from the point of view of methodology, it's a pain in the neck to have to take account of such differences, because this would mean that everyone would have to have a different questionnaire with their own salient beliefs listed, and this would then mean that we couldn't compare different people's answers anyway. If you want to predict behaviour, the best thing to do is to do some pilot research to find out what *most* people regard as salient consequences of buying a washing-machine or quitting smoking or whatever, and then choose a *single* set of beliefs – let's call them 'modal' salient beliefs – which we can then give to everyone in the reasonable expectation that this set will at least partly overlap what most people individually would select as salient beliefs for themselves. If you do this, you'll get pretty good correlations between the calculations of attitude (according to our formula) and behavioural intentions. Another thing that helps is that salience and extremity of evaluation may go together, i.e. people tend to give more extreme evaluations of things they personally regard as important. This means that such beliefs will be more strongly weighted in the calculations.

But this *still* doesn't answer the question. It just tells us how we can still get reasonable predictions even if we avoid committing ourselves to any explanation of what makes one belief more salient than another. Perhaps differences between individuals in their choice of salient beliefs are unsystematic and just reflect idiosyncrasies of background and experience. If so, then the fudge of 'modal salient beliefs' will not lead us too far astray. But suppose that individual differences in salience are systematic, suppose that there is a pattern to them. What then? Surely any such pattern would be suggestive of some process of selection. Perhaps we are dealing then with the same kind of selective process that we have seen to be implied in notions such as cognitive consistency and, indeed, in the principle of attitude measurement itself. And what if such individual differences in salience were not only patterned, but systematically related to the very attitudes we were trying to predict? Might this not mean that it is the global attitude that sometimes steers the selection of salient beliefs, rather than the other way round? Whatever the direction or cyclical nature of such relationships, surely attitudes must involve the *selective* use of feelings and beliefs, and the prioritization of different questions and uncertainties. If our thoughts were random, or unsystematically selective, we would not experience them as attitudes at all.

Attitudes involve selective information-processing

How can we try to understand the relationship between attitudes and the selective use of feelings and beliefs? A possible way forward is suggested by recent research on 'social information-processing'. Broadly, information-processing refers to the variety of forms of thought in which we can engage after receiving a given piece of information (verbal message, sensory input or whatever). We could ignore it as irrelevant ('Can't say I noticed anything'). We could recognize it immediately as (establishing the presence of) a familiar object ('Hello! That's Harry'). We could engage in further thought about how it related to other information we had previously acquired, or previous knowledge of the object in question ('Harry doesn't usually wear hats with purple feathers'). We could try and fit it into some more general schema or personal theory about the world ('People like Harry don't wear hats with purple feathers unless they're going to a fancy-dress party'). We could ponder the information and make a special effort to remember it in detail ('I'll try and come to the party too. Where did you say it was?'). We could use the information to make an evaluative judgement ('Harry's a twit'). Or we could let our thoughts lead us off in any of a myriad of different directions.

There has been a great deal of experimental work looking at factors that influence the different kinds of thinking in which we may engage when presented with particular kinds of information. If the information is uncertain or probabilistic, what kinds of inductive procedures will we use when drawing inferences? It turns out that we seem to depend on some rough-and-ready rules that make some sense in many everyday contexts but ignore a number of basic statistical principles (Tversky and Kahneman, 1974). How do we deal with information concerning some topic in which we are especially interested or on which we already have a strong opinion? Involvement with a topic – i.e. regarding it as important and personally relevant – tends to lead to more thorough information-processing, as we might expect. Work by Petty and Cacioppo (1986) shows that this has implications for persuasion and attitude change. If we are involved in a topic, and hence process the information more thoroughly, we are more likely to be persuaded by complex, informative arguments. On the other hand, if we are not especially interested or involved, we are more likely to be influenced by simple messages (for instance, some kinds of commercial advertisements).

Do we deal differently with information that contradicts, rather than supports, our pre-existing attitudes? Earlier work (from the Yale studies) suggests that we may discount as unreliable or incredible information that is highly discrepant from our own opinions. Cognitive dissonance theory would also predict that we should reject discrepant information (which would otherwise produce an unpleasant state of dissonance). Such rejection might take various forms, such as a refusal to listen to what we were told, a reinterpretation of it to render it consistent with our viewpoint, or a 'suppression' of it in memory so that it will not be available for recall at a later time. In fact, there is little consistent evidence for such biases in terms of *recall* of information. People do *not* tend to be better at remembering arguments which are favourable, rather than unfavourable, to their own opinions (Pratkanis and Greenwald, 1989). Instead, it seems that having a clear opinion on an issue means that one has some kind of structure, or set of concepts and hypotheses, in terms of which relevant information, whether favourable or unfavourable, can be more easily and thoroughly 'encoded' (i.e. interpreted and committed to memory).

One of the most important themes in such research is that information that has been more thoroughly encoded at the time of its presentation will be easier to retrieve from memory at a later stage. This provides a possible clue into the relationship between attitudes and salience of beliefs, discussed in relation to the Ajzen and Fishbein (1980) work. If we learn about an issue in terms of one particular theme (e.g. if we define a war, or some other international dispute, in terms of our *own* country's national interest), then this is the theme we will remember and find it easiest to structure our thoughts around at a later stage. Thus belief salience is a function of selective definition. According to Fazio (1986), it is to this principle of selectivity that we should look in order to understand the relationships between attitudes and behaviour: attitudes 'guide' behaviour by leading to selective definitions of the meaning of issues and situations, and hence to the selective recall or construction of particular behavioural plans. If people feel that the salient aspect of an international crisis is that their country's national interest and/or prestige is threatened by the aggressive acts of another nation, they are more likely to think of responding directly to such aggression. If the same situation is interpreted as just another dispute in another part of the world, this is likely to guide behaviour in the direction of staying out of trouble. On a smaller scale, much the same analysis could apply to scraps in a school playground.

Affect and cognition can influence each other

Much work on social information-processing seems to emphasize the importance of cognition over other kinds of psychological processes. But is such an emphasis altogether justified? Someone who thinks otherwise is Zajonc (1980). In a paper entitled 'Feeling and thinking: preferences need no inferences', he argues that our affective reactions – feelings of attraction or aversion and such like – are essentially spontaneous, rapid and unmediated by any complex inferential or ratiocinative process. He explicitly denies that such spontaneous evaluations are 'based on a prior cognitive process in which a variety of content discriminations are made and features are identified, examined for their value, and weighted for their contributions' (p. 151). This description of a supposed 'cognitive process' certainly fits with that proposed by Ajzen and Fishbein (1980), and a number of other models also fall victim to the same criticism. For example, probably the most influential social psychological theory of the seventies – attribution theory – (see Hewstone, 1989, for a recent review) maintained that the way we evaluate other people (and ourselves) depends our *causal explanations* for behaviour and its outcomes. These explanations, in turn, reflect our assumptions about the actor's intention, vulnerability to coercion, and various other personal and situational factors.

The crucial issue is that of how *aware* we are of the various factors influencing our judgements and decisions. Theories of the kind criticized by Zajonc may still be correct or at least informative in specific contexts. But do we *need* such theories to account for a broad range of simple, basic preferences? On this point, Zajonc is adamant: we do not. We can have a host of gut reactions that are very powerful, very quick, and frequently controlled by stimulus conditions of which we have no intuitive awareness. For instance, just becoming familiar with a stimulus (such as a meaningless shape or symbol) through repeated exposure can make that stimulus appear more attractive than less familiar ones. Although this effect is found only under certain conditions, it suggests that we may come to like or dislike some things without being aware of the origins of our feelings.

Another example is provided by recent work within the tradition of attribution theory. Weiner (e.g. 1985) has studied people's reactions to success and failure. Within a narrow conception of attribution theory, how we feel about doing well or badly in an examination (say) should depend on how we *explain* such success or failure in terms of such factors as our ability and/or effort (or the lack of either), luck with the questions, bias of the examiner, etc. Such explanations do indeed make a difference. We may feel more ashamed than angry if we attribute our failure to our lack of effort, more relieved than proud if our success seems due to special luck with the questions we were asked. Inferences clearly *can* influence our feelings. But this influence is essentially a colouring-in of less contemplative reactions which, in Weiner's terms, are 'outcome-dependent, attribution-independent'. Quite simply, success generally makes us feel happy and failure makes us feel unhappy, regardless of whether we put these outcomes down to chance, other people's interventions, or see them as our just deserts.

The proposal is, then, that we can feel good or bad about things, happy or unhappy, attracted or repulsed, without (or at least before) being able to work out *why* we have these feelings. It is tempting to look for evolutionary links here to the approach and avoidance reactions shown by other species. And why not? Some of the most important decisions for our survival (or at least well-being) may need to be made very quickly. But do these feelings qualify as attitudes? This is a trickier question than it sounds. On the one hand, it is clear that an attitude that was devoid of any such affective associations would be a pretty bland affair. Would one need a concept of attitude (rather than mere belief) if no feelings or preferences were implied? Surely not. On the other hand, we should hesitate before assuming that we are dealing *just* with raw emotion.

Of critical importance is the fact that we express our attitudes as being *about* something – we say what it is that we like or dislike. In other words, attitudes involve what philosophers call 'intentionality' – a confusing term with no close connection with the everyday concept of 'intention'. I shall be going into this issue in more detail later, but basically what is involved is that statements which express attitudes are *about* objects whose existence is independent of the attitudes themselves. In other words, they involve some kind of representation – in thought and/or language – of an attitude object. If I say 'I admire Gorbachev' this implies, as a minimum, that there *exists* (at least in my imagination) a person called Gorbachev; beyond this minimal level, it implies that this person has qualities of a kind that I (at least) admire.

What this amounts to is that we do not tend to regard 'raw emotion' as an attitude if it is seen as free-floating and unconnected with any target. The step from 'feeling emotional' to 'feeling an emotion *about* something' is crucial. It involves some form of cognitive connection. Likewise, *reporting* or *expressing* an attitude involves some form of evaluative judgement and it seems difficult to resist the conclusion that such a judgement must involve some kind of cognitive process. But what kind of cognitive process? It is here that the information-processing approach described in the last section may prove more helpful – and may leave more room for the influence of emotion – than the earlier, more rationalistic, theories which were the primary targets of Zajonc's (1980) criticism.

One reason for this is the importance, within contemporary research, of the concept of *associative memory*. The basic idea is that what we store in memory are traces or records of previous thoughts and experiences *and the connections or associations between them*. These connections are assumed to be organized in terms of a kind of 'network'. In terms of some models (e.g. Bower, 1981), such networks represent the different strengths of association between different pairs of concepts, depending, for instance, on how similar

they are to each other in meaning or evaluation. A consequence –
or indication – of these links is that one concept will 'activate'
another, if the two are closely associated. In other words, thinking
about the one will make us think about the other (for example, 'fish'
can make us think of 'chips'). We can also postulate that some of
the links between concepts will be inhibitory (rather than facilita-
tory), so that thinking about one concept will make it less likely
that we will think about another. More recently, this kind of approach
has blossomed into the field of research known as 'connectionism'
or 'neural networks' about which I will have a great deal to say in
chapter 9. (An important respect in which connectionism differs
from some other 'network association' research is the idea that we
form connections, not just between 'concepts' to which we can give
words or names, but between more rudimentary 'units' which are
not by themselves representative of any single concept. But more of
this later.)

Part of the appeal of this view of memory is that anything can in
principle be associated with anything else, depending on various
factors such as shared attributes and previous experience. All it
takes therefore for emotional and cognitive responses to influence
each other is that there should be associations formed between
them. One experimental effect which illustrates this is that people
who are in a good mood, or have been asked to think about something pleasant, will tend to show a variety of more positive judgements and behaviours (e.g. describing another person in positive
terms, or showing friendly or helpful behaviour) than will people
who are in a bad mood or have been asked to think about something unpleasant. The notion is that a positive mood can 'prime'
(i.e. activate, or render more accessible from memory) more positive thoughts and behavioural plans. Conversely, unpleasant feelings can 'prime' unpleasant thoughts – an effect that may underlie
many aspects of psychological depression.

As I hinted earlier, though, there are important differences between *having* thoughts and feelings, and *reporting* them. We often
report our feelings and attitudes in response to questions (Is your
headache better today? Did you like the film? What do you think of
the election results?). We therefore need to place our feelings into
a communicative context. We need to scan our feelings and memories for information that will help us answer the question that has
been (explicitly or implicitly) put to us. Within such a communicative context, our mood state will provide one source of information. How could you be feeling happy with a bad headache, after

a bad film or after a bad election result? But the trouble is, your happiness might be – indeed is most likely to be – the combined effect of many factors, including many of which you may be only dimly or indirectly aware. There is evidence that events that produce a temporary elevation or suppression of mood can lead people to rate their lives *generally* as more positive or negative (Schwarz *et al.*, 1987). In other words, mood can be used as a source of information on which more general inferences are based. (This effect depends partly on how the questions are asked. If respondents' attention is specifically directed to the temporary cause of their mood change, they may be more able to discount their present mood when rating their happiness in general.) Set alongside what Zajonc has to say, such data imply that gut reactions may indeed 'need no inferences'. On the other hand, there are also considered and articulated judgements of preference that *do* need inferences. Expressed judgements of preference can sometimes involve considerable thought, which is not to deny that such thought can also be highly emotional.

What thoughts and feelings are involved when we express our attitudes? This is not *quite* the only question with which attitude research should be concerned, but it is certainly a fundamental one. It is also a question which highlights some of the inadequacies of current attitude theories and encourages us to look for a wider range of ideas in other specialties and other disciplines. To express our attitudes is to communicate something about our feelings. But these feelings are *about* something, so we are also expressing something about things which exist apart from our feelings. We are saying something about how *we* stand in relation to these things and so we are making some judgement of ourselves. How then can we know our attitudes without knowing ourselves? But what does it mean to 'know' oneself, or even to 'have' a self that could be known? Can we have a 'self' outside an *interpersonal* network of communication and shared experience? I believe that these questions are very close – far closer than has generally been recognized – to the question of what it is to have an attitude. They are some of the classic questions of philosophy, and it is to that field of thought that I now shall turn.

2
Mind and Body

Knowing oneself

To ask the question 'How do we know ourselves?' is to enter the arena of some of the most significant philosophical contests of (at least) the last three-and-a-half centuries. In this and the following chapter, therefore, I shall concentrate on the work of three philosophers of the seventeenth and eighteenth centuries: Descartes, Locke and Hume. These all approached the question of personal identity and knowledge of the self from the standpoint of a far more general concern with the question of how we can claim to know anything at all. This defines a context in which their contributions should be understood, and without which the purpose of their arguments can be more difficult to grasp. Thus it is 'well-known' that Descartes considered the mind to be separate fom the body, and perhaps also that Hume considered it a 'bundle' of separate perceptions. It is difficult to make very much of such proposals, considered in isolation; still less is it easy to take them from their context, and set them alongside contemporary work in psychology and philosophy. But relevant they none the less are. The arguments that led up to these proposals are of more than historical curiosity. Many relate very closely to current debates over the nature of human consciousness and machine intelligence. They still deserve to be heard, and for this reason, I have allowed myself the indulgence of quoting at some length from the original texts.

Reason and evidence

In terms of our modern version of common sense, it may seem trivial to assert that we decide matters of truth and falsehood by appealing to a combination of reasoning and evidence. We *know*, through the use of reasoning, that the square root of 87 must be less than 10. (It *must* be so, since the square of 10 is 100 and 100 is greater than 87). We *know* that boiling water turns to steam, through our own experience of boiling kettles (and we can deliberately allow kettles to boil dry). We *know* that the defendant must be innocent if it can be shown conclusively that he was elsewhere at the time of the crime. Yet this view is obviously incomplete. Much of our 'knowledge' is obtained second-hand, from individuals or recorded authorities whose expertise on specific matters we believe to be superior to our own. (Indeed, there are many social psychological experiments that show we may even conform to other people's opinions or behaviour when we have no reason to assume that they are any better informed than we are ourselves). Part of our 'knowledge' consists in what we have worked out for ourselves, and part consists in what we have been told, or inferred from what others seem to know. What is far from trivial is to assert that the former part of our 'knowledge' is in principle more authentic and dependable than the latter, and that appeals to authority cannot give us 'real' knowledge – cannot 'really' settle the truth or falsehood of any matter – unless that authority is itself demonstrably based on reason and evidence.

It has not always been so, within the histories of our own societies, nor is it always so now, within our own age. Appeals to holy writ, ideological manifestos, pronouncements by popes, ayatollahs and party leaders, claims of contact with the spirits of the dead, have all been and are treated as revealed 'truth' by millions of 'believers'. For a long time, university students could be punished for daring to question the works of Aristotle. (Nowadays, of course, universities are much more democratic, and occasionally students can even get away with criticizing the works of their own lecturers!) But however confident or however cynical we may be about 'progress' – and perhaps especially if we see it as vulnerable and insecure – the assertion of the priority of reason and evidence over conventional authority is a value claim of the highest importance. On it are founded the freedoms whose 'truths' we hold to be self-evident or, more prosaically, let ourselves so often take for granted. This assertion is neither a truism nor a piece of academic cleverness. It is not politically neutral. What is at stake is nothing less than the battle between bigotry and enlightenment.

The greatness of the great philosophers is in pointing us in the direction of at least some form of that enlightenment, and we should resist feeling short-changed if they each take us only part of the way along the roads they choose. If our own reason and evidence cannot then take us further, that is perhaps the point at which we should retrace our steps and choose a different road. Furthermore, the hoped-for enlightenment is *not* a mystical revelation, not a piece of propositional pyrotechnics, but something graspable by ordinary minds, through the application of appropriate methods of enquiry and conceptual analysis. It is, in short, a democratic and sharable enlightenment. The philosophers who have most to teach us here are those who make only modest claims concerning their own intellectual capacities, and we need not take their modesty as pretence. Take, for instance, the following remarks with which Descartes starts his *Discourse*:

> Good sense is, of all things among men, the most equally distributed . . . the power of judging aright and of distinguishing truth from error, which is properly what is called good sense or reason, is by nature equal in all men; and the diversity of our opinions, consequently, does not arise from some being endowed with a larger share of reason than others, but solely from this, that we conduct our thoughts along different ways, and do not fix our attention on the same objects. For to be possessed of a vigorous mind is not enough; the prime requisite is to apply it. The greatest minds, as they are capable of the highest excellences, are open likewise to the greatest aberrations; and those who travel very slowly may yet make far greater progress, provided they keep always to the straight road, than those who, while they run, forsake it.
>
> For myself, I have never fancied my mind to be in any respect more perfect than those of the generality; on the contrary, I have often wished that I were equal to some others in promptitude of thought, or in clearness and distinctiness of imagination, or in fullness and readiness of memory . . .

Or listen to Locke in his 'Epistle to the reader' with which he prefaces his *Essay Concerning Human Understanding*:

> . . . searches after truth are a sort of hawking and hunting, wherein the very pursuit makes a great part of the pleasure. Every step the mind takes in its progress towards Knowledge makes some discovery, which is not only new, but the best too, for the time at least.
>
> This, Reader, is the entertainment of those who let loose their own thoughts, and follow them in writing; which thou oughtest not to envy them, since they afford thee an opportunity of the like diversion, if thou wilt make use of thy own thoughts in reading. It is to them, if they are they own, that I refer myself; but if they are taken

upon trust from others, it is no great matter what they are, they are not following truth, but some meaner consideration; and it is not worth while to be concerned with what he says or thinks who says or thinks only as he is directed by another . . .

I pretend not to publish this *Essay* for the information of men of large thoughts and quick apprehensions; to such masters of knowledge I profess myself a scholar [i.e. student], and therefore warn them beforehand not to expect anything here but what, being spun out of my own coarse thoughts, is fitted to men of my own size, to whom, perhaps, it will not be unacceptable that I have taken some pains to make plain and familiar to their thoughts some truths which established prejudice, or the abstractness of the *ideas* themselves, might render difficult . . .

The commonwealth of learning is not at this time without master-builders . . . it is ambition enough to be employed as an under-labourer in clearing ground a little, and removing some of the rubbish that lies in the way to knowledge . . .

Or Hume, who thus commenced the most succinct of autobiographies, in the last year of his life:

It is difficult for a man to speak long of himself without vanity; therefore I shall be short. It may be thought an instance of vanity that I pretend at all to write my life, but this narrative shall contain little more than the history of my writings, as, indeed, almost all my life has been spent in literary pursuits and occupations. The first success of most of my writings was not such as to be an object of vanity.

Descartes and the search for certainty

In looking at how many present-day issues concerning the nature of mind have developed, the influence of René Descartes (1596–1650) is hard to overestimate. It is tempting nowadays, from some points of view, to regard much of this influence as antiscientific and much of his thesis – particularly his insistence that the mind and body are separate – as untenable in view of the obvious fact that we cannot think anything without a brain. But even if we come to share such a negative verdict in the end, it is not one that should be arrived at too quickly. And while it is undeniable that we cannot think without a brain, it is still far from clear *exactly* how we can think even *with* one.

To understand Descartes's arguments, one must try to appreciate what he saw as the purpose of his philosophy. This is most easily gleaned from his *Discourse on Method*, or to give it its full title, *Discours de la méthode pour bien conduire sa raison et chercher la verité dans les sciences*. The 'method' involved a discipline – i.e. a controlled procedure – for using one's *reason* properly. Reason, according to Descartes, is not a rare capacity. On the contrary (as we can see from the earlier quotation), it is equivalent to 'good sense' (*le bon sens*) and thus 'equally shared' by all human minds. Distinguishing truth from falsehood is thus a matter of properly conducting or using one's reasoning capacity – a capacity that is entirely ordinary. But Descartes was not simply interested in emancipating what we now take to be philosophy. He was offering a method for *research*, for seeking *scientific* truth. In short, he was not offering merely an 'abstract' philosophy, but one applicable in principle to all forms of knowledge. And though one might suggest that he held a rather 'pure' view of science, with mathematics at its centre, he unequivocally took the position that truth and knowledge were attainable. In his own estimation, he was *not* a sceptic – that is, someone who regards *everything* as doubtful and disputable. Indeed, his 'method' was intended as a defence of knowledge against scepticism. (None the less, he was prepared, as we shall see, to concede so much to the sceptics that many later critics have regarded him as a sceptic himself.)

It is far from evident, even so, that Descartes regarded his 'method' as the only route through which truth was attainable. Rather, he presents it in these terms:

> My present design, then, is not to teach the method which each ought to follow for the right conduct of his reason, but solely to describe the way in which I have endeavoured to conduct my own . . . this tract is put forth merely as a history, or, as you will, as a tale, in which, amid some examples worthy of imitation, there will be found, perhaps, as many more which it were advisable not to follow . . . (*Discourse*, Part I)

Such disclaimers notwithstanding, it makes little sense to arrive at a judgement of Descartes's conclusions except in the context of the method he was following. The most crucial passages are presented in Part IV of the *Discourse*. This starts by distinguishing philosophical from practical certainty: '. . . in relation to practice, it is sometimes necessary to adopt, as if above doubt, opinions which we discern to be highly uncertain . . .' For the 'search after truth', on the other hand, 'exactly the opposite was called for', so that 'I ought to reject as absolutely false all opinions in regard to which I could suppose the least ground for doubt.' If anything remained of knowledge after such brutal pruning, this could then be taken as a foundation or first principle of a philosophy. Note that Descartes is *not* saying that anything that can be doubted in any way is *actually* false, only that it cannot be used as a basis for the discovery of truth.

Descartes then notes that our senses can sometimes deceive us, and therefore he 'was willing to suppose that there existed nothing really such as they presented to us'. Similarly, even the demonstrations provided by reasoning are to be doubted 'because some men err . . . even on the simplest matters of geometry' (note Descartes's change to the third person!). Likewise, he claims, we can have the same thoughts when asleep as when awake, and so cannot be absolutely sure that our thoughts are not dreams or illusions.

> But immediately upon this I observed that, whilst I thus wished to think that all was false, it was absolutely necessary that I, who thus thought, should be somewhat; and as I observed that this truth, *I think, hence I am*, was so certain and of such evidence, that no ground of doubt, however extravagant, could be alleged by the sceptics capable of shaking it, I concluded that I might, without scruple, accept it as the first principle of the philosophy of which I was in search.

Thus, through trying to doubt everything, Descartes discovered something that he could not doubt, a simple truth which he felt he could take for certain, and from which other truths could be derived. But how simple is this truth? Perhaps applying Descartes's own method by imitation, later commentators have found much that is ambiguous in this 'first principle'. What exactly does he mean by 'I', what does he mean by 'think', what does he mean by 'hence' (*donc*), what does he mean by 'am', are the two 'I's the same? What, in other words, is the certain truth – the proposition 'I think' (*je pense*), the proposition 'I am' (*je suis*), or the link between them? And if the link, how is this any more secure than any other 'reasoning taken for a demonstration', such as in geometry? Let us leave these questions hanging, at least for a moment, and see how Descartes himself develops the argument from his first principle.

His next step was to observe that he could apply his method of doubting anything of which he could not be absolutely certain to

his own *physical* existence. Thus, he found he could suppose
(*feindre*) that he had no body and there was no 'world nor place'
in which he existed, but he could *not* suppose that he did not exist
at all:

> . . . on the contrary, from the very circumstance that I thought to
> doubt the truth of other things, it most clearly and certainly followed
> that I was . . . I thence concluded that I was a substance whose whole
> essence and nature consists only in thinking, and which, that it may
> exist, has need of no place, nor is dependent on any material thing;
> so that 'I', that is to say the mind [*l'âme*] by which I am what I am,
> is wholly distinct from the body, and is even more easily known than
> the latter, and is such, that although the latter were not, it would still
> continue to be all that it is.

This short but famous passage has had a huge influence on
subsequent theoretical development in the philosophy of mind and
hence in psychology, in setting the scene for what is commonly
tagged the 'mind–body problem'. It is therefore worth keeping things
in perspective and remembering that Descartes's principal concern
was not – or not simply – with describing the nature of mind (or
the 'soul', since the same word would apply), or of personal identity or even of existence (although he certainly is putting forward
some strong hypotheses about these questions). Rather his interest
was with defining the basis of *knowledge*. He was seeking a form
of knowledge so certain that it would be unaffected by even the
slightest imperfection of information, inferences or evidence. For
practical purposes, he did not actually believe he had no body or
that there was no external world; but he found that he could *suppose*
or 'pretend' that these things did not exist, without, in his view,
falling into logical incoherence. Since he could not coherently apply
the same pretence to doubting the existence of his own mind, he
concluded that he was dealing with two qualitatively different forms
of knowledge, the one being fallible, the other certain.

'Clear and distinct' ideas

That the basis of knowledge was Descartes's main priority seems
clear from the way in which his argument immediately develops:

After this I inquired in general into what is essential to the truth and certainty of a proposition . . . And as I observed that in the words *I think, hence I am*, there is nothing at all which gives me assurance of their truth beyond this, that I see very clearly that in order to think it necessary to exist, I concluded that I might take, as a general rule, the principle, that all the things which we very clearly and distinctly conceive are true, only observing, however, that there is some difficulty in rightly determining the objects which we distinctly conceive.

Descartes was thus throwing down gauntlets in more than one direction. From the standpoint of contemporary psychology, with our interest in questions such as how brains perform their functions and whether computers really 'think', it is easy to regard Descartes's notion of an immaterial mind or soul as the most challenging aspect of his philosophy. But to many philosophers of his own and subsequent generations, this was probably only mildly controversial, granted its consonance with established Christian doctrine of life after death. Far more bothersome was the proposal that certainty was reducible to a kind of 'feel' – a 'clear and distinct' conception – which was not *necessarily* dependent either on some independently determinable state of affairs nor even on the application of formal logical rules, such as Aristotelian syllogisms. This is despite the point that *je pense donc je suis* can indeed be represented as a syllogism.

Descartes is therefore impelled towards justifying this criterion of a clear and distinct conception as the basis for truth, and like a classical Greek tragedian, he finds that a timely divine intervention can offer escape from the embarrassment of mortal folly. The argument, in summary, goes like this. In that I can doubt, my own being is imperfect, but this implies some concept of a nature more perfect than my own, which 'possessed within itself all the perfections of which I could form any idea; that is to say, in a single word, which was God.' Conveniently, God can allow things to be whose existence would otherwise be unnecessary. Being myself 'compounded' of a body and a mind is a form of imperfection, but since God is perfect, he cannot be 'compounded of these two natures'. Thus, 'if there were any bodies in the world, or even any intelligences, or other natures that were not wholly perfect, their existence depended on his power in such a way that they could not subsist without him for a single moment.'

Having (conceivably) got the world back on divine sufferance, Descartes uses God as the basis for the certainty of 'other truths' such as those of geometry. Here Descartes definitely has very 'clear and distinct ideas', e.g. that the sum of three angles of a triangle is the same as two right angles. But, as he observed, there is nothing in such a demonstration that provides assurance of the existence of any object such as a triangle. By contrast, the idea of a 'Perfect Being' entails existence – necessary truth – as part of the idea. Thus, the principle that 'clear and distinct ideas' must be true 'is certain only because God is or exists, and because he is a Perfect Being, and because all we possess is derived from him; whence it follows that our ideas and notions, which to the extent of their clearness and distinctness are real, and proceed from God, must to that extent be true.' By the same token, if we did not know that our clear and distinct ideas came from God, we could *not* assume that 'they possessed the perfection of being true'.

What are we to make of all this? Interpreted literally, it hardly seems very convincing. Anyone who found any basis for even *doubting* the existence of God could never know anything for certain. The whole notion of certainty of material or abstract thoughts being 'derived' from an idea of God's perfection is not articulated and smacks of mysticism. But there is perhaps a more sympathetic interpretation, which allows that Descartes was aware of the intellectual risk he was taking. 'Yes', we might imagine him saying 'I know about the methods of what you call science and I know about methods of mathematical proof – just look at my own work in the area. But the *feeling* that something is true, deep down, doesn't seem to me to be derived just from the use of such methods. This feeling is something far more direct and immediate than any conclusion from any rule-bound procedure or algorithm. For me the certainty that something is true is a kind of experience of perfection. If you ask me where this experience can come from, I can only assume it is from a Being more perfect than anything else I can conceive.' In other words – though please take this as a speculation on my part – Descartes's argument does not hold water as a proof of the certainty of knowledge precisely *because* he was prepared to assert the possibility of *certainty without proof.* Forget the invocation of the deity. Descartes was using the certainty of his own religious faith as a way of expressing (and indeed sustaining) a conviction that he could not reduce to any simpler rule. But even without his faith, or any other, we are left with a radical suggestion about the essence of human thought – that certainty and doubt are things which we *experience*.

If we push this suggestion to imply that *any* experience is a criterion for truth, then indeed we are on a very slippery slope indeed, and we might as well forget about scientific evidence or logical analysis. But Descartes is not saying this. Only 'clear and distinct' conceptions satisfy his requirements, even though he acknowledges the difficulty of defining what these terms mean. What I believe he is driving at is something quite similar to a contemporary problem in artificial intelligence, discussed at length by Roger Penrose (1989). This relates to whether all true propositions are 'computable', i.e. reducible to a form in which their truth can be settled by the application of some algorithm. The argument that some self-evident 'truths' (perhaps like Descartes's own example of the three angles of a triangle needing to equal two right angles) can be recognized directly *without* the use of an algorithm, raises the question of whether there may not always be something vital that is missing in algorithmic simulations of human intelligence. And perhaps it is no coincidence that the one truth that Descartes found the most self-evident and directly recognizable – awareness of his own existence as a thinking thing – is the very kind of thought or experience that we find it, rightly or wrongly, most difficult to attribute to a mere machine. I shall return to these issues in chapters 9 and 10.

A mind 'wholly distinct from the body'?

Unfortunately, what Descartes has to say about the subjective experience of knowledge has been largely overshadowed by his (now more controversial) claim that mind exists separately from the body. This position is referred to as *dualist*, since it implies a dual form of existence, with mental objects and events being wholly distinct from physical ones. For Descartes, the mind has a special status since its existence cannot be doubted without self-contradiction, whereas it is perfectly possible, he claims, to doubt the existence of any material object, even our own body. This 'first principle' of Descartes's, however, is quite limited in what it offers, even if we accept it as it is stated. Although we may not be able to doubt that we ourselves think, it is perfectly reasonable, by Descartes's account, to doubt the existence of any mind other than our own. If certainty is the benchmark for existence, we are alone in the universe. Or if there are other minds, they are unknowable by us and incapable of knowing us. The *je pense donc je suis* argument is presented in the

first person singular, so that all I know is *me*. Other people can be
convinced of their own existence by virtue of *their* own thoughts (if
they are good Cartesians), but this is of no help to me, since their
thoughts are not my thoughts and thus I can never directly experience them.

It can also be argued that the indubitability of a thinking act does
not entail that whatever does the thinking (the so-called '*res cogitans*',
or 'thinking thing') persists with any kind of continued existence
or identity from one thinking act to the next. (As we shall see,
Hume would later argue that the mind or self does not constitute
a distinct category of *experience* over and above the momentary
contents of a person's consciousness). It is therefore one thing to
argue that we cannot doubt the existence of an 'I' when 'I think'. It
is quite another thing to attribute to this 'I' the status of a 'mind' –
let alone a 'self' or 'person' – that has any kind of continued identity, or about which *anything* can be said, other than 'I think' (or 'I
am thinking now'). Thus, even if we take the existence of a thought
as indubitable, Descartes fails to demonstrate the existence of a
mind to which any thought *belongs*.

Disembodied thoughts?

The idea of thoughts somehow existing without actually belonging
to anyone in particular is disturbing, but it cannot be dismissed out
of hand. We can, for instance, talk of information or knowledge
existing, without being too specific about who possesses it. Even
if we want to claim ownership of our 'own' thoughts, our hold on
them can sometimes seem rather tenuous. I can say 'A thought just
came to me' – as though the thought had a kind of 'mind' of its
own, and was just visiting me as a favour. Or I can say 'I've lost my
train of thought' – as though my thoughts come and go according
to their own rules, over which I have little control. These are metaphors, of course, but there is an important idea underlying them.
This is that we can (at least partly) say what a thought *is* – i.e. state
the content of a thought – without specifying who is having that
thought. This allows us to adopt a manner of speaking in which *our*
having a particular thought is treated as almost incidental, and
frequently as less important than the content of the thought itself.
This manner of speaking, furthermore, is familiar and useful in
very many contexts. The validity of Pythagoras's theorem (about

the square on the hypotenuse), for example, does not depend on Pythagoras actually having been the person who proposed it. One might even take the line that the theorem in some sense already existed, before it was proposed; it just took Pythagoras to recognize it. All of this points to the fact that we frequently *do* distance ourselves from our thoughts, and others' thoughts from their authors.

But there seems to be something different between talking of thoughts in formal or abstract terms, and suggesting that my subjective or sensory experience just 'exists' by itself, and is in no sense 'had' by me. This is very disturbing, but perhaps less because of what it implies about the experience itself than because of what it implies about *me*. Quite simply, a 'no-ownership' theory of thought undercuts our concept of self. Far from demonstrating the existence of a mind distinct from a body, Descartes's argument makes the concept of mind redundant. Once we allow for the possibility of disembodied *thoughts* and experiences (or indeed insist that these thoughts are the only things of which we can be certain), we add nothing by trying to insist that these thoughts belong to a disembodied *mind*. Descartes ascribed thoughts to a disembodied mind, rather than leave acts of thought without an agent, but of this mind we are effectively told nothing, except that its essence is to think.

In fact, the incoherence of the 'disembodied mind' position follows rather directly from some of the issues already raised. The claim that my ability to think of something 'without logical contradiction' establishes the 'something's' existence is wrong on numerous counts. It is clear that my ability to imagine flying saucers is no kind of proof whatsoever that they exist; imaginability is not a sufficient condition of reality. Nor is imaginability a necessary condition of reality − a first test that must be passed before other criteria are satisfied. Most of the phenomena of quantum mechanics (as we shall see in chapter 5) are quite unimaginable on the basis of our ordinary experience and require descriptions of physical reality which, on any classical account, would be logically contradictory. Indeed, contradictoriness itself may depend on different criteria within different contexts, broadly defined.

A mind that 'has need of no place'?

To argue that a 'disembodied mind' can exist, we must do more than say that it is all we are left with when we have got rid of everything that we could doubt. We have to say what kind of existence we are claiming for it, if not in the real physical world of space and time. In practice, our test of the reality of anything is to demand that it interacts in some way with other things that we already take to be real. A mirage of a great lake across the desert plain is *not* a real lake, since it recedes and disappears as we move towards it. The tests on which we rely are not infallible, as any good conjurer can demonstrate. But if we see a cherry *and* touch it *and* taste it, we are as sure as can be that it is a real cherry. With slightly more difficulty, we can think of an electric current as 'real', since it powers the 'real' light we see. But can a mind be 'real', or 'exist', in the same way as a cherry or (perhaps more comparably) an electric current?

If we allow the mind to interact with real occupants of space–time, then it must in some sense be real. If so, however, it must be *part* of space–time; it must have *some* physical instantiation. We can remain agnostic, for the time being at least, over the form of this instantiation: whether we are talking about a 'thing', a 'process', a 'pattern of events', a combination of 'particles' or of 'waves', or in the language of quantum theory, a superposition of alternative states or descriptions. But we cannot account for such interactions and still claim that the mind is disembodied, in the sense of belonging to a separate world. If, on the other hand, the mind does not interact at all with anything else we take as real, we will simply be unable to describe it at all, to say in what sense it 'exists', or to make any sensible statement regarding the content of our thoughts.

We can only describe our thoughts, and hence our mind, by reference to a shared physical reality. We cannot shunt our mind off to some separate 'spirit world' and still keep physical reality as something we can think about. Furthermore, the *way* we think about physical reality is manifestly from the dominant perspective of our (that is, our body's) location in space and time. So where else could we possibly locate our mind, except in our body?

'But surely,' you may say, 'the answer's obvious. Our minds are in our brains. What's all the fuss about?' Well, once upon a time there could have been some fuss over whether it was the brain, or the heart, or stomach, or spleen, or some other bit of innards. Even now it is far from agreed exactly what functions are performed by each *part* of the brain. But the real fuss is not over whether physiological knowledge is useful; it is over whether it addresses the conceptual point at issue. If we want to regard mental events as distinct from physical ones in some fundamental sense, it is just as difficult to locate them *physically* in the brain as, say, under one's left knee-cap. (Indeed, it would not be entirely facetious to argue that part of your mind *is* under your left knee-cap, as well as in all other parts of your body with neural connections to your brain). We are also left with a host of problems (about which philosophers have written at great length) concerning how anything that happens in physical space can cause an event in the mind (i.e. 'outside' physical space). Likewise, there is the question how we can lift our arm (thus producing a change in physical space) through some kind of 'act of will'. In short, if the mental and the physical are distinct worlds, how can they impinge on one another?

Mind–brain identity

Nowadays, we like to think of ourselves (in psychology at least!) as more sophisticated and less prone to spiritualist superstitions. When asked what the mind is, or where it is, one of the commonest strategies is to attempt to *identify* the mind with the brain. To say 'Our minds are *in* our brains' may be a step in the right direction, but it still seems to contain the vestiges of a dualistic way of thinking. If we were actually to look *inside* a brain (assuming, for the sake of argument, that we could do so without killing the person concerned), there would be no single piece of tissue that we could pick up with our tweezers and say 'Look, here's the mind!'. All we would see would be parts of the brain to which neuroanatomists have given long and colourful names. The inescapable conclusion has to be that we can find no separate physical *thing* called a mind, over and above the parts of the brain (or body) already identified by other names. So (no great surprise!) we say that the mind *is* what we have already identified as the brain – they are one and the same thing.

Thus, instead of talking loosely about our minds being *in* our brains, we tend to assert more strongly: 'Our minds *are* our brains' or 'Mental events *are* brain events'. Often it is unclear exactly what kind of identity is being claimed in such statements. There is a non-doctrinaire form of the claim, however, which can be accepted easily without further ado: we need our brains to be able to think, and thinking is what our brains do. I could wheel in a whole mass of evidence to show that people and other animals think differently if their brains are damaged or altered in some way (e.g. through the use of drugs), but this is not a general text on neuroscience. If all we sought from such observations was an answer to the general question of whether 'minds' could exist and operate independently of 'brains', the response would be an emphatic, repetitive and boringly predictable 'No'.

Would anyone seriously have imagined anything different? Well, Descartes might have done, for one. But even if such physiological evidence might have given Descartes some pause for thought, it is unlikely that it would have changed his fundamental point of view. To disprove the dualist position *empirically* is as impossible as offering empirical proof of a universal proposition (All minds are brains), or, if you prefer, of a negative proposition (There is no mind that isn't a brain; or, more familiarly: There are no such things as ghosts). There is an asymmetry in the burden of empirical proof. It only takes one ghost (but it has to be a *real* one!) to prove the claims of spiritualists and hence of dualists. Descartes, though, did not look for empirical proof, but depended instead on the notion that, if you can *think* of the mind distinct from the body (or brain), then the mind and body in some real sense *are* distinct. Descartes might well have looked at the recent evidence and accepted that *living creatures* think with their brains in the same sense that they see with their eyes, but *still* have argued that the mind was distinct from the brain *conceptually*.

I have argued, though, that Descartes places too much existential weight on this conceptual distinction. To say that brain and mind are different *concepts* does not mean that they are different *things*, still less that one is material and the other immaterial. It certainly does not commit us to placing the mind outside the real world of space and time. Nor does it preclude the possibility that finding out more about the brain may tell us something about the mind that we could not as adequately explain before. But it does, quite rightly, imply that *the things we can say about our mind* are very different kinds of statements indeed from the kinds of things we can say about our bodies, or even our brains. There have been a variety of attempts to reconcile this observation with the position that mind and brains are somehow the same.

Levels of description

Within philosophy, a more recent tradition has argued for the view that 'mental' statements can describe the same events as 'brain' statements, but at a different level of conceptual analysis. Descriptions at different levels are a familiar feature of everyday language. A statement such as 'I'm getting myself a cup of coffee' describes a whole series of separate sequences of physical acts and movements that could be specified at a more miniscule level of detail (I'm going to stand up out of my chair; turn towards the door; put my right foot forward . . .). There is a sense in which the higher-order description depends on the lower-order description: if I make no movement from my chair (barring undeserved assistance from someone else!), I will not get my coffee. Similarly, the phrase 'getting my coffee' does not describe anything *other than* my movements in terms of rising from my chair, etc. (although some of these movements will certainly be more specifically identifiable as to do with coffee-getting than will others).

This approach offers an apparently neat way of handling the fact that thought is a physical as well as mental activity without needing actually to describe thought in physical terms. The firing of neurons stands to thought in the same relation as my walking across the room (etc.) stands to my getting some coffee. It is absolutely essential in a causal or physical sense, and absolutely superfluous (or so it is claimed) to the logic of the higher-order description. In short, I can accept that it happens, and then happily ignore it. There is little incentive (for philosophers) to 'reduce' mental statements to brain statements, since brain statements are simply not available at anything like the level of analysis required. Furthermore, no philosopher will be held responsible if the required brain statements fail to be provided.

There is another, closely related, reason why mind–brain identity poses no real threat to those who prefer to talk about thought at a different level of description from the brain (as indeed we almost all do, almost all the time). This is that the brain is, for most practical purposes, at least as unobservable and unfathomable as is the mind in any dualist philosophy. We can claim that we have put thoughts and feelings into the real physical world and located them in space and time. But we are still not much better off, if at all, when it comes to *observing* them, or indeed accounting for the whole classical collection of mind–body interaction problems, such as my ability to move my arm through an act of will.

Brain functions and mental statements

Within psychology (broadly defined), opinions vary regarding the priority that should be attached to explicit descriptions of the

workings of the brain. As a consequence, the route beyond acceptance of the central thesis of mind–brain identity can take a number
of different directions. One of these, which might be characterized
as the 'brain-reading' route, seems to rest on an article of faith that
research in the neurosciences will lead us, sooner or later, to the
point where we will be able to translate statements about a person's
thoughts precisely into statements about his or her brain activity,
and *vice versa*. In other words, it is assumed, not just that any
mental event is also a brain event, but that any such brain event
will be readily identifiable for what it is. A one-to-one correspondence is assumed to exist, and be in principle discoverable, between
every electrically recorded piece of brain activity and every subjectively reported thought or feeling.

We should pause and consider just what is required here. It is
not just a matter of being able to tell whether someone is awake, or
dreaming, or in a more or less dreamless sleep. It is not a matter of
using measures of brain activity to identify possible neurological
damage or psychiatric disorder. It is not even a matter of detecting
how tense or relaxed someone is when answering the questions
of an interrogator. It is like being able to look at a brain-scan and
determine the *contents* of someone's thoughts, to be able to put
electrodes onto your head and get an interpretable read-out of your
visual images or inner speech. To anyone who seriously thinks this
is possible, there is only one answer: try it and see!

Another popular route is to accept that what the mind is and can
be depends on what the brain can do, but thereafter ignore all
neurophysiological considerations. Mental states and events are
to be described in their own terms, without 'reference back' to
descriptions in terms of brain processes. This is similar to the 'levels
of description' position held by many philosophers. A strong version of this approach is a belief that it is psychologically irrelevant
to establish quite *how*, in physical terms, the brain goes about the
business of being a mind. Sigmund Freud (1922, p. 329) provides
an eloquent example of this point of view when distinguishing his
approach to the study of anxiety from that adopted by 'academic
medicine':

> Interest there centres upon the anatomical processes by which the
> anxiety condition comes about. We learn that the medulla oblongata
> is stimulated, and the patient is told that he is suffering from a neu-
> rosis in the vagal nerve. The medulla oblongata is a wondrous and
> beauteous object; I will remember how much time and labour I devoted

to the study of it years ago. But to-day I must say I know of nothing less important for the psychological comprehension of anxiety than a knowledge of the nerve-paths by which the excitations travel.

A weaker version rests on the view that the brain is so flexible that all plausible hypotheses about mental processes are equally permissible on neurophysiological grounds. An analogy is often drawn with the distinction between computer software and hardware: the brain is the hardware, and can accept programs in a whole variety of alternative (software) languages if set up appropriately. Theories of mental processes can therefore confine themselves to descriptions of the software alone. This is appealing from a pragmatic point of view. We can get on with the business of describing thoughts and behaviour without worrying how the brain makes it all possible. This is the approach taken in many areas of psychology. However, it has one limitation: we cannot use anything we know about the brain to distinguish between different theories, or to help us build better ones.

In search of post-dualist theories

But what counts as a 'better' theory? In terms of the software— hardware distinction, computer programs are not 'true' or 'false', they merely produce accurate or inaccurate output. The only way of distinguishing whether one logically coherent program is 'better' than another is to see if it makes more correct predictions with respect to a particular criterion within particular contexts. This implies that there is no basis for preferring one psychological theory to another, unless their predictions differ. Indeed this is how we test theories most of the time (or at least how we claim to do so). However, it is not uncommon to come across circumstances where an effect is equally well predicted by two different theories. When this happens, we tend to consider one theory to be preferable to the other because it is more general and parsimonious, and makes fewer *ad hoc* assumptions. Such a choice can feel at least as aesthetic as it is empirical, and is perhaps not unlike computer programmers deciding that one program is neater and more economical than another. There are times, however, where the problem may not be just one of writing a better program within a given language, but of developing a radically new programming language for a particular set of problems. In these circumstances, some regard for the capabilities of a given hardware system must surely be advantageous.

The issues raised by Descartes's assertion of a mind–body distinction are therefore still very much alive, although the debate has moved on in a number of different directions. For most of us nowadays, there is less investment in establishing the existence of minds and/or bodies on the basis of principles of reason. The basic thesis of mind–brain identity is taken very much for granted, religion and other superstitions notwithstanding. How we should *use* such knowledge of mind–brain identity, however, is far less agreed. Even if minds and brains have an identical *physical* reference, our knowledge of brains as brains is neither similar in kind nor comparable in extensiveness to our knowledge of minds as minds. The task of translating the one kind of knowledge into the other is so difficult – both technically and conceptually – that, for most purposes, it is almost certainly not worth the effort. We might as well act as though our knowledge of the mind were wholly distinct from our knowledge of the brain. Descartes goes further than this, of course, in asserting that the mind is *actually* distinct from the brain. Perhaps, though, this extra step of his makes little difference when it comes to communicating such knowledge: we anyway need to talk about thoughts at a different level of description from when we talk about bodies.

There is a vital difference, none the less, between merely communicating knowledge and accounting for its possibility. To report, or even explain, a thought is not the same as to explain how thought occurs. Explaining processes of thought (or trying to do so) is psychologists' stock in trade. Diagrams abound to represent how one particular kind of thought can lead to another. But what kind of processes can such diagrams or models reflect, if not physical ones, dependent ultimately on connections between different brain events? If we take the thesis of mind–brain identity seriously, then a theory of thought, and hence a theory of self, or of attitude, must also be a physical theory. This does not mean that the descriptive language or terminology of these theories need or should be neurochemical (any more than a neurochemical theory need or should be defined within the terminology of attitude research). Different levels of description will still be needed, but these will not pertain to 'wholly distinct' objects and events. Sometimes, even, descriptions at one level may help clarify problems at another. But these are implications that have rarely been taken to heart. There has been less emphasis than one might expect within psychology on *using* the 'fact' of mind–

brain identity, or more generally of the instantiation of ourselves as physical objects in time and space, in order to build better theories. For much of what it conventionally does, psychology might as well be dualist or Cartesian, and might indeed be better for admitting it. But this is not where the future lies.

3

Experience and Identity

Truth and observation

Although much of psychology may be closer to Descartes's dualism than it would readily admit, it is in the philosophy of empiricism that the intellectual roots of the discipline are mainly to be found. If psychology is the study of thought and action, where do our thoughts 'come from' and where do our actions 'go'? If we have knowledge, how do we come by it, and what is it knowledge *of*? Descartes sought to distinguish truth from doubtful supposition, but found himself able to doubt so much, even the evidence of his senses, that he fell back on the notion of 'clear and distinct ideas' to account for his own feelings of certainty and uncertainty. Where could such ideas and feelings come from? Judging from their perfection, no doubt from God. To the empiricists (even those among them who espoused orthodox religion), this still smacked of an appeal to a higher authority, rather than to reason and experience, as a criterion for judging truth: it could thus undercut the very enlightenment to which Descartes himself was so committed.

The revolution had to be carried further, and the supremacy of reason and experience asserted even more emphatically: what we know is what we have learned, truth is a matter of evidence, and evidence is provided by our senses. If we want to establish whether or not something is the case, we go and look. We use observation, with all its faults, to determine the truth of things; so any statement we take to be true must be based in some way on our observations. With this established, we can go further and investigate how observational knowledge may be organized to form more general categories and higher-order concepts, including our concepts of self and identity.

Locke and the reality of experience

John Locke (1632–1704), though far from being a full-time academic, can legitimately be regarded as the founding father of empiricism. His major work, *An Essay Concerning Human Understanding*, was published quite late in his life (1690). It was composed over a long period of time, and is comparatively loosely structured. Indeed, Locke himself admits (in his Epistle to the Reader) 'I will not deny but possibly it might be reduced to a narrower compass than it is ... But to confess the truth, I am now too lazy, or too busy, to make it shorter'.

The principal aim of the *Essay* was to distinguish between different forms of knowledge and belief. For Descartes, nothing could count as knowledge that could not be derived deductively from some self-evident, or *a priori*, premise. What everyday 'good sense' takes as knowledge about the external world is open to doubt and hence only properly regarded as a form of 'belief'. For Locke, this was far from good enough. Distinctions still needed to be drawn between different forms of knowledge and belief about the world, and not simply between *a priori* knowledge and everything else. To this end, he was prepared to acknowledge the existence of *intuitive knowledge* 'when the mind perceives the agreement or disagreement of two ideas *immediately by themselves*, without the intervention of any other' (Book IV, chapter II) – possibly the kind of certainty which Descartes was striving for. He also allows for *demonstrative knowledge*, in which the agreement or disgreement of ideas is not immediately apparent, but requires demonstration or proof (and interestingly, he includes Descartes's example of angles of a triangle within this category).

But by far the most important message of the *Essay* is the assertion that there are no 'innate' ideas or principles in the mind and that all our knowledge and certainty are attained through the use of our 'natural faculties'. While allowing the possibility of 'intuitive knowledge', he disputed the suggestion that we have specific 'clear and distinct' ideas that are universally accepted and from which all other certainty can be derived. His attack on the notion of innate principles seems motivated by a fear of the authoritarian implications of treating such principles as true without demonstration. In other words, he seemed to take it for granted that conceding the innateness of any idea, i.e. its independence from reasoning and evidence, would be tantamount to conceding that it was necessarily true. This is quite different from the way in which 'innate' processes are viewed in modern psychology, where the important question is the contribution of such processes to survival. Likewise, although many researchers in the field of human cognition are prepared to allow for some kind of 'hard-wiring' facilitating the development of particular cognitive skills (e.g. language), this is a long way from any commitment to the notion that any thought influenced by innate processes must be 'true'. One could take the view that we are (sometimes) 'innately' disposed to think along certain lines without taking this to entail anything about the truth of any thoughts we thereby have, but Locke does not seem to make this distinction.

The term 'idea' is probably the most important in all of Locke's writings but is – perhaps for this reason – left loosely defined. Many critics have found fault with Locke by making out that he regarded 'ideas' as pictorial representations of the outside world, perceived through our senses. Such a definition would invite the question of how these representations were themselves 'perceived' and represented, leading to an infinite regress, where we have to represent our representations of representations of representations, and so on. But at least as fair and defensible an interpretation is that Locke was simply using the term 'idea' to refer to the content of thought (whether imagistic or otherwise). Book II of the *Essay* starts in these terms:

> Every man being conscious to himself that he thinks, and that which his mind is applied about being the *ideas* that are there, it is past doubt that men have in their minds several ideas, such as are those expressed by the words 'whiteness', 'hardness', 'sweetness', 'thinking', 'motion', 'man', 'elephant', 'army', 'drunkenness', and others . . .

This identification of ideas with the ordinary meaning of language, so familiar to twentieth-century philosophy, seems to have been a position that Locke almost fell into, without perhaps fully realizing the significance, or need for explication, of what he was saying. In later correspondence with his critic, Edward Stillingfleet, Bishop of Worcester, he affirmed more explicitly that 'the new way of ideas, and the old way of speaking intelligibly, was always, and ever will be, the same thing.' He then defines 'speaking intelligibly' as involving a person using signs of the 'objects of his mind in thinking', combined into propositions and thence into coherent discourse, so that these ideas ('objects of mind') can be made known to another. First, however, Locke was concerned with how we come by the ideas that we have. He had argued that there were no innate ideas, so what was left? The argument of Book II develops:

> Let us then suppose the mind to be, as we say, white paper, void of all characters, without any ideas; how comes it to be furnished? . . . To this I answer, in one word, from *experience*. In that all our knowledge is founded, and from that it ultimately derives itself. Our observation employed either about external sensible objects, or about the internal operations of our minds perceived and reflected on by ourselves, is that which supplies our understandings with all the materials of thinking. These two are the fountains of knowledge, from whence all the ideas we have, or can naturally have, do spring.

The parting of the ways from Descartes could hardly have been more sharply stated. The only kind of knowledge we can have is the very kind that Descartes strived so strenuously to deny. Knowledge provided by empirical observation *and by reflection on such observation* (through relating ideas to one another) is not only the best kind of knowledge that is practically available to us, it is also the *only conceivable* kind of knowledge there can be. This position affirms *empirical* inquiry and observation as the basis for advancement in science, a principle which we now, often too complacently, take for granted. It also has many more specific implications for psychology, for issues such as the nature of learning, of cognitive development, and of mental representations.

Continuous existence and identity

Within this approach, then, how do we come to have ideas of *ourselves*? For Descartes, as is well known, our idea of ourself is an immediate, certain, conception of our own conscious mind as something whose essence consists only in thinking, and is entirely separate from our body or any material thing. Locke, by contrast, builds up a view of our understanding of personal identity developing directly out of our understanding of the identity of physical objects. The relevant argument is to be found in Book II, chapter XXVII of the *Essay*, which is entitled 'Of Identity and Diversity'.

Locke starts from the notion that everything exists in a particular time and place, and that no two objects of the same kind can share exactly the same time and place. If something continues in time within the same place, without alteration, we easily regard it as the same thing. This applies to singles atoms and also to collections of atoms to form a single mass: if nothing is added to or subtracted from this mass, it remains the same 'let the parts be never so differently jumbled'. But, as Locke quickly acknowledges, the more difficult problems start when we stop talking about just 'jumbling' atoms, and address the issue of the identity of more complex objects, such as living creatures:

> For in them the variation of great parcels of matter alters not the identity: an oak growing from a plant to a great tree, and then lopped, is still the same oak; and a colt grown to a horse, sometimes fat, sometimes lean, is all the while the same horse . . . The reason whereof is that in these two cases – a mass of matter and a living body – identity is not applied to the same thing . . .
>
> We must therefore consider wherein an oak differs from a mass of matter, and that seems to me to be in this, that the one is only the cohesion of matter however united, the other such a disposition of them . . . in which consists the vegetable life. That being then one plant which has such an organization of parts in one coherent body, partaking of one common life, it continues to be the same plant as long as it partakes of the same life, though that life be communicated to new particules of matter . . .
>
> The case is not much different in *brutes* . . .
>
> This also shows wherein the identity of the same *man* consists: viz. in nothing but a participation of the same continued life, by constantly fleeting particles of matter, in succession vitally united to the same organized body. He that shall place the identity of man in anything else, but, like that of other animals, in one fitly organized body . . . will find it hard to make an embryo, one of years, mad and sober, the same man . . . For if the identity of *soul alone* makes the same *man* . . . men, living in distant ages, and of different tempers, may have been the same man; which way of speaking must be from a very strange use of the word *man*, applied to an idea out of which body and shape are excluded . . .
>
> For I presume it is not the idea of a thinking or rational being alone that makes the idea of a man in most people's sense, but of a body, so and so shaped, joined to it . . .

Thus, identity for Locke depended on *material* existence within time and space, and across time and space, insofar as *material* continuity was satisfied. The continued life of living creatures depended somehow on the 'organization of parts' of their bodies – something which he may not have felt in a position to explain more precisely (he talks in places of life as a 'motion'), but which he clearly thought of in *material* terms. He none the less took the view that, where 'ideas' (and this implied, words) can be different, so can be the criteria for identity. He therefore proceeded to draw a distinction between the identity of a *person* and that of a *man* (having distinguished both from the idea of a substance), while acknowledging that 'in the ordinary way of speaking', these 'stand for one and the same thing'. Essential to the identity of a person was the notion of consciousness, and particularly consciousness of oneself and of one's own past experiences:

> ... to find wherein personal identity consists, we must consider what person stands for; which I think, is a thinking intelligent being, that has reason and reflection, and can consider itself as itself, the same thinking thing, in different times and places ... For, since consciousness always accompanies thinking, and it is that that makes everyone to be what he calls self, and thereby distinguishes himself from all other thinking things, in this alone consists personal identity, i.e. the sameness of a rational being; and as far as this consciousness can be extended backwards to any past action or thought, so far reaches the identity of that person ...

Locke then toys somewhat discursively with problems of interrupted consciousness, waking and dreaming, and even the possibility of reincarnation, in ways that come near to undercutting his previous insistence on the importance of a continuing living body (for the identity of a man). The more recurrent themes, however, are those of what it *feels* like to be oneself, the ownership of one's own thoughts and emotions, and the question of personal responsibility for one's actions. All these require 'consciousness' – which sounds more and more like a form of memory rather than momentary awareness – to link past existence with the present. This leads him to the following conclusion, rich in half-explored suggestions:

> Wherever a man finds what he calls himself, there, I think, another may say is the same person. It is a forensic term, appropriating actions and their merit, and so belongs only to intelligent agents, capable of a law, and happiness, and misery. This personality extends itself beyond present existence to what is past, only by consciousness ... All which is founded in a concern for happiness, the unavoidable concomitant of consciousness ...

Thus, Locke proposes a materialist basis for the 'identity of man' as a continuously living creature, but grapples more speculatively with the notion of 'personal' identity, which he regards as bound up with concepts of the self and of consciousness. Since consciousness can manifestly be interrupted, there are problems – which Locke recognizes more clearly than does Descartes, but to which he fails to offer a real solution – of talking about the *same* continued consciousness existing across different times. Although he regards the mind as 'joined' to the body, he does not seem to go as far as treating the mind itself as a living thing, or as 'partaking of one common life' with other parts of the body. Hence, in trying to define the identity of the person or self, he does not rely simply on continuous bodily existence, but, insisting on his man–person distinction, invokes the notion of conscious awareness, together with an implication of some kind of 'ownership' of one's thoughts, actions and memories.

Hume and the principles of association

David Hume (1711–76) is probably the greatest of the empiricist philosophers and certainly the most congenial in his approach from the point of view of modern research into human cognition. Frustratingly, however, he was rather unforthcoming with regard to issues of the self and of personal identity, with the exception of a famous passage (which I shall discuss shortly) in his first book, *A Treatise of Human Nature*. He was far less concerned with what the mind can be said to be than with what it *does* and how it does it. Human understanding depends upon the experience of our senses and the operation of our reason, the latter depending on the association or connection of ideas, which themselves are derived from experience.

Hume lists three principles whereby ideas can be associated with each other: *resemblance*, *contiguity*, and *causation* (also referred to as cause and effect). The last of these is the most difficult, but also the most important. Taking a similar starting point to Locke's, Hume distinguishes abstract reasoning, concerning 'relations of ideas', from experimental reasoning concerning 'matters of fact'. The first enables the truths of mathematics to be 'intuitively or demonstratively certain' (*Enquiry Concerning the Human Understanding*, section IV, chapter I). Evidence for matters of fact, however, do not have the same kind of certainty, since their contraries (e.g. 'the sun will not rise tomorrow') can be asserted without logical contradiction. ('Whatever *is* may *not be*. No negation of fact can involve a contradiction'). Our acceptance of matters of fact as true therefore depends on a form of inference, that is, inductive rather than deductive reasoning.

Despite his regarding all empirical knowledge as inferential, Hume is very sparing in his scepticism, and the lengths to which he allows his doubts to lead him. Of some matters, such as religious dogma, he was extremely doubtful, but not of the existence of material things. Excessive scepticism, such as of the Cartesian variety, he regards as 'entirely incurable' and self-defeating. Thus an excessive sceptic 'must acknowledge, if he will acknowledge anything, that all human life must perish were his principles universally and steadily to prevail' (*Enquiry*, XII, II). Instead of the principle of 'universal doubt', he proposes a 'mitigated scepticism' directed at emphasizing the probabilistic or relativistic nature of our beliefs. 'The greater part of mankind are naturally apt to be affirmative and dogmatical in their opinions... nor have they any indulgence for those who entertain opposite sentiments' (*Enquiry*, XII, III). The probabilistic basis of our beliefs about material objects resides, for Hume, not in the possibility of doubting whether they exist at all, but in the indirectness of experience, wherein 'nothing can ever be present to the mind but an image or perception' (*Enquiry*, XII, I). His scepticism extends to the point of asserting that there is nothing in an image or sensation *per se* that establishes the existence of a material object that is perceived. Such existence can only be inferred from the relations of ideas and perceptions to each other, in particular from observed relations of cause and effect:

> The existence, therefore, of any being can only be proved by arguments from its cause or its effect, and these arguments are founded entirely on experience. If we reason *a priori*, anything may appear able to produce anything. The falling of a pebble may, for aught we know, extinguish the sun, or the wish of a man control the planets in their orbits. It is only experience which teaches us the nature and bounds of cause and effect and enables us to infer the existence of one object from that of another. Such is the foundation of moral reasoning, which forms the greater part of human knowledge and is the source of all human action and behaviour. (*Enquiry*, XII, III)

What then is this relation of cause and effect? According to Hume, causation is inferred when 'An object being followed by another, and where all objects similar to the first are followed by objects similar to the second.' In other words, what is essential is the constant succession of one class of objects upon another. Recognition of this relation is facilitated if similar causes have been observed to lead to similar effects ('resemblance') and if the cause and effect occur close to each other in time and place ('contiguity'). But – and this Hume stresses – there is nothing logically necessary about this inferred connection; put differently, it is a product of inductive rather than deductive reasoning. Hume's main logical point is that there is no basis, *a priori*, for asserting that 'a cause is always necessary', i.e. that nothing can exist without an antecedent cause. In that we can conceive of a cause and an effect as distinct, we can, without contradiction, imagine one existing without the other. Therefore, the existence of a cause for any given effect is a *matter of fact* that can only be asserted on the basis of experience.

A common misconception of Hume's thesis is that he was *defining* causality as merely the constant succession of one object upon another. A fairly standard critique then runs along the following lines: there is more to our concept of causality than mere succession (e.g. concepts of physical force or of deliberate intention) and his 'definition' is therefore incomplete. Furthermore, lots of objects or events may follow one another without being causally related (and resemble each other, or occur together, as a matter of mere coincidence), so his 'principles' have no justification in logic. Most importantly, his 'principles' remove the possibility of knowledge of the external world, since the causal dependence of experience on reality can never be established *by* experience.

Granted, one of the shakiest sections of Hume's philosophy is his discussion of sensory impressions as 'images' which are 'present to the mind', and especially his notion of the 'resemblance' of impressions to material objects. But, to a large extent, the standard critique merely reiterates points that Hume himself was making. Causality *as ordinarily conceived*, with its connotations of some kind of motive force, is not *entailed* by experience, that is, by any empirical evidence. That is precisely the point of Hume's denial of a 'necessary connection'. Similarly, Hume himself accepts (e.g. *Enquiry*, XII, I) that neither reason nor experience can establish, as necessary and beyond the reach of any *philosophical* doubt, the existence of a material world corresponding to the impressions of our senses.

It is Hume's response to this impasse, however, that is simultaneously so infuriating to many philosophers but so engaging to many psychologists. If these philosophical doubts are incurable and unanswerable, *we shouldn't try to answer them*, since nothing follows from them. Indeed any proposed answers 'can contain nothing but sophistry and illusion' (as he robustly concludes the *Enquiry*), except where they are derived from 'abstract reasoning concerning quantity or number' or 'experimental reasoning concerning matter of fact and existence'.

Abstract or *a priori* reasoning concerning fact and existence was a route down which Hume was not prepared to travel. His interest was not in 'pure reason' or 'universal truths' (unlike Kant), but (borrowing phrases from his titles) in *human* nature and *human* understanding. The question Hume *was* prepared to tackle was 'how experience gives rise to such a principle [of causation]' (*Treatise*, I.III). *How* we think is an empirical – indeed a psychological – question, a 'matter of fact'. Hume's principles of association are his proposed answer to this question, and the adequacy of this answer must be judged, according to his own criteria, by *experimental* reasoning.

No simple idea of self

Hume was very much concerned, therefore, with both the processes and the products of human thought. However, he differed sharply from both Descartes and Locke in refusing to accept the notion of the mind or the self as a distinct entity whose existence was immediately apparent and beyond the possibility of doubt. The crucial argument is presented in the *Treatise* I.VI, but is not reproduced in the *Enquiry* (which in most other respects is a reworking of the *Treatise*). This is what he has to say:

> There are some philosophers, who imagine we are every moment intimately conscious of what we call our Self; that we feel its existence and its continuance in existence; and are certain, beyond the evidence of a demonstration, both of its perfect identity and simplicity . . .
>
> Unluckily all these positive assertions are contrary to that very experience, which is pleaded for them, nor have we any idea of *self*, after the manner it is here explained . . . If any impression gives rise to the idea of self, that impression must continue invariably the same, through the whole course of our lives; since self is supposed to exist after that manner. But there is no impression constant and invariable. Pain and pleasure, grief and joy, passions and sensations succeed

each other, and never all exist at the same time. It cannot therefore
be from any of these impressions, or from any other, that the idea of
self is derived; and consequently there is no such impression.

But farther, what must become of all our particular perceptions
upon this hypothesis? ... After what manner ... do they belong to
the self; and how are they connected with it? For my part, when I
enter most intimately into what I call *myself*, I always stumble on
some particular perception or other, of heat or cold, light or shade,
love or hatred, pain or pleasure. I never catch *myself* at any time
without a perception, and can never observe any thing but the
perception ...

We are therefore left with

nothing but a bundle or collection of different perceptions, which
succeed each other with an inconceivable rapidity, and are in perpetual flux and movement ... The mind is a kind of theatre, where
several perceptions successively make their appearance; pass, re-pass,
glide away, and mingle in an infinite variety of postures and situations. There is properly no *simplicity* in it at one time, nor *identity*
in different; whatever natural propension we may have to imagine
that simplicity and identity. The comparison of the theatre must not
mislead us. They are the successive perceptions only, that constitute
the mind ...

Hume then asks:

What then gives us so great a propension to ascribe an identity to
these successive perceptions, and to suppose ourselves possessed of
an invariable and uninterrupted existence throught the whole course
of our lives?

His answer, depending as we might expect on his principles of
association, covers much of the same ground as Locke's, but arrives
at a different conclusion. Like Locke, Hume uses the example of
continuity of biological life ('An oak, that grows from a small plant
to a large tree, is still the same oak'), but he links this 'continuity'
with his own principles of association. Thus, the identity we ascribe to 'the same oak' depends on the association of *ideas*. This
enables him to assert, unlike Locke, that the issue of personal identity
can be settled in the same way as the issue of biological identity.
In other words, he does not follow Locke into the 'man-person'
distinction, but insists that the identity of self or mind is to be
decided in the same way as that of other living things. The price he

pays is accepting that all such forms of identity are 'fictitious', that is, a product of thought.

> The identity, which we ascribe to the mind of man, is only a fictitious one, and of a like kind with that which we ascribe to vegetable and animal bodies. It cannot, therefore, have a different origin, but must proceed from a like operation of the imagination upon like objects.

This 'operation of the imagination' is described as a running of 'several different perceptions into one', but this does *not* require the assumption that there is 'something that really binds our several perceptions together'. This is part of Hume's more general argument that 'the understanding never observes any real connexion between objects, and that even the union of cause and effect, when strictly examined, resolves itself into a customary association of ideas.' However, Hume does not seem to regard identity as merely a subjective matter, as is shown by how he deals with the issue of memory. Although he did not share Locke's view of the self as something of which we are constantly and unproblematically aware, he was none the less prepared, unlike Locke, to attribute a continuity to personal identity that was *not* vulnerable, as Locke had argued, to lapses of memory and awareness.

> As memory alone acquaints us with the continuance and extent of this succession of perceptions, it is to be considered, upon that account chiefly, as the source of personal identity. Had we no memory, we never should have any notion of causation, nor consequently of that chain of causes and effects, which constitute our self or person. But having once acquired this notion of causation from the memory, we can extend the same chain of causes, and consequently the identity of our persons beyond our memory, and can comprehend times, and circumstances, and actions, which we have entirely forgot, but suppose in general to have existed . . . In this view, therefore, memory does not so much *produce* as *discover* personal identity, by showing us the relation of cause and effect among our different perceptions.

In order to interpret, and not overinterpret, what Hume is saying, we must remember the context in which he was developing his argument. The major issue for him was not as such with what it feels like to be a person, or with the nature of consciousness. Like other philosophers of his own, and most other, periods, his principal concern was with the nature of knowledge and the basis for distinguishing truth and falsehood. A major part of this concern is with the status of sensory perception as evidence of reality. Locke, Hume and other empiricists were not prepared to accept Descartes's line that philosophical advance required the distrust of all sensory evidence. On the other hand, there is an important distinction between trusting or accepting evidence, and regarding the empirical knowledge so acquired as beyond the reach of any conceivable contradiction. Hume had no patience with attempts actually to doubt the reality of the external world, and was less prepared even than Locke to entertain the possibility of minds existing apart from bodies. But he was still at pains to stress that empirical evidence did not carry the force of logical necessity.

It is perhaps difficult for us to appreciate the importance, at the time, of such an emphasis. We take it for granted that knowledge about the world, albeit imperfect, can be acquired, not only from our own experience, but also from scientific experiments and statistical inference. We do not (hopefully) have to argue with people who maintain that truth can *only* be found through reading the bible or constructing syllogisms according to the rules of Aristotle. Hume proposed his principles of association as his answer to the question of how we come to have such (albeit imperfect) knowledge of 'matters of fact'. This is where many of his critics have been in a rush to dismiss his approach as obviously flawed: if you can't logically derive truth from an idea, you can't do so either from any combination of ideas in association with each other, and you can't take any particular form of association as more representative of truth than any other – thus we are left no nearer empirical truth than we were before. But such criticisms miss Hume's point. He was the first to accept that he was offering no logical derivation, no *guarantee*, for 'matters of fact'. What he was trying to do was to *explain* how we come to have the kinds of beliefs we do about matters of fact. In other words, he was attempting something that deserves to be taken seriously as a piece of *psychology* rather than what has often passed as philosophy.

So when Hume talks about personal identity, the mind or self, as 'fictitious', he is essentially denying Descartes's first principle, that our mind, self or soul is something of which we are immediately and distinctly aware and whose existence it is impossible to doubt. From this denial, Hume takes us in two, far from obviously compatible, directions. The first is to assert that we can only conceive of consciousness in terms of its contents – that there is nothing that we can recognize as our conscious mind apart from our conscious thoughts themselves. The second is to treat personal identity as a matter to be settled on the same basis as the identity of any other living thing, animal or vegetable. If one can assume continuity of cause and effect, one can ascribe identity, regardless of the imperfection of memory. And although Hume still regards cause and effect as a customary association of ideas, this is no more damaging to the identity we ascribe to minds than to that which we ascribe to bodies.

The self: distinctive or elusive?

Thus, we see in the work of Descartes, Locke and Hume an unfinished debate concerning the nature of the self and of self-knowledge. Descartes took as the first principle of his philosophy the certainty of his own existence, that is, of the existence of his own conscious mind whose essence was to think. Beside the clearness and distinctiveness of this certainty, all other knowledge was open to doubt. But Descartes was not really on the track of his self, or mind, or soul, when he hit upon this principle. He was searching for something – anything – of which he could 'see' the truth with an immediate, non-inferential, and non-derivative certainty. One might even regard his dualism – his insistence on the separation of body and mind – as a serendipitous by-product of this search. At any rate, it would allow a much easier reconciliation of his approach with contemporary ways of thinking, if such an interpretation were sustainable.

As one benefit of such a reconciliation, renewed respect could be given to his suggestion that we can be certain of at least some truth without deliberate invocation of analytic or empirical procedures. However, it is far from obvious that this something must be our own personal identity or self, in the *full* sense in which these concepts are more often used. Indeed, Descartes was saying just this, in denying the necessity of our bodily existence. Likewise, he was not claiming that it was self-evident that the mind continued to exist, as the same mind, beyond the instant of awareness. Paradoxically, he was not saying anything very particular about the mind or the self at all. But he *was* claiming that it makes sense to talk about self-evidence, as distinct from evidence.

The empiricists, by contrast, start by acknowledging the possibility of 'intuitive' knowledge, as in mathematics, but then direct their efforts to the defence and understanding of *evidence*. The proposition that any statement on 'matters of fact' could be accepted as true in the absence of evidence was, for both Locke and Hume, not only wrong but sinister. Locke insisted that we could have no ideas, or thoughts, except on the basis of evidence of our senses. Digressing (almost) into the question of identity, he inferred that some notion of continuity could provide a basis for the idea of objects and creatures retaining an identity despite change in their physical constituents. When faced with the issue of personal identity (as opposed to the 'identity of man'), he goes some of the way with Descartes in assuming 'consciousness' to be a necessary part of thinking, and seems to imply that such consciousness involves self-reflection. Locke is less clear, however, regarding what idea of self it is upon which one can reflect. Moreover, where consciousness (and hence 'ideas') are absent or interrupted, so, for Locke, is the self.

Hume takes Locke's argument further, to ask if there is any 'self' of which we have a simple, or clear and distinct, idea. He concludes that we do not. We have conscious thoughts, and being conscious means having thoughts. However, he is not prepared to allow an infinite regress in which we are conscious of our consciousness of our consciousness, and so on. We do *not* have a distinct conception of our having thoughts, over and above the thoughts that we are having. A mind, without the thoughts that fill it, is not a self-evident truth. In fact, it is something of which we have no idea or immediate conception whatsoever. None the less, Hume was fully prepared to accept that we actually ascribe an identity to ourselves, and for this he sought to offer what I have argued is an essentially *psychological* explanation. His principles of association are easily reconciled with psychological principles of learning and cognition. We do not have a clear and distinct idea of our *selves*, at least, not just like that. Any notion of personal identity we have is 'fictitious', that is derived from our processing of information and our own learning history. It takes work to derive an identity or self-concept that generalizes at all beyond the specificities of the immediate and fleeting here-and-now, and of the product of such work we should not demand too great a consistency.

The self and the stream of consciousness

At the start of this chapter, I characterized psychology as an empiricist discipline, and have done my best since then to dub

Hume an honorary psychologist. Even so, the actual and potential contributions of the empiricists to psychological theory have typically been underestimated. By contrast, 'everyone knows' that the mind–body problem is one that has stimulated a considerable amount of psychological research. I shall argue, in later chapters, that there is a close affinity between Hume's notion of association of ideas and modern 'connectionist' approaches to cognitive science. Humean features are also recognizable in more established theories of learning and conditioning.

A more explicit bridge between the empiricists and the beginnings of modern psychology, however, is provided by the writings of William James (1842–1910). I shall have more than one occasion to refer to James, so the following is only a brief introduction to some of his more relevant arguments, as put forward in his *Principles of Psychology* (1890).

A dominant theme in James's writings (and one to which contemporary psychology could well pay more attention) is the importance of *time*. In other words, a major task for psychology is to account for change, over time, in our thoughts and feelings. James is almost Cartesian when declaring his starting point:

The first fact for us, then, as psychologists, is that thinking of some sort goes on. (p. 224)

Quickly, though, he moves into an empiricist vein by characterizing how 'thought goes on' in terms of the following five principles:

1 Every thought tends to be part of a personal consciousness.
2 Within each personal consciousness thought is always changing.
3 Within each personal consciousness thought is sensibly continuous.
4 It always appears to deal with objects other than itself.
5 It is interested in some parts of these objects to the exclusion of others, and welcomes or rejects – *chooses* from them, in a word – all the while. (p. 225)

Of these principles, the second and third are most relevant to this chapter. Of the others, the first relates directly to the problems with 'no-ownership' or 'disembodied thought' positions discussed in chapter 2. The fourth and fifth will come into play especially from chapter 6 onwards, although parts of the argument have already been foreshadowed in the mention of selectivity in chapter 1.

The argument that 'thought is in constant change' is elaborated in the following remarks:

> ...no state once gone can recur and be identical with what it was before. (p. 230)
> ...there is no proof that the same bodily sensation is ever got by us twice. What is got twice is the same OBJECT...The sameness of *things* is what we are concerned to ascertain; and any sensations that assure us of that will probably be considered in a rough way to be the same with each other. (p. 231)
> Experience is remoulding us every moment, and our mental reaction on every given thing is really a resultant of our experience of the whole world up to that date. (p. 234)
> No doubt it is *convenient* to formulate the mental facts in an atomistic sort of way, and to treat the higher states of consciousness as if they were built out of unchanging simple ideas...But...we must never forget that we are talking symbolically, and that there is nothing in nature to answer to our words. A permanently existing 'idea' or 'Vorstellung' which makes its appearance before the footlights of consciousness at periodical intervals, is as mythological an entity as the Jack of Spades. (p. 236)

James proceeds to argue that 'thought feels continuous' so that:

> ...even where there is a time-gap the consciousness after it feels as if it belonged together with the consciousness before it, as another part of the same self; and likewise...changes...in the quality of consciousness are never absolutely abrupt.(p. 237)

It is significant that James slides with so little difficulty from talking of the continuity we ascribe to objects, despite changes in our sensations, to the assertion of continuity of the consciousness, or self. The feeling of continuity *in experience of objects* is thus, by implication, what gives consciousness its 'stream-like' quality, and hence the feeling of self-identity. He comes nearer to making this explicit when he writes:

> The words ME, then, and SELF...are OBJECTIVE designations, meaning ALL THE THINGS which have the power to produce in a stream of consciousness excitement of a certain peculiar sort. (p. 319)

Identity and change

Like Hume, James regards memory as vital to the sense of personal identity. James describes the process in the following terms:

Remembrance is like direct feeling; its object is suffused with a warmth and intimacy to which no object of mere conception ever attains. This quality of warmth and intimacy is what . . . *present* thought also possesses for itself. So sure as this present is me, is mine, it says, so sure is anything else that comes with the same warmth and intimacy and immediacy, me and mine . . . whatever past feelings appear with those qualities must be admitted to receive the greeting of the present mental state, to be owned by it, and accepted as belonging together with it in a common self. (p. 239)
The sense of personal identity . . . is the sense of a sameness perceived *by* thought and predicated of things *thought-about*. These things are a present self and a self of yesterday. The thought not only thinks them both, but thinks they are identical. The psychologist . . . might prove the thought wrong, and show there was no real identity . . . but it would exist as a *feeling* all the same . . . (p. 332)
The sense of our own personal identity, then, is exactly like any one of our other perceptions of sameness among phenomena. It is a conclusion grounded either on the resemblance in a fundamental respect, or on the continuity before the mind, of the phenomena compared. (p. 334)

Despite the richness of introspective description, it is hard to see that James is claiming anything new here that is not covered by Hume's principles of association (particularly that of resemblance). Nor does James address here the problems (discussed by Locke and Hume) which lapses or loss of memory raise for concepts of personal identity. What interested him most was the *feeling* of identity that could be expressed in statements such as 'I am the same I, that I was yesterday'. Indeed, James's analysis could be said to remain at an experiential, rather than conceptual, level. None the less, James is frequently at pains to distance himself from Hume:

. . . a necessary consequence of the belief in permanent self-identical psychic facts that absent themselves and recur periodically is the Humian doctrine that our thought is composed of separate independent parts and is not a sensibly continuous stream . . . this doctrine entirely misrepresents the natural appearances . . . . (p. 237)
Consciousness, then, does not appear to itself chopped up in bits. Such words as 'chain' or 'train' do not describe it fitly as it presents itself in the first instance; it flows. A 'river' or a 'stream' are the metaphors by which it is most naturally described. (p. 239)

But how deep really is the division between James and Hume? Hume, it is true, talks of 'that *chain* of causes and effects, which constitute our self or person'. He also talks of 'successive' and 'different' perceptions. But this hardly justifies the claim that Hume sees consciousness as 'chopped up in bits'. Although Hume describes the contents of consciousness as 'nothing but a bundle or collection of different perceptions', he immediately qualifies this by insisting that these perceptions 'succeed each other with an inconceivable rapidity, and are in perpetual flux and movement'. They likewise 'pass, re-pass, glide away, and mingle'.

It seems difficult to make much of a distinction between mental events that are '*sensibly* continuous' and ones which succeed each other with an '*inconceivable* rapidity'. If the rapidity of succession is so fast that it cannot be *conceived*, how could it be *perceived* as discontinuous or 'chopped up in bits'? How many frames per second are required before the pictures on a film appear to *move*? Not that many, as we now know. The distinction between a 'perpetual flux' and a 'continuous stream' seems even more difficult to sustain. Hume also talks of the imagination running 'several different perceptions *into one*' and of personal identity being similar to the kind of continuity of life ascribed to 'vegetable and animal bodies'.

Yet James, who quotes the famous passage from the *Treatise* ('There are some philosophers who imagine . . . etc.'), after commending Hume for a 'good piece of introspective work', promptly rebukes him for defining the self entirely as 'diversity, abstract and absolute' (p. 352). He then pursues his complaint against Hume's followers:

> The chain of distinct experiences into which Hume thus chopped up our 'stream' was adopted by all of his successors as a complete inventory of the facts. The associationist philosophy was founded. Somehow, out of 'ideas', each separate, each ignorant of its mates, but sticking together and calling each other up according to certain laws, all the higher forms of consciousness were to be explained, and among them the consciousness of our personal identity. (p. 353)

But is this talk of 'chopping' fair? Both James and Hume acknowledge that the contents of consciousness are always changing. The stream-like quality of such change is what gives us a sense of identity, according to James. The properties of contiguity, resemblance and constant succession are what allow Hume to ascribe a continued existence to personal identity. Such continuity is, for Hume, a product of the imagination, using the principles of association; but he never claimed that such association was *random* or unpatterned. For James, it is a feeling; but this feeling arises from selectively recognized resemblances between the past and present *objects* of consciousness.

Metaphors are important, none the less. Hume was dissatisfied with his own metaphor of the mind as a theatre. James's metaphor of a 'stream of consciousness' (though anathema to the behaviourists who followed him) has been one of psychology's most enduring catch-phrases. But what physical processes might such a 'stream' represent? Within the framework of modern cognitive science, it could be said to reflect patterns of activation within neural networks. Fair enough, but what kind of patterns? The message from both Hume and James is that these patterns must represent succession or continuity over *time*. They must, in other words, be *dynamical systems*.

Hume's talk of a 'succession' of causes and effects reflects, perhaps, a physics of 'bodies' (or, as we might now say, particles) acting on one another. James's talk of 'streams' seems closer to a 'wave' description of physical energy. As we shall see in chapter 5, however, 'particle' and 'wave' theories may provide complementary accounts of the same physical reality. By analogy (and perhaps it is more than an analogy), the notion of one thought leading to another may be a necessary complement to the notion of a single, continuous consciousness. As James expresses it (sounding more conciliatory towards Hume than he perhaps intended):

> The unity of parts of the stream is just as 'real' a connection as their diversity is a real separation; both connection and separation are ways in which the past thoughts appear to the present Thought – unlike each other in respect of date and certain qualities – this is the separation; alike in other qualities, and continuous in time – this is the connection. (p. 353)

4

Mind and Behaviour

A penny for your thoughts

How can I ever know what you, or any other person, is thinking? If I offer you a penny and you tell me, I surely have a bargain. No amount of psychological observation or philosophical analysis would give me an answer anywhere nearly so quickly, or in nearly such rich detail. When it comes down to it, you know what is in your own mind better that anyone else conceivably can. In the jargon of philosophers, you have *privileged access* to your own thoughts and feelings. If you insist that you were remembering your last telephone conversation with your mother, I have no right to contradict you. So much seems obvious, but it is far from being the whole story. Privileged access is not necessarily exclusive access. Your mind is not always the private mystery you might wish it to be. Perhaps without realizing it, you may be giving others glimpses of your thoughts. Perhaps other people can often be quite good at predicting when you are tired, or hungry, or anxious for company.

There are other difficulties that undermine the bastions of privacy of thought. Does it make sense to suppose that you yourself only have a partial view of what is 'in your mind'? Could you be engaged in some processes of thought of which even you are unaware? The answer is almost a parody of the standard academic response to all philosophical questions: it depends what you mean by words like 'thought', 'mind', 'awareness', etc. And so it does; but the problem is more than a matter of words. The question is whether it makes any sense to adopt a notion of mental processes that extend beyond the thoughts and feelings that comprise the contents of your immediate consciousness. If it does, then privileged access may apply to the contents of immediate consciousness but not to the totality of your mental states and happenings. If some of what you can tell me about your thoughts is based on inference rather than conscious experience, then the reliance I place on what you tell me depends on *my* inferences about whether *your* inferential reasoning is sound. I can disregard what you tell me if I have reason to suppose you lack insight into the influence of some crucial factor. All of this points to the fact that thought, mind and consciousness are difficult concepts. We may know the contents of *consciousness* directly, immediately and beyond the possibility of doubt, but if our concept of *mind* is to do all that is required of it, we will need to define it more extensively.

Just suppose, however, that we allow mind and thought to be defined coextensively with the concept of consciousness. If I offer you a penny for your thoughts, I am asking for the contents of your immediate consciousness *and nothing else.* Does this make it easier for you to answer me? Perhaps yes, but herein lies an even greater mystery: how is it, if your thoughts are the private contents of a private consciousness, that you can communicate them to me in any language that I can ever hope to understand? There are a number of separate issues involved here. One is how we can use words to express thoughts and feelings. Closely related is the issue of how these words could be understood by anyone else. With the possibility of understanding there may also be the possibility of misunderstanding. This distinction in turn raises the question of the criteria by which we should judge the truth of any expression of thought or feeling.

And behind all of this is the question of whether we have yet succeeded in discarding the legacy of Descartes's thesis that the mind is wholly separate from the body – or indeed whether we should even attempt to do so. We may 'know' that brains and minds are somehow the same, but in practice we cannot do much with this knowledge when we come to make statements about what people think and feel. If I want to tell what you're thinking, the best I can do is still to offer you a penny for your thoughts: no amount of recordings of your brain activity will come anywhere near to providing so good an answer.

The behaviourist challenge

The two best-known traditions of psychological thought throughout the first two-thirds of this century could not have been more different from one another. Psychoanalytic (or psychodynamic) theory, stemming from the work of Sigmund Freud and his collaborators, seeks to explain human behaviour in terms of deep-seated drives and motives buried in our unconscious. This world-view continues to enjoy wide popularity, mainly outside academic and scientific circles. Behaviourism, associated especially with the names of J. B. Watson and B. F. Skinner, is a far more ascetic faith, whose followers have mainly been the missionary-founders of experimental psychology laboratories in many universities of the western world. Over the last quarter-century, this has been largely supplanted within academic psychology by what is sometimes known, rather grandly, as the 'cognitive revolution'.

The first tenet of behaviourism is that claims concerning mental states and processes are superfluous to any causal analysis of behaviour. What this means is that we should not, and do not need to, explain observable behaviour in terms of anything that is in principle unobservable. On the contrary, we can explain observable behavioural responses entirely by reference to observable antecedents, that is, the person's (or animal's) previous experience and the stimulus environment. Learning, the process most studied within this tradition, is viewed as the acquisition of behavioural responses conditional on the presence of particular stimulus configurations (hence the term 'conditioning'). Examples of conditioned responses are those which are set up to be 'instrumental' in the acquisition of a reward (as when pressing a lever delivers a food pellet) or in the avoidance of a punishment (as when moving to another part of the cage prevents the occurrence of an electric shock).

It is important to recognize that behaviourists do not deny the existence of thoughts. They would not even deny that rats have feelings, of a kind. But what is crucial is that the *kinds* of feelings (such as hunger or fear) *that are relevant to the prediction of behaviour* are, according to this point of view, entirely describable in terms of stimuli and responses. Thus, hunger can be 'operationalized' (i.e. defined for the purposes of the experiment) in terms of the length of time the animal has been deprived of food. Simply stated, if we know that a rat has had no food for twenty-four hours, we don't need to ask how the rat feels about it! Nor did behaviourists confine their (theoretical) endeavours to simpler forms of behaviour. Skinner's most ambitious project – but the one that provoked the most sustained counter-attacks, especially from the linguist Noam Chomsky – was to try to account for human language in terms of principles of instrumental conditioning.

There are many facets to the rise and fall of behaviourism, including sometimes fierce and frequently unedifying debates over what is acceptable as 'scientific' or 'empirical' research within psychology, and what is the 'proper' subject-matter of the discipline. Not all of these questions need detain us here. What cannot be dismissed as a previous generation's folly, however, is the behaviourist account of how mental statements are to be *understood*, if they are to be understood at all. The premise of this account is that any meaningful statement about a person's mental state must be *reducible* to some statement about that person's behaviour.

If correct, this approach is far more threatening to our ordinary way of talking about thoughts and feelings than is any mere identification of mind and brain. No one would seriously propose replacing statements about thoughts and feelings with mathematical descriptions of electrical activity in the brain. Even if the events described were in fact identical, talking about them in 'electrical' terms would never be as convenient for ordinary conversation. The behaviourist claim, however, is not that we need an expanded vocabulary or terminology for talking about minds, but a reduced one. We should, so the story goes, get rid of any figures of speech that make unverifiable assumptions about unobservable aspects of people and their behaviour: these figures of speech add nothing to the meaning of what we are trying to say.

There is thus a close affinity between behaviourism and the philosophical position known as 'logical positivism': the meaningfulness of a statement depends on our being able to state the criteria for its truth or falsehood, so that unfalsifiable statements are regarded as meaningless. If we put behaviourism and logical positivism together, we end up with the following syllogism:

Mental events are unobservable.
Statements referring to unobservable events are meaningless.
Hence, statements referring to mental events are meaningless.

And there matters might be allowed to rest, were it not for the fact that such a conclusion appears highly counter-intuitive. We *seem* to communicate about mental events all the time. The following elaboration is therefore offered by way of explanation:

Statements referring to mental events are meaningless.
Statements ostensibly referring to mental events appear
    meaningful.

Hence, such statements must actually refer to something else (which is observable).

The 'something else' in question is purportedly the behaviour and the stimulus context in which it occurs.

How much do I get for a penny?

This century has witnessed many assaults by philosophers on earlier 'mentalistic' views of the mind as something with a distinct and private existence. One of the most influential and strongly-worded of these was Gilbert Ryle's (1949) book *'The Concept of Mind'*. Although Ryle accepted the label 'behaviourist', he discussed psychology only as an afterthought, and then dismissively. His line was that the notion that there are distinct entities called 'mental phenomena' deserving of scientific study in their own right is a fallacy and hence that claims for a distinct science of psychology rest on unsound foundations. Ryle's treatise is, quite simply, that 'mental phenomena' have *no* qualitatively distinct existence, that the idea of a 'mental' world distinct from the physical one is a 'myth', 'dogma' or 'legend', and that the mind itself has no more reality than that of a 'ghost in the machine'. He then moves on to argue that what I have called 'mental statements' – that is, statements that appear to deal with thoughts and feeling – do not, in fact, refer to 'mental' states or events at all, at least in any sense that can be separated from particular kinds of behavioural performance. Thus:

> ... when we describe people as exercising qualities of mind, we are not referring to occult episodes of which their overt acts and utterances are effects; we are referring to those overt acts and utterances themselves. (p. 26)

This undermines any claim for people to have 'privileged access' to their own mental states (since there is nothing 'privileged' about the so-called 'mental'). Ryle still allows, for reasons that are not altogether obvious, that people can describe their own thoughts and feelings, and be understood when they do so. But he insists that such subjective reports have only limited value:

Certainly there are some things which I can find out about you only, or best, through being told of them through you ... If you do not divulge the contents of your silent soliloquies and other imaginings, I have no sure way of what you have been saying or picturing to yourself. But the sequence of your sensations and imaginings is not the sole field in which your wits and character are shown; perhaps only for lunatics is it more than a small corner of that field. I find out most of what I want to know about your capacities, interests, likes, dislikes, methods and convictions by observing how you conduct your overt doings ... (p. 60)

The concept of volition is condemned to the scrap-heap of (now) 'illegitimate and useless' technical concepts, along with phlogiston and animal spirits:

We do not know in daily life how to use it, for we do not use it in daily life and do not, consequently, learn by practice how to apply it, and how not to misapply it. It is an artificial concept. (p. 61)

Ryle gives considerable space to discussion of concepts of attention or 'heeding' as well as of consciousness. He does not deny that people can attend to, or be conscious of, what they are doing or feeling, but rather that such terms do not refer to any *extra* occurrence. Performing a task attentively (for example, 'driving with due care and attention') does not, in his view, imply the 'coupling of an inspecting or researching operation with the performance of that task' (p. 141). Likewise 'The myth of consciousness is a piece of para-optics' (p. 153). In this respect, Ryle is not too dissimilar from Hume, and is emphatically opposed to any notion of an 'inner eye' observing performances on a private stage.

Unlike psychological behaviourists, however, Ryle does not regard the 'black box' of supposedly mental processes as something best left well alone. He is perfectly prepared to talk of people having sensations and feelings, arguing, reasoning, thinking, and performing all the other operations with which philosophy has been traditionally concerned. He attempts to classify different forms of emotions in terms of 'propensities', 'conditions' and 'occurrences' (p. 81). He talks, more than once, of 'silent soliloquies'. In this respect, he is more of a traditional philosopher than his rhetoric might suggest; but where he breaks from tradition, or claims to, is in denying that describing these operations as 'mental' affords them the kind of special status implied by the dualist 'myth'.

We may none the less wish to argue that such operations *are*

special in a slightly different way, not because they are set apart
from physical existence, but because they are performed by those
special inhabitants of the physical world to whom we have given
the title of *persons*. Much recent philosophical work has considered the question of what if anything is special about persons, and
how they might differ from 'lower' animals on the one hand, and
artifical intelligence systems on the other. All this is post-behaviourist
in the sense that it is a deliberate attempt to look inside the 'black
box', but it is just as emphatically post-dualist, in that it does not
attempt to examine thoughts and experience in a manner split off
from what the organisms or systems in question can 'have' or 'do'
or 'be'.

Attribution and inference

How, then, can we tell from people's actions, how they feel or
think, or what they are like in terms of character? Fools, it is said,
rush in where angels fear to tread. Without wanting to characterize
philosophers as angels or, still less, my social psychological colleagues as fools, a large body of research in social psychology has
treated this question as an apparently simple one and has led to
conclusions that are more complicated than they first appear. The
field in question is known as 'interpersonal attribution' and the
notions around which the research has been organized are identified by the umbrella term 'attribution theory'.

   Attribution theory is regarded conventionally as the brainchild
of Fritz Heider (1958), although his own statement of the theory is
somewhat informal, and a number of continuities can be found
with the work of earlier authors (including William James). At a
time when social psychology was looking for a new direction,
however, Heider's voice was influential. Heider appealed for attention to be paid to what he called 'commonsense psychology',
that is to say, to ordinary people's 'naive' theories or explanations
of human behaviour. In other words, he started from the position
that we all seek to *explain* what is going on around us, and that our
interpretations of what happens, including particularly our own
feelings and others' behaviour, depend on implicit causal 'theories'.
Thus, we supposedly make sense of events by 'going beyond the
information given' so as to infer the *causes* of what we observe.
Subsequent research has largely been concerned with identifying

the conditions under which people tend to prefer one kind of explanation over another and, much more recently, with the consequences for one's own behaviour of explaining events in one way rather than another.

Attribution research has traditionally rested on two assumptions: first, that people can *infer* one another's thoughts, intentions and character from observable behaviour, granted certain conditions; and second, that such inferences are *causal*, in the sense that the behaviour is seen to occur *because* of such conceptually distinct mental events and attributes. 'Explanations' of a person's behaviour as 'caused' by their feelings, intentions or character, are termed *personal* or *internal* attributions. Some writers also call them 'correspondent inferences', on the grounds that they imply a 'correspondence' between the behaviour and the actor's attitudes or character. These are distinguished from *situational* or *external* attributions, where the 'cause' of the behaviour is seen to reside in some environmental pressure or coercion.

Internal and external attributions show a kind of trade-off relationship. Where there is strong evidence of environmental pressure to make an actor behave in a given way (so that one would expect all or most other actors to behave similarly), the standard experimental finding is that observers are *less* likely to draw inferences concerning the actor's attitudes or character. In contrast, where the situation appears to be one where the actor was free to choose, the behaviour is taken as reflecting personal or 'internal' characteristics. In other words, the implicit 'commonsense psychology' is that individuals have a variety of 'propensities' (to use Ryle's term) which reflect themselves directly in behaviour, so long as the situation permits free choice.

An especially important area of attribution research concerns how we think about and describe ourselves. The proposition is that 'self-attributions' follow much the same logic as the attributions we make about other people. In other words, statements about our *own* mental or personal characteristics do not reflect any 'privileged access' (except perhaps to fuller information about our past behaviour), but are simply *explanations* of our own observable behaviour, no different in principle from those that could be made by a fully-informed outside observer. We see ourselves, so the story goes, as we think others see us – or more precisely, as *we* would see someone else who behaved as we did in the same situation. (Actually, the data do not support quite so simple a story. For instance, it has been shown that we are relatively more likely to explain other people's behaviour in terms of their personal characteristics, but to explain our own behaviour as an adaptive response to situational demands.)

Self-attributions are important for behaviour because they are associated with differences in feelings of self-confidence and expectations of future success or failure. For instance, a student who puts a poor examination performance down to inadequate revision is likely to try harder next time, since removing the cause of failure should improve the chances of success. On the other hand, a student who has made an 'internal' attribution for his or her failure as being a sign of lack of academic ability is unlikely to try harder, since effort would make no difference to the outcome. Much the same can be shown for a number of challenges that people face in the field of health. For example, cigarette smokers who see themselves as more 'addicted' have lower expectations of their ability to stop and may be less likely to make such an attempt. Thus, the way we describe ourselves will reflect what we think others expect, or are entitled to expect, of us as well as what we expect of ourselves.

Dualism and behaviourism in attribution theory

Despite the huge number of empirical studies conducted within this framework, attribution theory remains conceptually confused. In fact, it seems to achieve the remarkable distinction of being both dualistic and behaviourist at (almost) the same time. Part of the reason is that it is not just a theory, but a theory about theories. The subject matter of the field is not behaviour *per se*, but ordinary people's explanations or 'theories' of it. Such *implicit* theories are supposedly dualistic through and through. The story is that we see behaviour as either forced by 'external' constraints and temptations, or as arising form 'internal' motives, impulses or personality traits.

The whole 'internal–external' distinction seems to exemplify the idea of mind which Ryle called 'the ghost in the machine'. On the one hand there is a world of observable actions, on the other hand a world of unobservable thoughts which have to be 'inferred' from their observable corollaries. Yet at the same time introspection is typically treated as an empty exercise for the purpose of self-attributions. What matters is the observable behaviour and the features of the situation to which it is a response. According to Bem's

(1967) critique of cognitive dissonance theory (see chapter 1), apparent reports of our feelings, preferences and such like are *actually* reports of our behaviour. Bem, indeed, termed himself a 'radical behaviourist'.

A possible route out of this morass would be to claim that ordinary people (poor benighted souls!) are dualists who accept the dogma of 'the ghost in the machine', but that attribution theorists know better and adopt a behaviourist view of human action *and of how ordinary people talk about action*. Unfortunately, this interpretation cannot be consistently imposed on the literature. Almost without exception (Bem is an exception), attribution theorists have shown themselves ready to use or introduce facile concepts of 'correspondence' or 'covariation' between behavioural *consequences* and 'internal' or 'external' *causes*. Now, of course, these concepts are introduced to show how people supposedly *think* behaviour should be explained, and it can be shown that such 'naive' explanations are vulnerable to a number of biases. Even so, the theorists themselves have hardly sought to distance themselves from the implicit dualism which they attribute to their subjects.

This is not an argument for guilt by association. If 'common sense' is dualist, but dualism is wrong, then the errors of 'common sense' demand an explanation. The issue here is not just that of what is wrong with a widely-accepted idea, but why a wrong idea should be accepted so widely. Attribution theorists remain essentially silent on this issue. Indeed, they assume that people *can* process information relating to the covariation or correspondence between mental causes on the one hand and behavioural consequences on the other, and imply that it will often be quite rational for them to do so. We seem to be back with the incoherent demand that people should be able to observe correlations between observable effects and unobservable antecedents.

The escape offered by behaviourists is that the antecedents of observable behavioural effects are themselves observable. How then should we account for the apparent dualism of 'common sense'? One set of reactions starts from the view that 'common sense' is dualist, and wrong to be so, and therefore many ordinary-language explanations and descriptions of behaviour will make misleading assumptions. Many philosophers seem to take this line, being content to show *how* such assumptions are misleading. A psychologist who took this line, however, would need to show *why* such assumptions are appealing, even though they may constitute a 'myth'. This would in many ways be a more difficult question, and I know of no substantial programme of empirical research which points towards an answer. Behaviourist accounts (including Bem's) sidestep this issue by treating apparently mentalistic descriptions as just another form of observable verbal behaviour, under the control of antecedent environmental stimuli. To a behaviourist, the fact that such descriptions seem to talk about mental states is completely irrelevant. They might as well refer to configurations of planets and stars (as indeed, they sometimes do). Thus, to use Bem's example, my saying that I like brown bread depends (only) on the antecedent observable fact that I always eat it.

This approach leads us quickly into new difficulties. We are still inclined to think of a statement such as 'I like brown bread' as meaning something more than 'I always eat brown bread even if I am not forced to do so'. We may account, by appropriate behavioural principles, for when such a statement is likely to be uttered. We have not thereby accounted for what that statement means, or could be taken to mean, within the context in which it is made. Expressive behaviour is not only behaviour, it is expressive. But if we insist that what is expressed (by statements such as 'I like brown bread') is something unobservable and uncommunicable over and above what is observable and communicable, we seem to be back where we started.

Another approach, however, is to consider whether 'common sense' might in fact be less dualistic than it appears (at least to attribution theorists). That is to say, attribution theory may offer a false picture of the reasoning processes underlying ordinary people's accounts of their own and others' behaviour. There are certainly findings which point in this direction. The emphasis on explanation of past events rather than the prediction of future conditions seems inappropriate (and maladaptive) in many contexts. Under many circumstances, particularly when events confirm one's expectations, it is difficult to find evidence of people making explicit causal attributions at all. When explanations are sought, different kinds of causes may not be 'traded off' against one another quite as the theory predicts. All this suggests that the theory may have limited generality. But suppose that attribution theory is not just limited, but wrong in its fundamental assumptions. Suppose that people don't typically use an implicit theory of human action in which mental events are regarded as distinct and split off from behavioural and physical events. Perhaps instead 'common sense' psychology regards these events as complementary parts of a single whole. The challenge for psychology is then to explain how such a conception of unity can be acquired from the complex sequencing of experience. This was Hume's problem too.

Inferring feelings: A fallacy in one act

The fact that we can communicate our thoughts is paradoxical if we take the dualist line and regard thoughts as private mental events. If mental events are private, how can we use words as symbols of 'things in our minds'? On the other hand, if we take the behaviourist line, the 'fact' of communication is quite uninteresting, or even no fact at all. All we are doing when we make a 'mental' statement is exhibiting a piece of verbal behaviour. Prior conditioning may make this behaviour situationally appropriate, but it does not make it meaningful.

For instance, imagine the following scene: a dualist (Dorian) and a behaviourist (Bruce), deep in philosophical argument, walking through a park. The former is tall and elegant, with long white hair and a red silk bow-tie. His companion is shorter, with an uneven brown beard and a tweed sports jacket, faintly discoloured by sawdust. They decide to sit down and rest on a conveniently placed pile of clothes. Actually, this pile of clothes contains the body of a sleeping gardener (George). Coming up more quickly behind them is a fresh-faced young woman (Angie), wearing stone-washed jeans and an over-sized tee shirt with the insignia of a university somewhere in the prairies, and carrying a pile of computer print-out under one arm. Approaching from another direction is Clarissa, a well-coiffured but somewhat intense-looking woman of forty-something, whose left hand grips a document case with a combination lock. How should they all react, to be consistent with their philosophies? One might imagine the following exchange:

GEORGE: (*waking up*) Hoy! Get off! You're hurting me!
DORIAN: Now that's very interesting! This person – it must be a person I suppose – has just made a proposition that superficially appears to be predicating *our* behaviour. He says that we are 'hurting him'? But all that can be physically observed of our behaviour is that we are sitting down on him. So what does he mean? All I think he can be talking about is some internal state of his own mind that he is somehow confusing logically with our behaviour. What he should really

have said is 'You are sitting on me *and* I am being hurt'.
Then it would have been clear that he is actually making
not one proposition, but two. The first is undoubtedly correct.
The second is more mysterious, because we have no way of
knowing what this phrase 'being hurt' refers to.

BRUCE: Look, I really think we should stop sitting on him.

DORIAN: Why?

BRUCE: Well, he said 'Get off'.

DORIAN: So what?

BRUCE: Well, maybe it's my upbringing, as you'd call it – I
prefer to call it conditioning – but I can't help feeling that,
when I hear words such as 'Get off', I really ought to *move*.
In fact, I've been strongly reinforced in the past for making
particular movements in response to things people say. I
guess you'd say that I've learned to do what I'm told.

DORIAN: OK, but *I'm* telling you now to *sit down* . . .

BRUCE: (*uneasily*) Well, if you say so . . .

DORIAN: . . . and tell me what you think of what this person
just said.

BRUCE: (*much more comfortable now*) I frankly don't see the
mystery in any of this. Saying things like 'Get off' and 'You're
hurting me' are just behaviours that this person exhibits
when other people sit on him.

DORIAN: But why does he 'exhibit such behaviours', as you
put it?

BRUCE: Presumably because he's learned that doing so makes
whoever's sitting on him get off, and that's reinforcing.

DORIAN: What do you mean by 'reinforcing'?

BRUCE: It makes him more likely to exhibit the same behaviours again under the same conditions. I guess it must happen
to him quite often.

DORIAN: You mean that if people get off him, this gives him
pleasure, or reduces pain?

BRUCE: That's your interpretation. I'm making no assumptions
about what other people feel.

DORIAN: So you're not at all puzzled by what he might *mean*?

BRUCE: No. As far as I'm concerned, the question's irrelevant.

DORIAN: Ah, but that's where we differ. I'm extremely puzzled
by what he could mean. You see, I know what *I'd* mean if
I said someone was hurting me – I'd be having such and
such feelings, which, incidentally, wouldn't be nice at all –
but I've no way of looking inside his mind to discover the

feelings to which *he*'s referring when he talks of 'being hurt'. For all I know, the feelings he's talking about could be completely different from the kind I refer to when *I* say I'm being hurt.

(*By this time, Angie and Clarissa have both arrived and have stopped to witness the scene. Clarissa adopts a pose of somewhat disdainful sympathy. Angie, by contrast, is bubbling with excitement as she waits for a chance to join in the conversation.*)

ANGIE: Hi! Do you mind if I say something? I'm a social psychologist – an attribution theorist to be more precise – and, the way I see things, you're both right, or almost. All we've got to go on is this person's behaviour – that's all the information we've got. We don't really *know* for certain what he's feeling – or even whether he's feeling anything at all. But perhaps we can go beyond the information given and *infer* that he must be feeling pain. After all, feelings of pain covary with being sat on. That is to say, when I'm sat on (though it doesn't happen very often), I find it hurts, and when other people are sat on, they find it painful too.

DORIAN: Hang on – how do you know?

ANGIE: (*sheepishly*) Well, that's what they say.

BRUCE: Precisely!

DORIAN: Forgive me, my dear. I know that's what they *say*. But the question is, what do they *mean*? What *kinds* of feelings are they talking about?

ANGIE: (*more defiantly*) But what else could they mean? What other kinds of feelings could there be?

DORIAN: (*airily*) Who knows?

BRUCE: (*snidely*) Who cares?

CLARISSA: *I* care. I'm a *clinical* psychologist and I spend all day long listening to people describe their feelings; and what I want to say is that you have to deal with the *whole person*, and that way you can really empathize with clients' problems and form alliances with them to help them deal with the pain they are feeling...'

GEORGE (*who has listened to all of the above in quiet bemusement*): Listen, sweetheart...

CLARISSA: I'm not your sweetheart...

GEORGE: I know, but listen anyway. If you want to form an alliance to deal with the pain I'm feeling, just tell these idiots to shove off. It's not my whole person that's hurting, it's my right leg. They're squashing it.

DORIAN: This is fascinating. If someone sat on *my* right leg, I might describe *my* feelings in just the same way.

ANGIE: That's what I was trying to say.

GEORGE: Go to hell!

BRUCE: (*standing up*) I'm going.

CLARISSA: Look, I really feel it would be better if we respected my cli . . . I mean, this gentleman's privacy and we continued this discussion elsewhere . . .

(*Bruce exits right, Dorian, Clarissa and Angie left; George resumes his slumbers.*)

This little drama illustrates, I hope, how so many conceptual muddles in psychology arise from paying dualism too much respect. According to psychological forms of dualism, we understand others' feelings by *inferring* their mental states from what they say and do. This notion of 'inference' implies a kind of probabilistic or inductive reasoning, but the logical basis of such induction remains vague. The notion of covariation is scarcely helpful if we are called upon to observe covariations between observables and unobservables.

A possible escape from this dilemma (towards which our dualist in the drama sounds as though he is being led) is to assume that we understand other's mental states and experiences by analogy with our own. Because we understand what 'hurting' means in our own experience, we 'infer' that it means the same in other people's experience. Another example often used is the interpretation of colour terms: how can we know what someone else means by 'red'? We assume, the same as what we mean ourselves. This approach has a ring of plausibility, but we need to be very careful. The notion of 'inference' still implies a rift between what can be known for sure and what can be only inferred. On the latter side of this rift are the referents of statements about feelings and sensations. But what are these referents? The quick answer is, just the feelings and sensations themselves, but this answer may be too quick. If these are the only referents, how can feelings be described – not just by other people so that I can understand what they say – but by myself so that I can understand what *I* say? How can I learn the words to express my feelings, if no one else can ever know the feelings I am trying to express? For what is obvious, yet of the first importance, is that I do not make up such words all by myself.

Ryle, for one, was clear that such talk of 'inference' was misleading. As he puts it:

I discover that there are other minds in understanding what other people say and do. In making sense of what you say ... I am not inferring to the workings of your mind, I am following them. Of course, I am not merely hearing the noises that you make, or merely seeing the movements that you perform. I am understanding what I hear and see. But this understanding is not an inferring to occult causes. It is appreciating how the operations are conducted. (1949, p. 59)

Are our feelings real?

But we are left, even (or perhaps especially) after Ryle, with the problem of specifying the referents of the statements wherein we express our feelings and experiences. How do I *follow* someone else's thoughts and feelings, by listening to what they say? What is involved when we express our thoughts and feelings so that other people can *follow* (and not just infer) them? These are vital questions for theories of attitudes, which are concerned, for much of the time, with accounting for verbal expressions of thoughts and feelings. Perhaps we have paid too much respect to behaviourism as well. When we express our feelings, it does seem to be our feelings, and not just our behaviour, that we are talking about. The impasse seems to arise from the insistence that, because my thoughts cannot be actually *had* by anyone else, they cannot be intelligibly talked about, in the same way that we can talk to each other about physically observable objects such as trees, and cats and cherries. But perhaps this insistence is unjustified. Perhaps, after all, we really can describe our feelings directly, and not just through some kind of implicational double-talk, according to which what we *really* mean by 'I like cherries' is 'I'm going to eat the lot'. But if we can do so, how do we manage it, and what are we *really* describing? For sure, we cannot re-espouse dualism and claim that we are describing purely 'mental' phenomena, without any logical connection to the outside world; but neither does it seem that mental statements merely report statistical *inferences* from more public goings-on, as the attribution theorists suggest.

We shall return to this issue in chapter 6. First, though, we need to put another common assumption under the spotlight. According to attribution theorists, our 'subjective' impressions stand to 'objective reality' as effects stand to causes. Sometimes we may even look for explanations of our thoughts and feelings in terms of some alternative 'cause' (e.g. in terms of the effect of some intoxicant) to account for why things may not be 'really' as we think they are. In a number of forms of psychotherapy, people are encouraged to reappraise their current feelings (e.g. of their own worthlessness) as open to alternative, and happier, interpretations. All this points to an implicit distinction between subjective 'appearance' on the one hand and an independent, objective 'reality' on the other: between impressions 'in here' and things 'out there'.

This distinction presents us with a dilemma. If, on the one hand, we assume there is an 'objective reality' independent of our observations, we face the problem that we can only describe this reality in the form we (or others) have observed it (as both Locke and Hume argued). Mostly we can operate efficiently enough by treating our impressions as the best guide we have to this reality, without needing to assume that they tell us the whole story or that others' impressions might not tell a different one. This stops short of claiming that our impressions and observations are the only reality, but leaves us with the puzzle of how reality can ever be truly known. If, on the other hand, we define reality as the content of our observations and experience, we can know it in its entirety, but it will be a 'reality' with no necessary existence independent of ourselves. In short, reality depends on observation and there is no such thing as an independent, objective world. It is a disturbing suggestion, but it has been made, and on apparently excellent authority.

5

Observation and Reality

Is there anything out there?

We take it for granted that we observe objects in the world, and that
the world is real. From this starting point, we can base the study
of attitudes on common-sense assumptions: we are all part of the
same 'reality', but sometimes we perceive things differently from
one another, attend to different things, and form different evaluative judgements. We may frequently disagree about things, but there
are still 'things out there' about which we disagree. Likewise, we
can form attitudes about what *other people* may say, do or feel, and
in so doing we assume obviously that these other people also exist
'out there' and have their own thoughts, independently of (though
not necessarily isolated from) our own. We can *influence* the objects of our perception by our actions (we can pick up a book or put
it down). We can *influence* other people's thoughts by what we say
or do ('Please read this book!'). But we cannot bring such objects
into existence simply by thinking about them. Our attitudes depend
on the existence of some 'reality'; but the existence of that 'reality'
does not depend on our having an attitude towards it.

In the following chapter, I shall be arguing that this 'common-
sense' approach is essentially correct, although it is evident that
people with different attitudes can interpret and describe 'reality'
in very different ways. In this chapter, however, I shall confront a
more fundamental challenge: that 'reality' does not exist until it is
observed. As a general proposal about our place in the universe,
this idea is quite crazy, but this is less than fatal to its popularity,
even now. And *showing* that it's crazy, I should warn you, will be
far from easy. Perhaps, indeed it won't turn out to be *completely*

crazy after all: even in arguing against it, we may come to redefine what 'reality' is, in ways that 'common sense' would certainly not predict.

Berkeley's cherry

Many readers may have been surprised at the omission of George Berkeley (1685–1753) from the list of philosophers considered in chapters 2 and 3. The reason for his exclusion was simple: Berkeley has almost nothing of interest to say about our concepts of personal identity. He has a great deal to say, however, about the relation of perception to reality. His *Essay towards a New Theory of Vision* (1709) is a quite remarkable piece of writing, anticipating many of the issues of modern experimental research on visual perception. But his greatest influence is attributable to his extreme version of philo-sophical empiricism, which he pursued with a single-mindedness unmatched by his amateur predecessor, Locke, or his more secular and political successor, Hume. For Berkeley, it was not enough to assert that our perceptual experience provides us with evidence of an 'external' reality. Rather, we cannot conceive of any reality except in terms of our own experience. Reality is not just something we happen to experience: it *is* our experience. To be perceived and experienced is what existing, what being real, *means*.

His argument starts from a conviction that Locke was correct in asserting that we can have no knowledge other than through the senses, but wrong in asserting that we could form 'abstract ideas' of attributes of objects, over and above our sensations of them. We cannot think of pleasure or pain as existing independently of our experience, so by the same token we should not attribute an in-dependent reality to sensations of colour, size and such like. Thus, *reality is all in the mind*. We have no justification for assuming anything to exist, other than our sensations or ideas. But Berkeley is not a sceptic (he would be easier to understand if he were). He does not conclude from this that there *is* no reality, or that our sensations are all illusions (since they cannot be proved to be otherwise). He argues, instead, that the world of our experience really exists:

> Look! are not the fields covered with a delightful verdure? Is there not something in the woods and groves, in the rivers and clear springs,

that soothes, that delights, that transports the soul? . . . What treatment then do those philosophers deserve, who would deprive these noble scenes of all reality? How should those principles be entertained, that lead us to think all the visible beauty of the creation a false imaginary glare? (Berkeley, *The Second Dialogue between Hylas and Philonous*)

However, the real existence of the world *consists in* its being perceived and experienced. If something was never observed, it is not that we would be *ignorant* of its existence; it is rather that the attribution of existence to it would be completely meaningless. The cherry of the title is just one of a number of examples which Berkeley uses to illustrate this point:

> I see this *cherry*, I feel it, I taste it: and I am sure *nothing* cannot be seen, or felt, or tasted: it is therefore *real*. Take away the sensations of softness, moisture, redness, tartness, and you take away the cherry. Since it is not a being distinct from sensations; a *cherry*, I say, is nothing but a congeries of sensible impressions, or ideas perceived by various senses . . . Hence, when I say I see, and feel, and taste, in certain sundry manners, I am sure the *cherry* exists, or is real; its reality being in my opinion nothing abstracted from these sensations. But if by the word *cherry* you mean an unknown nature distinct from all those sensible qualities, and by its existence something distinct from its being perceived; then indeed I own, neither you, nor I, nor anyone else can be sure it exists. (Berkeley, *The Third Dialogue between Hylas and Philonous*)

But surely there is something in the notion of reality that implies the cherry was there before I saw it, picked it up, and tasted it? Surely somebody else could have seen the *same cherry* (but not, for reasons that are more obvious to common sense than to Berkeley's philosophy, have eaten it)? Berkeley wants to be able to answer 'yes' to these questions. He wants to have a real cherry, not just the illusion of one. But how can he, if nothing exists unless it is perceived? His 'solution' is that *there must be some other mind* in which cherries and everything else exist without interruption, and the 'mind' in question is God. Reality therefore depends on existence in the mind of God. Berkeley was Bishop of the Irish diocese of Cloyne from 1734 onwards, and so was at least as concerned as Descartes to make his thesis consistent with his faith. He was even prepared to use the argument the other way around, that is to use our belief in the reality of what we experience as 'proof' that God exists. But this leaves us with no guarantee that we are part of a reality that is in any way *shared* by any other mind – even a god's – or that the continuity which we attribute to our *own* experience of reality corresponds in any way to the kind of continuity that may be apparent to some other mind, or to ourselves in a different time and place.

Granted Berkeley's premise, it might have been simpler for him to go the whole hog and argue that there is *no* real world, or at least none that can be shared by different minds. Berkeley, however, was not a sceptic. Alternatively, he might have argued that there are as many different worlds as there are different minds, or even occasions of observation of the world by any single mind, but he was not a mystic either. Newton had published his *Principia Mathematica* in 1687, and descriptions of the material world were henceforth to be made on the basis of physical observation, not abstract speculation. Berkeley was possibly less in awe of the new physics than Locke had been. In the *Third Dialogue*, he scorns the possibility that 'laws of motion' applied to 'inert bodies' could ever 'reach the production of any one animal or vegetable body', or that 'physical principles' could account for 'the aptitude and contrivance, even of the most inconsiderable parts of the universe'. Unlike Locke and Hume, he was not prepared to talk of 'continued life' in (quasi-) materialistic terms. Of the lawful observability of physical reality, on the other hand, he had no doubt. Paradoxically, it was from physics, not from philosophy, that such doubts would eventually re-emerge.

The discontinuity of energy

Let's jump the best part of 200 years. The year is 1900, and physicists are attempting to make sense of new findings and concepts relating to atoms, electrical charges and radiation. Among the many unresolved puzzles is one concerning the amount of radiation from hot objects. Objects (such as metal rods or pokers) can feel warm without visibly glowing; this can mean that any radiation of light energy is in the low-frequency range of the spectrum called infrared, which is invisible to the human eye. As these objects are heated further, they can glow red; still further, and the colour becomes brighter and brighter until we talk of the metal as 'white hot'. If we measure the emission of radiation at different frequencies, the peak of the distribution rises with an increase in heat. However, this rise does not continue indefinitely, but tails off as one passes into the very-high-frequency (ultra-violet) region. A plausible hypothesis is that all this had something to do with the energy of oscillation of electric charges within the atom. But the trouble is that established theory predicts that one should find more and more energy at higher and higher frequencies, instead of the observed cut-off. In Berlin, Max Planck proposes a mathematical solution with bizarre conceptual ramifications: the energy (E) of the electrical charge associated with radiation at a given frequency (*v*) is given by the formula:

$$E = hv$$

where *h* is a new fundamental constant, derived from experimental observation.

The central message of this equation is that energy exists only in exact multiples of *h* (henceforth known as Planck's constant). In-between energy levels are not 'allowable'. This resolves the paradox of the tail-off of radiation at high frequencies, in that the 'interval' between one allowable energy level and the next increases directly with frequency. Thus, at very high frequencies of radiation, the 'jump' from one level to the next may require more energy than is available. But the price of solving this one small puzzle in this way was the requirement to think of energy as discontinuous – as existing only in discrete packets or *quanta* – and to think of change as consisting of interrupted 'jumps' from one 'quantum state' to another.

Quantum theory was soon extended to a bewildering range of physical phenomena. Within a few years, Albert Einstein showed that light could be described, not necessarily as a continuous wave, but in terms of discontinuous packets of light quanta, or photons. At any given frequency or wave-length, all photons have the same energy (consistent with Planck's formula) with light intensity being a function of the number of photons emitted. In 1913, Niels Bohr started to describe the structure of atoms on the basis of there being only a limited number of 'allowable' ways in which electrons could (according to the imagery of the time) 'orbit' around the nucleus of an atom, and within ten years had revolutionized chemistry with a theory to account for the periodic table of the elements: atoms can only combine to form molecules in a limited number of 'allowable' ways. And almost coincidentally with all of this, Einstein was proposing his special theory of relativity in 1905 and his general theory of relativity in 1915.

All of this presented a fundamental challenge to the deterministic model of the universe that had been dominant at least since the time of Newton. Not only are the apparent fundamentals of time and space relative, but physical laws take on an uncertain, statistical, flavour. Take a physical energy system that is at the borderline of one 'allowable' state and another, and it is impossible to determine its future state, except on a statistical basis. All we can do is to predict *probabilistically* that, say, half the time the system will be found in state A, and half the time in state B, the 'choice' between states appearing essentially random. This implication of quantum theory was one by which Einstein, for one, was deeply disturbed. Another implication, with which Einstein identified as eloquently as anyone, was that descriptions of physical systems in terms of particles (or matter) on the one hand and in terms of waves (or energy) on the other, are essentially complementary and interchangeable. At the scale of the atom, particles can behave like waves, and waves like particles. This property is often known as 'wave–particle duality'. There was thus uncertainty at the very heart of physical reality.

The uncertainty principle

Perhaps even more worrying than the idea that we cannot exactly predict physical events was the conclusion that we cannot even *measure* or observe them, except in ways that must interfere with the events themselves. Any experiment becomes an interaction with the physical world, so that the physical world is not just observed, but changed. We cannot know exactly what form the physical events would have taken if we had made no attempt to interfere with them by observation. There is a temptation to talk of the observation 'creating' one kind of physical reality rather than another, and this is a temptation that the more mystically inclined of popular science writers have been unable to resist.

The 'uncertainty principle' was proposed by Werner Heisenberg in 1925, and was developed over the next few years (in collaboration particularly with Born, Schrödinger and Dirac) to provide the basis for quantum mechanics. At the heart of the problem is the fact that energy exists only in discontinuous quanta. This means that a finite limit must always be set to the discriminability of any physical measurement. If it is energy we are measuring, we cannot divide up

our units of measurement *ad infinitum* so as to produce ever finer
and finer discriminable intervals. Eventually, we will come to a
stage where finer discriminations imply subdivisions of the intervals between quanta; but since no energy levels are to be found
within these intervals, no measurement can be made. By the same
token, the discontinuity of energy quanta limits the fineness of the
'grain' of any other kind of measurement we may wish to make, e.g.
of position or time. Why? Simply because there will always be
some kind of energy transfer whenever any physical event is recorded. Just as energy is discontinuous, so must be the measurements
we make using energy. 'Uncertainty' can therefore be expressed
mathematically as an interval within which further accuracy cannot be achieved.

What Heisenberg's principle states is that, if we multiply the
'uncertainty' involved in measurement of the position of an electron (say) by the 'uncertainty' involved in measurement of its momentum (i.e. mass times velocity), the product must always be greater
than a constant $\hbar$ (which is in fact Planck's constant h divided by
2π). What this amounts to is that there is a trade-off between the
potential accuracy of different kinds of measurements. The more
accurately we measure the electron's position, the less accurately
we can measure its momentum, and *vice versa*. This ties in with
the 'wave–particle duality' already mentioned. Just as 'particle' and
'wave' descriptions (e.g. of electrons) are essentially complementary, there is a trade-off between the 'uncertainty' associated with
each of these descriptions. (An equivalent trade-off can be shown
to apply between uncertainties of energy and of time.)

It is important to stress that the 'uncertainty' in Heisenberg's
principle is not a reflection of any technical flaw in the instruments
we use to measure physical quantities (although, obviously, faulty
instruments produce even more uncertainty). It is simply an inescapable fact about the physical world, reflecting the 'grain' of the
quantities we have to deal with, the complementarity of wave and
particle descriptions, and the probabilistic behaviour of the waves
or particles so described. It should also be remembered that we are
dealing with incredibly tiny quantities when put alongside those of
our everyday experience.

One inference that is sometimes drawn is that quantum theory
is therefore inapplicable on the scale of the objects we can see and
handle, which we can understand quite well, thank you very much,
on the basis of the more 'familiar' rules of Newton's 'classical'
mechanics. (This is a dangerous line of argument, though. It works

well enough for bicycles and billiard balls, but the technological applications of modern physics, from nuclear power stations to light-pens at supermarket checkouts, are also increasingly 'familiar' parts of everyday experience. It seem vain to suppose that common-sense views of physical reality are inevitably fixed in the Newtonian mould.)

A more helpful interpretation is that the uncertainty still applies to measurements on the scale of human experience, but is incredibly tiny in proportion to the mass and size of the objects we ordinarily perceive. In other words, we can measure the size and position of a book on a desk say, with all the precision anyone could reasonably demand (although even in this example, we may be 'uncertain' if we are asked to make our measurements of length, say, accurate to within 1 mm). If, however, we inspected the boundaries of the solid object we are measuring (either the book or the desk) under greater and greater magnification, we would find that the edges were not solid at all, but fuzzy. By now, we would have already reached the stage where the dimensions of the book or desk could only be described probabilistically within a margin of error or uncertainty. And even this 'fuzzy' stage comes extremely early in the process of magnification. If we were able to continue our journey to the level of locating atoms, or particles within atoms, what we would 'see' would be an emptiness comparable to that of outer space.

Quantum metaphysics

So, by the very nature of things, we are never able *completely* to eliminate uncertainty in any description we make of a physical system. So, we live in a probabilistic, not a deterministic, universe. Perhaps this can provide some metaphysical comfort for anyone who felt that their free will was compromised by science. At a day-to-day level, though, surely it makes no practical difference. If we do not know our fate, and are incapable of predicting it, does it really matter whether there is such a thing as fate or not? We might as well organize our lives on the basis of the choices that seem most reasonable to us. (This seems to have been the line taken by the ancient Greeks, even though the concept of 'fate' was one which they were prepared to treat quite seriously. Indeed, even those who could afford to consult the oracle had to be satisfied with forecasts at least as guarded and ambiguous as any horoscope.)

But suppose a different interpretation were to be put on such indeterminacy or uncertainty. Let's consider two states of affairs that are alternatives to each other, for example, that a coin would come down heads or tails (ignoring the tiny, but non-zero, possibility of its balancing on its edge). I might say 'Either it will be heads, or it will be tails'. This presents no problem. Or I might say 'The probability that it will be heads is one-half, and the probability that it will be tails is also one-half'. Again, there's no problem. But suppose I offered 'The probabilities of it coming down heads and tails both exist'. 'Hang on,' you might say, 'what do you mean by *exist*?'

To this I might reply 'I mean what actually *is*. Right now, before I toss the coin, the alternative states of heads and tails *coexist* as equal possibilities "superposed" on each other (as in a double-exposure photograph). To describe this coin as it *is*, I can only say it is a heads-and-tails: both descriptions are equally correct. It is only when it hits the ground and stops rolling, so that we can look at which side it's come down, that one of the coexistent possibilities will cease to exist (for purposes of this one toss), and it will become a heads *or* a tails. I can give you a mathematical description of this superposition of possibilities if you like . . .'

'No thanks', you might say 'I don't want an equation. Just explain this: you're surely not claiming that the coin itself undergoes any fundamental change when it's tossed, that it turns from being one kind of *thing* into another. Surely, you just mean that you don't know whether it'll be a heads or a tails. But it's still the same coin, isn't it, whatever you can say about it? It surely can't be two things at the same time. It has to be one thing or another.'

At this point, responses come in different flavours. The flavour I prefer myself goes something like this:

A   Of course there's only one coin. But the point is that it isn't just that I don't know whether it will be a heads or a tails. It's that *in principle* the outcome of the toss is unpre-dictable. No one could predict it. Yes, of course it's the same coin, whatever, as you put it, I can say about it. But what *can* I say about it? Only that, right now, there is *both* a 50 per cent probability of it being a heads *and* an equal probability of it being a tails and that these aspects are com-plementary so that a description which mentioned the one without implying the other would be incomplete (and non-sense). The uncertainty is a property of the coin, not a matter of my own ignorance. Now, after I toss the coin – say it comes down heads – it's not that I now know something that I didn't know before *but was there to be known*. It's rather that the observable reality I'm describing has changed. The coin is still the same coin, in all normal senses of 'same' (I certainly haven't doubled my money!). However, its history has changed: a certain amount of energy has been applied to it, it will probably no longer have exactly the same temperature or size, and it now needs to be described as occupying a different position in space–time. The relevant aspect of this change in position is that only the 'heads' side can now be seen. But I'm not suggesting that the 'tails' side has magically disappeared for ever.

But there are other flavours of response which, at the risk of caricature, go something like this:

B   It *can* be two things at the same time. At least, if it was an an electron rather than a coin, it would be. It would have a dual existence as a wave and a particle, and we can represent this duality as the superposition of two alternatives, just like the heads and tails of the coin. But we can only observe physical events in the form of particles or in the form of waves. According to the uncertainty principle, if we determine the correct particle description of an event, we can know nothing about its wave description, and *vice versa*. So it is the *act of observation* that turns an event with a dual existence into one with a single existence in either of its possible forms. By analogy, a tossed coin doesn't become a 'heads' until we *observe* it to be so. If you say to me, a tossed coin must *be* one thing or another, whether or not I've observed it so, I would answer: empirical statements can only refer to what has been *observed to be*.

This second flavour is probably closer to Heisenberg's own interpretation of the uncertainty principle (although I am not suggesting that he saw no relevant differences between coins and electrons). But stranger is yet to come:

C   Not only can the coin be two things at once. It can be a whole number of different things, coexisting in different universes. The mathematics of quantum theory allows us to suppose a multiplicity of universes, and a multiplicity of identities for objects including ourselves. Every wave–particle duality implies, not just the complementarity of different descriptions of a single reality, but a splitting of reality into alternatives *all of which may continue to exist*, whether or not they are observed. Observation is relevant because we cannot experience the coexistent universes simultaneously, and hence can never meet alternative versions of electrons, coins, or even of ourselves.

Is there anything to be said in favour of this last point of view, beyond the encouragement it offers to science fiction? It is like me saying that I have an identical twin who follows me around, but if ever anybody looks at one of us, either I will disappear or he will (and I can't tell which!), and then both of us will go spinning off into different regions of 'superspace'. If I made such a claim with all apparent sincerity, you'd be entitled to assume that something was seriously wrong. And probably what is wrong is a misunderstanding of what the physicists in question are really proposing. (Even so, some approaches to quantum theory, particularly the 'many worlds' hypothesis of Hugh Everett, seem vulnerable to such extravagances.) Perhaps none of this is quite as implausible when considering something as mysterious as a quantum, but then we are still left without an explanation of why quantum uncertainty should imply something different about reality than is implied by the uncertainty of heads and tails.

The two-slit experiment

We can hardly blame quantum theory itself for the fantasies that have been constructed around it. Nor do we need such fantasies; the facts themselves are fascinating enough. Among the most intriguing are the findings of the so-called 'two-slit' experiment, which illustrates the importance both of the wave–particle duality and of uncertainty. Suppose we have a source of light (such as a monochromatic light bulb producing light of a single frequency), a light-sensitive screen and, between the light and the screen, a partition. If we open a single thin slit in the partition, what we will see on the screen is a single band of light, the most intense point of which will lie on a direct line from the light source through the slit.

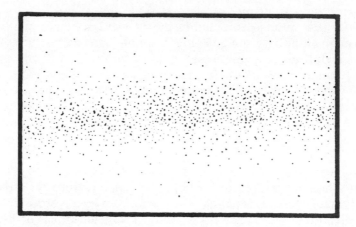

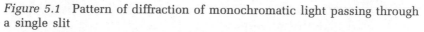

Figure 5.1 Pattern of diffraction of monochromatic light passing through
a single slit
Source: R. Penrose (1989) *The Emperor's New Mind*, Oxford University Press

However, the edge of the band will be softened, as though the light
beam fanned out symmetrically on either side of the central band
after passing throught the partition. This is just the kind of picture
you would expect if you thought of a beam of light as a shower of
light *particles* (photons), some of which were diffracted, or bounced
sideways, as they passed throught the slit (see figure 5.1).

Now we open a second slit, parallel and quite close to the first.
What we now see is a 'zebra-like' pattern of bright bands, separated
by bands of shadow (see figure 5.2). This is just what we would
expect if we pictured light as consisting of *waves*, that is, oscillations with peaks and troughs coming at regular intervals (wave-
lengths). Depending on the point on the screen, the waves of light
coming through the two slits will be either in-phase or out-of-phase.
By in-phase is meant simply that the peaks of one wave always
coincide with the peaks of the other (and since we are dealing with
a single wave-length light, all other parts of the wave will coincide
too). Where the waves are in-phase, the light on the screen will be
brightest. However, at some places on the screen, the waves will
arrive from the two slits so that the peaks of one wave always
coincide with the troughs of the other, and *vice versa*. When this
happens, the oscillations cancel each other out. The result is a band
of shadow.

Suppose, however, we reduce the intensity of the light source (by

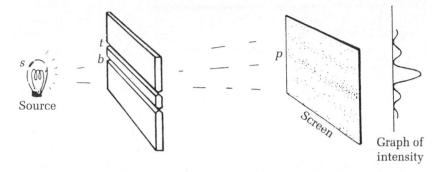

Figure 5.2 Pattern of Diffraction of monochromatic light passing through two slits
Source: R. Penrose (1989) *The Emperor's New Mind*, Oxford University Press

many million million millions!) so that it just emits a *single photon* at a time. When just one slit is open, the photon hits the screen on (or close to) a straight line from the source through the slit. If we keep repeating this so that the number of photons builds up over time, we will get the same single-band pattern that we would get if we fired a large number of photons simultaneously through a single slit. What happens with both slits open? A sensible guess would be that, if we repeat the experiment a number of times, the photon will sometimes go through one slit and sometimes through the other. We may not be able to predict the outcome of a single observation deterministically, but we can predict the statistical shape of a series of observations. In this case it should consist of *two* single-band distributions alongside each other, the one in line with the first slit, the other in line with the second, but each accumulating independently of the other. Indeed, this is very much what happens with two slits open, but *only* if we add another refinement; this is to place a particle detector at one of the slits so as to detect whether the photon has passed through the partition by one or the other of the two possible routes. But if we dispense with the detector, so that we cannot tell which route the photon takes, the outcome is eventually the zebra-like pattern of alternating bands of light and shadow typically produced by waves that reinforce and interfere with each other. The conclusion is that each single photon acts like a wave, passes through both slits at once (although we can never observe its passage) and interferes with itself.

There are therefore two very strange messages. The first is that even *single* particles can behave like waves. The second is that such wave-like behaviour is destroyed by any attempt to *observe in particle form* the passage of each photon en route from the source to the screen. (The point is that a detector at either of the slits can only record the passage of a whole *particle*, whereas the screen can record the arrival of light in either wave or particle form.) By introducing a means of removing uncertainty (on the question of route, i.e. spatial position), we actually change the photon's behaviour and make it behave like a particle (and only like a particle). Only if we remain ignorant on the route question do we allow the photon to behave like a wave.

If we take such findings as the basis for interpreting reality on a more everyday scale, the inferences one might draw are stranger still: *reality only exists in a particular form because we observe it so; if we left it unobserved it might be quite different* (and maybe it would then be more than one thing at once) . One can imagine Berkeley chortling 'I told you so!' – although even he would not have been prepared for the suggestion that perception *altered* reality, or that the world can only be determinate in one way at the price of being indeterminate in another. But how far can we push this inference? Must we restrict our uncertainty to physical events on the scale of a single photon, or can such indeterminacy extend even to matters of life and death? It is time to meet a remarkably long-lived animal.

Schrödinger's cat

The animal in question is part of an example presented by Erwin Schrödinger in 1935 to illustrate his dissatisfaction with the apparent implications of the uncertainty principle for the reality of everyday 'macroscopic' objects. We can accept, surprising though it may be, that electrons may be both particles and waves at the same time, but the objects of our visible environment surely can't be two things at once. A cat, for instance, can't be *both* alive *and* dead at the same time – or can it?

Schrödinger proceeds to describe an imaginary 'thought experiment' in which a cat is placed in a steel box, so that it is invisible to anyone outside. Inside the box is also a device containing a tiny amount of radioactive material. The radioactivity is so weak that there is a 50 per cent chance that one atom will decay within an

Figure 5.3 Schrödinger's cat
Source: P. Davis (1986) 'Time asymmetry and quantum mechanics' in R. Flood and M. Lockwood (Eds) *The Nature of Time*, Blackwell

hour, and a 50 per cent chance that no atom will decay. If one decays, this will be registered by a Geiger counter inside the box which will then trigger a hammer which will break a container of cyanide, and the cat will die. With no radioactive decay, the cyanide container will remain unbroken and the cat will live. When we open the box after an hour, we will discover what has happened.

Schrödinger was appealing to a common-sense view of what we could mean by indeterminacy at an everyday or 'macroscopic' level. At any time within the hour, the cat is *either* definitely alive or definitely dead (or dying) – *even though we can't tell which*. We can't easily imagine a 'blurred' reality in which a live cat and a dead cat are 'superposed' on one another (see figure 5.3). But the problem is that such a 'blurred' reality is just what the uncertainty principle seems to imply. The reason for this is that quantum-theoretical descriptions of physical events *are* in the form of combinations (superpositions) of different probabilistic functions. Radioactive decay is just the kind of process that can be so described, and the probabilistic (or 'blurred') description reflects our inability *in principle* to determine in advance whether a given atom will decay or not. Somehow, though, we don't feel comfortable about carrying over the same indeterminacy from the level of the atom to the level of the cat: but why not? Another aspect of the paradox is that we cannot look inside the box until the experiment is over. Does this matter? Surely not, we might say: a transparent airtight box would do just as well, as long as the radioactive decay and the trigger mechanism were not tampered with. According to the uncertainty principle, however, we *can't* necessarily assume that any observation leaves the process unaltered.

Schrödinger was very wrong if he believed that his example would discourage further speculation about the indeterminacy of reality. On the contrary, the conventional response of most defenders of quantum theory has been that his cat must live or die (or more accurately, live *and* die) according to the same laws that govern everything else in the universe. From their point of view, the cat too must be described as a 'superposition' of alternative states, analogous to the 'wave-function' of the atoms or subatomic particles on which its life depends, unless some interference can be specified which 'collapses the wave function'. The following are some of the suggestions that have been made about the reality of our quantum cat:

1 The cat continues to exist, as a superposition of dead and live states, even after we open the box and observe one of these states without the other.
2 The 'collapse of the wave-function', which leaves us with one alternative but not the other, is a consequence of *conscious observation*. Therefore the cat only becomes unequivocally alive or dead when we (as conscious observers) open the box.
3 We could, however, insure that the cat died immediately the atom decayed (if it decayed at all), by building the box large enough for a human observer with a gas-mask to sit in it too.
4 But maybe we don't need a human observer. Perhaps the *cat's* consciousness is strong enough to collapse the wave-function (but we'd better be careful, or we may end up predicting something different for an ant).

How seriously should we take all of this? Is it anything more than (as Hume certainly would have had it) 'mere sophistry and illusion'? The answers depend on what fundamental assumptions one is keenest to defend, and at what price. One such assumption is that cats can't be both alive and dead at the same time. The consequences of questioning that assumption are mind-boggling, and if we are going to redefine our categories of experience to such a radical extent, the arguments had better be good ones. Another assumption is that the uncertainty principle and quantum mechanics generally describe a universal truth about physical reality, at least at the level of subatomic particles. Nobody should lightly question this assumption either, unless they have a better theory to account for the stupendous amount of experimental evidence in its favour.

I am quite sure that *both* these assumptions should be accepted as true (the first necessarily so, the second contingently, so long as no better theory is suggested). The paradox arises because somehow they *seem* to be incompatible with each other, at least in the context of Schrödinger's imaginary experiment. This apparent incompatibility appears to derive from additional assumptions which, though appealing, must, in view of the paradox, be called into question. One is that the laws of physics apply in the same way to cats as to quanta. Another is that descriptions of physical reality cannot refer to anything other than what is directly observable.

Why Schrödinger's cat has been given no peace is that it implies a challenge to the underlying assumption of the uncertainty principle: that alternative descriptions of the same reality are complementary and *both true*. Whereas many 'quantum metaphysicists' have got very excited about what extrapolations we can draw from atoms to cats, quantum *physicists* have been more concerned with what they see as invalid extrapolations from cats to atoms. For what Schrödinger seems to be suggesting is this: that the uncertainty attached to our description of the cat is merely a confession of our own ignorance, not an account of what actually *is*. By analogy (but probably more than an analogy is being claimed), when we offer descriptions of physical events at the quantum level in terms of 'superposed' probabilities (e.g. wave or particle descriptions), it *isn't* that the alternative or complementary descriptions are both correct – it's that only one of them is, but we can't tell which. In short, the uncertainty principle only describes *our* ignorance, not the *actual* state of subatomic reality. Such a suggestion would be viewed as nothing short of heresy by most other quantum physicists.

But must the price of accepting quantum theory be an abandonment of common-sense notions of the reality of cats? Let's hope not, but if not, what has gone wrong? The answer may be partly the physics, and partly the philosophy. Schrödinger's thought experiment includes a number of red herrings. The first is the elaborate use of the Geiger counter to trigger the mechanism. From the point of view of the consequences of the triggering, it is completely irrelevant that the device relies on the emission of a radioactive particle. Any procedure resulting in a 50:50 probability would do just as well. We could link the device up to a pseudo-random number generator on a microcomputer. Or we could stay in the 'steam age' with two buttons on the outside of the box (without, of course, any indication which would trigger the hammer); we could then simply toss a coin to decide which button to press. Any such set-up would produce the required state of indeterminacy.

If designed in this way, however, the experiment would tell us nothing about *quantum* indeterminacy. This is why the Geiger counter and radioactivity are included, so as to imply that it all has something to do with quantum processes. But a Geiger counter is still a macroscopic object, so we are still left with the need to explain how a change in this object and a change at the quantum level may interact. This *may* relate to the need for reappraisal of the place of quantum mechanics within a more unified physical theory which could integrate concepts such as gravity and relativity (see, for instance, Hawking 1988, Penrose 1989), but let us leave even these important considerations aside. The point is that the Geiger counter is a measuring instrument and *no* measuring instrument can simultaneously resolve *all* aspects of the uncertainty inherent in any physical description of a quantum state; nor (as shown by the two-slit experiment) can such an instrument be introduced without affecting the quantum state itself. Thus, the mechanical linkage which Schrödinger introduces between the uncertainty of the cat's life and the uncertainty of the radioactive decay actually *prevents* any extrapolation from cats to atoms, at least with regard to the indeterminacy of quantum states in the *absence* of any measurement intervention.

Another red herring is the construction of the box so that nothing can be seen until it is opened. This is probably the most distracting aspect of the whole story, in that it confuses the indeterminacy of an unmeasured quantum state, which is (according to the uncertainty principle) a necessary feature of physical reality, with a purely contingent state of human (if not feline) ignorance. Even if the quantum uncertainty of the radioactive decay were unaffected by all the mechanical linkage, we could never know that this was so. Thus, we could not resolve *this* uncertainty by any observation of the *cat*. In short, we could put in as many video-cameras or windows as we wanted, and we still would not be able to observe directly what was happening at the quantum level. In fact (at great risk of mixing metaphors beyond repair!), the cat itself is a red herring too – as indeed is the cyanide, the hammer, and all the mechanical linkage back to the Geiger counter itself. All that matters is that a physical event has been recorded in a way that is in principle observable. We are still faced with the difficulty of inferring a correct description of the event in quantum terms, however, even if we have made that observation.

All this suggests that we should be able to give honour to the Caesars of quantum physics, and still sustain our commonsense beliefs about the impossibility of dead-and-alive cats continuing a 'blurred' existence for any *measurable* period of time. It is not that the uncertainty principle has *no* applicability to cats, or to life and death. (One could certainly imagine applying it to problems such as determining the *precise* time at which a cat, or indeed a person, dies. Even 'moments of death' cannot be infinitely divisible; and when we arrive at the limit of divisibility, a 'superposition' of life and death may indeed be an accurate description of reality.) It is rather that Schrödinger's imaginary apparatus tells us far less about quantum uncertainty than he claims.

Before we can arrive at such a happy conclusion, however, we have to dispense with the legacy of Berkeley: to be is *not* necessarily to be perceived or known. Statements about reality are not simply interchangeable with statements about observability. The cat can *be* alive or dead, even though we cannot (because of the box) *observe* it to be either. The uncertainty concerning the life of the cat is an aspect of our *knowledge*, not an aspect of the *reality* of the cat. And this is no more than we would have always assumed, were it not for the fact that the relationship between reality and observability is different when we deal with quanta. The uncertainty of a quantum state is an aspect of physical reality, not of human knowledge (or ignorance); and futhermore, if we try to observe such quantum uncertainty, we alter its reality. But with both cats and quanta, knowledge and reality are logically distinct.

Common sense and common reality

One of the most enduring of philosophical questions, as we have seen, is that of how we come to have knowledge of the world – a world that both includes ourselves and lies beyond ourselves. For the main empiricist philosophers, Locke, Berkeley and Hume, the first level of response was straightforward – we gain such knowledge through sensory perception. If we had no sensory input, we would have no knowledge. The difficulties – and the divisions within the empiricist camp – come at the next level of response, when we start to ask about the logical status, or certainty, of the knowledge we gain through our senses. There is no simple answer to the question 'Can you prove the existence of a real world on the basis of perceptual information?' It depends on what one means by terms such as 'proof' and 'reality'. To the extent that 'reality' is conceived of as logically distinct from 'what we perceive' (as it most forcibly was for Descartes), and to the extent that 'proof' means a logically necessary deduction, perception cannot prove reality. So how can our common-sense belief in reality be justified, if at all?

One way forward, adopted by Locke and pursued more systematically by Hume, is to consider how we come to believe in matters of fact despite their lack of absolute logical necessity. This carries with it a tendency to talk of our knowledge of the world as indirect, abstracted or derived by processes of inference and association. There are dangers here, however. One is that our experience of the world (often) does not *seem* inferential. It feels as though we experience things (e.g. cherries) as they *are*. If we take away such experience, it is difficult, if not impossible, to imagine what kind of idea of a cherry would remain: this was Berkeley's argument. But Berkeley went further, to propose a radical redefinition of reality: what is real is what is perceived; hence perception *proves* 'reality'.

Nowadays, it would seem that we have learned to think of proof in a more relaxed way. Induction is a respectable form of reasoning and both the natural and social sciences have accepted ground-rules for deciding on the confidence to be placed in empirical evidence. However, the concepts of knowledge and reality – and particularly their relationship to each other – continue to present major difficulties. Berkeley started from the 'common-sense' position that we learn about reality through observation. This led to the claim that we could not think of anything existing without assuming it to be observable. The mere *possibility* of something being observed, however, was not enough for Berkeley; any object would have to be *actually* (and continuously) observed before we could say that it *actually* (and continuously) existed. Reality is not just what is observable; reality is what is *observed* (if not by us, then by some other mind). Thus, from the 'common-sense' empiricist starting point that we need observation for knowledge, Berkeley takes us to the radical conclusion that we need observation for reality. Not only is what we observe real, what is observed is the *only* reality. Reality thus *depends on* observation.

From a very different starting point, many modern physicists have drawn a conclusion that has enough superficial similarity to Berkeley's to get many philosophers excited. Yet there are some very important differences that are sometimes overlooked. For Berkeley, the dependence of reality on observation was an expression of an essentially logical relationship. The importance of observation within quantum theory, on the other hand, assumes some kind of *causal* process. It is very difficult to specify exactly what this causal process may be, but the point is that physical reality *changes* as a result of measurement interventions. Even more vital is the idea that there *is* a reality before it is observed, and that much that is physically 'real' cannot *in principle* be directly observed, or known with certainty: this is what the uncertainty principle tells us. All this, however, is a long way from any claim that 'observation' somehow *creates* reality out of nothing, or even out of 'nothing but waves'.

What kind of empiricism will then be sustainable, and useful to an understanding of human thoughts and feelings? There are real things of which we do not, and cannot have, any direct and unambiguous observational knowledge. Furthermore, even with respect to the things which are large or powerful enough for us to see or hear or feel or taste, our observational knowledge will be incomplete. Although it is certain that we perceive such objects, we perceive them only in a few of their aspects and only from one perspective at a time. This is no more than common sense, or at least a modern version of it. It can lead into psychological issues such as selective information processing, and differences of opinion concerning the 'same' events or issues. There is a common reality, but we experience it in different ways. But there is still a nagging question left over from the earlier concerns of the empiricists: what *sense* can we make of reality, if not in terms of our own experience? And if our experiences are necessarily personal and selective, how can we make sense of anyone else's, and come anywhere near to sharing *their* reality?

6

Expression and Shared Experience

Aboutness

In the last chapter, I defended a view of reality as something that is 'objective' and 'out there', even though we may not be able in principle to define it in its entirety and even though it may appear rather different when interpreted from different perspectives. So much seems common sense, so long as we do not push it too far and provided we acknowledge the relativity of our *own* perspective. This relativity of perspective will reflect the differential amounts of attention we pay to features of our environment. It will influence how we interpret new information as a consequence of previous experience and of our own position in time and space. But common sense is never without its hidden difficulties. There may be a world 'out there', but how can we come to *say* anything about it? How can we use language to describe reality in ways that other people understand, and how can we understand what other people say to us?

Over the last 100 years or so, a great deal of philosophy has been preoccupied with the meaning and use of language. The reasons for this are not immediately obvious, but seem to stem from a broad acceptance of the empiricist view of reality. We learn about the external world through the information provided by our senses: that is the first lesson of empiricism. The existence of language is also a fact. Each by themselves, these are things that we take for granted almost all the time. But put the two together and we have the makings of a mystery. Language – to be language – must have meaning, but how is this meaning determined? I have my subjective experiences and you have yours, but how can we each put these into words? If I cannot see with your mind's eye, how can I be sure that we have the same experiences when we use the same words? More basically, do I even need to assume that we have the same experiences, or is it enough to assume that our separate experiences, similar or dissimilar though they may be, stem from a common (objective) source? The debates, therefore, are not just about words, but about the relation of words to things beyond themselves. But how can such a relation ever be established?

The relevance of this question to our understanding of attitudes may seem a little distant, but is quite fundamental. When you express an attitude, what is it you are talking *about*? Are you just describing your 'feelings', and if so how can you manage do so in such a way that other people understand you? Or are you saying something special about the world of publicly observable reality? I shall argue unequivocally for the latter alternative. If we accept the empiricist position that we learn about the world through our experience, then, by a short step, we can say that the world is what our experiences are about. What is true of experiences in general is true of attitudes in particular. When we express our attitudes or report our experiences, we are saying something *about* the world *and our relation to it*. An attitude is more than just a state of mind. Every attitude we have is *about* something. If we express an attitude, we are making a comment on some object 'out there' in the real world. Moreover, this comment will be something which other people can understand, because the same object can be part of *their* experience too. Any attitude theory, therefore, must look at how expressions of attitudes can come to be about a shared reality.

The relation of words to reality has been considered by philosophers from a number of standpoints. A good deal of discussion centres around the concept of 'intentionality'. Associations with everyday concepts of intention are confusing. This is a technical term referring to the capacity of thoughts and statements to imply that something else exists. According to Franz Brentano (1874–1973), from whose work this use of the term is mainly derived:

> Every mental phenomenon includes something as object within itself, although they do not all do so in the same way. In presentation something is presented, in judgment something is affirmed or denied, in love loved, in hate hated, in desire desired and so on. This intentional in-existence is characteristic exclusively of mental phenomena. No physical phenomenon exhibits anything like it. We can therefore define mental phenomena by saying that they are those

phenomena which contain an object intentionally within themselves. (p. 88)

I shall use the term 'aboutness' to include much of what Brentano meant by 'intentionality' – the capacity of thought to refer to an 'object within itself' – but I am aiming for a broader concept encompassing our use of the word 'about' in everyday speech. For many philosophers, what is important is the logical relationship underlying this implied 'in-existence'. If such 'in-existence' can be shown to be logically necessary, then we have the opportunity to put a new twist on Descartes: 'I think, therefore what I think about exists.' This, in turn, raises new questions, such as how we manage to think (and talk) about imaginary objects. Presumably we do so by some kind of analogy, so that we think of unicorns as 'like' horses and soap-opera characters as 'like' real people. But such difficulties need not detain us here.

Nor need we be side-tracked by the concerns of the early empiricists with the *causal* dependence of our visual impressions on physical properties of objects (as well as the anatomy of the eye). Although such work fits comfortably into the history of perceptual psychology, it leads to some muddles of a more philosophical nature. The presumption gained ground that statements about mental phenomena could only be understood through an appreciation of their causal dependence on (and correspondence to) objects in the observable physical world. On a Cartesian view, no such causal dependence of the mental on the physical can be assumed. However, even if we steer away from dualism, we risk being drawn into the quicksand of questions about whether we see the world the way it *really* is, and whether our view of the world has any more to recommend it than the view held by, say, a bat (see Nagel, 1979). There are also difficulties over the definition of the 'physical'. It is very dangerous to treat thoughts as 'mental' and the world as 'physical', since on no sensible account can the 'physical' be said to end as we penetrate the cornea or the cranium. Thought is itself a physical process, and this process will vary somewhat in its physical details between bats and people and computers.

But this is to anticipate a later argument. For the present, we need not make any specific claims about the underlying causal process. But we do need to acknowledge that thoughts are about *something*, and that, when we express our thoughts, we are saying something about objects and events in the world, from the perspective of our own experience. I have risked labouring this point because there is an alternative line that one might take, that to express a thought is merely to report some kind of 'inner' feeling or impression – rather like offering a peep onto the private performance of 'successive perceptions' passing across the stage of Hume's theatre. This alternative, indeed, underlies much loose theorizing about attitudes. At issue is whether statements of attitude are merely communications of private feelings and impressions, or whether they make claims about the nature of objective reality.

Describing experience

A familiar argument in the philosophy of language is that the meaning, or sense, of a phrase or statement depends on more than the object which it points out or *refers* to (Frege, 1892). Meaning is not just achieved by pointing at something: it is achieved by conveying usable information. The question of the meaningfulness of any statement thus turns on whether or not it is informative; and whether or not it is informative depends on its 'aboutness'. So long as expressions of thoughts are about familiar things, they are generally quite easily understood, but it is important to be clear about *what* is understood. If I say 'This strawberry is red', I am probably experiencing some red visual image. The nature of such an image depends on the operation of my particular sensory apparatus, which will be different in detail from that of other people and extremely different from that of some other species. However, it is not the operation of my sensory apparatus that I am referring to. The word 'strawberry' is not inter-substitutable with 'a red visual image of such-and-such size', since then my statement would translate to 'This red visual image is red', which would be a tautology (and hence uninformative). Instead, I am asserting a *fact*. I am referring to a strawberry (or something I take to be one). The truth or falsehood of what I say depends on the strawberry and *not* on my sensory processes (although these processes are what provide evidence of the fact).

The example of colour vision relates to another classic philosophical dilemma: do we see objects in the same way? More specifically, how can I know if what I mean by red is what you mean by red? There are two parts to this. The first is a question about whether you and I apply the word 'red' in the same way. This is in principle easy enough to settle, although it may be extremely tedious to do so. But let us assume that we both agree perfectly on which objects we call red and which we don't. We are then left with the more experiential question of whether the visual images you 'get' from red objects are the 'same' as those that I 'get'. In other words, if we could somehow get a photographic print-out of our visual images, would they be the same? The positivistic response is that this latter question cannot be settled empirically, and is therefore meaningless. As long as we use the word red consistently in the same contexts, we are investing it with the same meaning. The issue of the quality our visual *experience* of redness, as distinct from the objects themselves, is irrelevant to the meaning of the word 'red'.

Now this is all very well if our interest is in accounting for *how* we use language to describe colour, but there seems something missing at the level of accounting for *why* we should want to develop a colour language in the first place. Quite simply, we would not develop, and would not use, a colour language unless we could assume that other people are sensitive to colour in broadly the same way as ourselves. The evidence supporting this assumption, however, is that different people use colour words in comparable ways. Of their (private) visual images or experiences we can say nothing directly. Thus, although the statement 'This strawberry is red' is *about* a strawberry rather than anybody's visual experiences, the *making* of this statement makes no sense unless one assumes some comparability at the level of private experience.

The relativity of experience

It is for such reasons that 'aboutness' must involve more than merely 'pointing at' the object of our experience. Expressions of thought are not just statements about things in the world, they are about our relation to these things. Indeed, this must be necessarily so, in that *all descriptions of physical objects and events are relative to a particular reference point or perspective in time and space*. This relativity may often be hidden in both our use of language and our customary ways of thinking, but it is there none the less. The redness of the strawberry is a fact, but not a fact about the attributes of the strawberry alone. It is also a fact about how it may be distinguished by perceivers sensitive to particular ranges of light frequencies. It is a statement, implicitly, about the relations of the perceived and the perceiver to each other at a given point in time.

So we cannot define what statements are about on the basis of explicit reference alone. Yet the relative perspective is often left so implicit that it is easy to miss the fact that it is assumed. When this happens, statements that express thoughts (as indeed, all statements do) come across as statements about the physical world, pure and simple, rather than involving any privileged information about our own mental experiences. There thus seems nothing very mysterious about the fact that such statements seem to be easily understood, since they are about things we can all observe. Problems of a private language describing 'inner' experiences simply do not arise. How can we understand each others' thoughts? Easily, because such thoughts are about *things*, and these things are public. And so they are, but this is not quite the whole story. Sometimes we make the relativity of our perspective more explicit. We add a level of reflexivity to our expression of thoughts: we not only express our thoughts, we attempt to describe them. We introduce a distinction between the way things 'are' and the way they 'seem' to be.

Consider the following exchange:

'This strawberry is red.'
'No it isn't, it's green.'
'Well, it looks red to me.'

The first two statements are explicitly about the strawberry, and they contradict each other. The same strawberry cannot be both red and green at the same time (at least, not all over). The third statement is especially interesting, however, in that it does not actually contradict the second. What is more, it succeeds in reconciling the first two statements with each other at the level of speech *acts*, if not at that of absolutist descriptions of reality. It achieves this by redefining the 'aboutness' of the statements and the exchange as a whole. Instead of being about the strawberry *qua* strawberry, the conversation is about the participants' respective experiences of it, which can well be somewhat different from each other. This kind of stratagem seems to be widely used to take the inter-personal heat out of discussions of attitude, where disagreements are more to be expected. The third statement makes salient, in a way that the first two do not, the relativity of the perspectives from which we have made our observations.

This redefinition is not achieved, however, by turning the conversation into one which is just about visual sensations *qua* sensations. The effect of the third statement would be quite different if it went:

> 'You mean, you're having a green visual sensation and I'm having a red one.'

This would imply that the strawberry could be disregarded altogether, which is not the case. Although sensations have been brought nearer the front of the stage, they are still (in the original exchange) sensations *of* (that is 'about') the strawberry. The first speaker does not just see 'red', but a red strawberry, and the second speaker sees *it* as green. Much of the dualist puzzle over private language stems from a misrepresentation of the 'aboutness' of sensory reports and of mental statements generally. Such reports and statements do *not* describe, as dualists claim or imply, 'inner' events whose meaning is contained entirely within themselves. Any such descriptions would indeed be impenetrable by anyone else. Rather, they describe (that is, are *about*) things and events *as experienced*.

Mental statements are thus *not* fundamentally different from statements which make no allusion to thought and sensory processes, except in the salience they attach to the relativity of perspective. This does not mean that the different types of statements are interchangeable, or that their truth is settled always by appeal to the same criteria. The statements 'This strawberry is red' and 'This strawberry looks red to me' are not logically entailed by one another. A blind, or blindfolded, person could probably tell that a strawberry was red by its smell, or touch, or taste. Likewise, it would be quite intelligible for someone to say 'This strawberry looks red to me, but it's just as likely to be green, because I'm red-green colourblind and I can't tell the difference.' Yet these statement are still *about* the same object. We do not have two classes of statements: those about the 'external' world on the one hand and those about our 'inner' experience on the other. We just have different ways of talking about the world from the perspective of our own experience, and we make use of these different ways of talking in different contexts.

Meaning and context

The importance of context in defining appropriate 'ways of talking' is a fundamental issue in the philosophy of language, to which I shall not even attempt to give fair coverage. The pre-eminent influence of modern times is that of Wittgenstein (1953), who regarded meaningful language-use as a kind of game played according to arbitrary and context-specific conventions. I mention this here only to help correct a possible misconception. Although statements are about things in the world, viewed from a particular perspective, this 'aboutness' does *not* depend on a universal correspondence between particular words and particular 'things'. Sometimes words may be *used* in such a way that there is some local one-to-one correspondence with things, but this is just one feature of conventional language-use.

This is the same point as I made earlier concerning the distinction between sense and reference. 'Aboutness' does not depend just on the 'things' identified within a statement, but on the ways in which they are talked about. Communication comes more easily if we are in fact talking about things in the same way – if, in Wittgenstein's terms, we are playing the same 'language-game'. There are, indeed, many language-games that require agreement on the referents of specific words and phrases. For example, in the exchange:

'This strawberry is red.'
'No it isn't, it's green.'

The 'it' in the second sentence is taken to refer to the same strawberry identified by 'this' in the first sentence. However, this agreement in reference is not given in any way by the words 'this' and 'it' considered in isolation (a dictionary would be no help at all). Rather, the reference of the words is implied by the context of the conversation, and hence by rules of language-use relating to the use of demonstratives and pronouns *within conversations*. Thus, the fact that, within conversations, different words can achieve a common reference is a *product, not a cause*, of the fact that conversations are language-games based on shared 'aboutness'. (In the same way, the game of football requires that both teams play with the same ball; it does not just *happen* because there is only one ball on the field.)

Agreement over reference, in broad terms, does not guarantee agreement over 'ways of talking'. Consider the following:

'These strawberries have an excellent flavour.'
'No they haven't, they're green.'

On the face of it, this is another contradiction (since we know that green strawberries don't taste nice). But it can, in fact easily be resolved, by:

'Yes I know they're green now, but they have an excellent flavour when they're ripe.'

The point is that a comment on the flavour of strawberries could be made *either* within the context of 'ready to pick now' *or* in the context of 'excellent variety'. One could, just about, argue that this implies that the referents of the first two statements were not quite identical, in that different *properties* of the (same) strawberries were being considered. But the more straightforward interpretation is that our two strawberry-pickers experienced a mild failure of communication because they were trying to have different kinds of conversation. That is to say, they were playing slightly different language-games. (A game of football does not just require that both teams play with the same ball; it requires that they both play by the same rules.) There is one important conclusion that can be drawn from this: we need to be attentive to the kinds of conversations people are trying to have when they make statements that seem to express their thoughts, feelings and attitudes.

Bodily sensations

You doubtless will remember George the gardener, whose encounters with philosophers and psychologists (in chapter 4) left him with a pain in his leg. Not all our mental experiences seem to be about events beyond ourselves. If being about something 'out there' is what matters, then how are we to be understood when we try to talk about things 'in here'? Part of the answer is that it often *is* very difficult to communicate our personal experience of bodily sensations, mood states, and such like, in ways which we are confident that other people will understand. But this does not require the reintroduction of any inner/outer-world distinction. What I believe contributes most to such difficulties of expression is that the focus of 'aboutness' has been shifted almost exclusively onto oneself as perceiver rather than the topic or object as perceived. We are still being asked about events as we experience them, but the emphasis can often be on saying what is special about our way of experiencing them, rather than what is special about the events themselves. It is clearly much easier to describe events which you feel others would experience in the same way. Being asked to say in what ways your feelings are different from everyone else's is almost like being asked in what ways your feelings are difficult to describe. If they can be easily communicated, they can't be special!

But this, as I said, is only part of the answer. By far the more important part is that the fact that the 'real world' does not end at the epidermis. Our bodies are part of it too. There is no essential difference between my talking about strawberries and talking about my right leg that could make the former kind of statement philosophically less problematic than the latter. On the contrary, I actually get a much richer, and more continuous, stream of sensory information from (and hence about) my right leg than I could get from (or about) a strawberry. Where there is a difference is that much of this sensory information is of a kind that simply is not available to me from objects other than my own body. There is thus a qualitative change of sorts as the focus of my sensory attention moves from under my skin to above it. This inner–outer distinction, however, is still a physical one, that is, one between different parts of physical space. It is *not* a distinction between an inner 'mental' world and an outer 'physical' one.

Thus, pain does not force us back into a dualistic account of expressions of feelings since pain is still an experience of a physical object, namely our own body. We can say 'My leg hurts' as intelligibly as we can say 'This strawberry is red', and we can be understood as immediately and non-inferentially. To claim 'Ah, but no one can have *your* pain' is as inconsequential as claiming 'No one else can have *your* visual image of a strawberry': it merely asserts that any two people's experiences will be numerically distinct. Whether their experiences will be qualitatively different is quite another matter, and will depend on a variety of factors, such as whether they are both looking at the same strawberry and whether they are both being sat on. Similarly, inferring that someone else's leg is hurting, say from the presence of a large bruise on it, is no more nor less mysterious than inferring that a strawberry is red from its smell. There is no dispute that our expressions of thoughts and feelings can depend on different kinds and amounts of information. But this does not mean our expressions must be about different kinds of 'worlds'.

Thinking about and thinking that

Towards the end of chapter 3, I mentioned William James's notion of the 'stream of consciousness'. An important feature of this notion is that what we are conscious of is objects, and that it is the continuity of our consciousness of objects which, above all else, gives us our sense of personal identity. Like Hume, James did not posit a 'self' as a distinct object of consciousness, over and above the things the self was conscious *of*. Notwithstanding special occasions when we are particularly 'self-conscious', we are conscious of *things*; we are not conscious of our consciousness. Thinking, though, does not merely imply that objects of thought *exist*, it implies that they exist in a particular way. In other words, thinking consists in the handling of information, or knowledge, about things.

Because of this, it might be argued that a notion of 'thinking about' is too woolly: what we should progress to is a notion of believing or of 'thinking that'. If this line is followed, we may want to characterize consciousness as consisting typically of what we *believe to be the case* at any given moment. An even stronger version of this position would be that conscious thinking consists of internalized belief *statements*, or propositions. The temptation to characterize thought (like truth) in terms of propositions, is one which many philosophers find hard to resist. For instance, Dennett has proposed that 'propositional episodes, these thinkings that *p*, are our normal and continuous avenue to self-knowledge . . . they exhaust our immediate awareness' (1986, p. 165). Much work in contemporary cognitive psychology has likewise looked to linguistics for its theoretical direction. Prototypical is Fodor's (1975) hypothesis that cognitive processes involve a 'language of thought' involving the manipulation of representative symbols to generate propositions.

But how explicitly are such propositions featured in on-going consciousness? If we think about some object, this seems to put us in a better position to say what we believe about it, if we are called upon to state our beliefs. But this only means that thinking helps us *arrive* at some belief or opinion, perhaps by helping us direct our attention, or search our memory for relevant information. The fact that conscious thinking *allows* us to formulate propositions does not mean that the 'stream of consciousness' consists entirely of 'propositional episodes'. Try asking yourself how many propositions fill your consciousness right now. Or let me make it possibly a little easier for my argument – stop thinking about this book (just for a moment!) and look out of the window; allow yourself to think freely about what you can see. (Or perhaps that's too restrictive – just look out of the window and think anything you want . . .)

If I look out of my window at this very moment, I can see a tree, with blue sky and a white cloud above. The tree is in shadow, but further off, there are other trees still lit by the sun. There is a light breeze which is moving the leaves. The silhouette of the leaves against the sky seems more and more intricate the more closely I look at it . . .

This little piece of introspection is, as well as I can express it, a fair account of what I was thinking about just now. Certainly it is all 'about things in the world and my relation to them'. It is about what you would see too, if you were here too, looking over my shoulder. But is it propositional? Doubtless, a logician could point to many *implicit* propositions: a tree exists, the sky exists and is blue, and so on. There are also some statements that have the syntactic form of explicit propositions: the tree is in shadow, the breeze is moving the leaves, and so on. I am not using words just for fun. I am saying what I believe to be *true*. But I do not feel I am 'making propositions' in the sense of asserting something that is anything other than self-evident to me. I am not 'proposing' that the tree exists; I can *see* it does. I am not 'thinking that' the white in the sky is a cloud; I recognize it as such.

If you insist on classifying the above introspection as 'propositional', I would accept that there are parts to it which could be so described, and so you may be correct, logically. But I would still feel uneasy about this, in that I didn't *feel* I was 'formulating propositions' in any elaborate way. This isn't to say that I couldn't do so, if I let myself, or if you asked me what I *knew* or *believed* about what I was looking at. I could ask myself what kind of tree the one in the foreground might be, and infer that it is some kind of oak, and that therefore the leaves will turn golden in the autumn. I can say that I know that there is a river between the foreground tree and those in the background, even though it is hidden by the leaves, because (among other reasons) I remember clearly how it looked from my window in the winter when the trees were bare. I am sure that the silhouette of the tree-top is what Mandelbrot (1983) would call a fractal curve, and I will be arguing later that consideration of such curves carries some important implications for attitude theory. Such 'propositional episodes' take over more and more of my consciousness as I elaborate my thoughts about the view. Such elaboration involves subjecting my impressions to a kind of critical analysis, and this analysis can involve explicit 'thinking that'. But before such elaboration, my thoughts seemed to me to be a consciousness *of*, not a consciousness *that*.

It may be tempting to see this difficulty as arising just from an ambiguity in the term 'propositional'. However, I believe it is more important than that. If we wish to say that statements can express thoughts and conscious experience, we need to have some view on what such thoughts and experience contain. Fodor's view implies that consciousness is shaped by a 'language of thought'; pushed further, this might suggest it is a form of 'inner speech' or (in Ryle's phrase) a 'silent soliloquy', to which we may, from time to time, give voice. Where better, then, to look for evidence of the nature of thought than in the structure of spoken *language*? Another view is that thoughts contain whatever they can be taken to imply. This involves treating thoughts primarily as *logical* structures. Thus, in thinking about the tree outside, I could be said to be thinking, by implication, that the tree outside exists. This view seems to have something going for it, in that my thoughts about the tree outside would at least be very different, if not entirely absent, if I believed that the tree did not exist. Both these views, however, seem to involve treating thought as something other than itself, as either a kind of linguistic structure or a kind of logical structure. They leave us, on the one hand, with the intuition that we may have thoughts that are difficult to put into words, and, on the other hand, with the difficulty that we often do not think through many of the possible implications of our immediate thoughts.

It is because our immediate thoughts have a quality of 'aboutness' that we can use language to express them. 'Aboutness' allows us to talk. If we think about an object (such as the tree outside), we can assert what we believe to be the case about it (such as that it is an oak). 'Aboutness' allows us to think *that* something is the case. But this does not mean that 'thinking about' is reducible to talking to ourselves or 'thinking that'. It has a greater immediacy (or, as James would have put it, 'warmth and intimacy'). It is not that I 'think that' there is a tree outside my window. I do not merely 'infer' or 'believe' that the tree is real. I see it; and this seeing, this consciousness, is, for me, inseparable from the grasping of its reality. So much would Berkeley also have argued. But whereas, for Berkeley, the presence of an object to consciousness is what constitutes its reality, for me (and I hope for you) reality is what consciousness is of and about.

Knowing that and knowing how

Introspective accounts of my immediate consciousness, however, leave at least one important question unanswered: how do I know that it is a tree that I see? Although my consciousness may be 'immediate', it clearly has a history. Among the relevant features of this history are that I have seen many trees before, and have learned that the name 'tree' can be applied to them. My *knowing* that it is a tree that I see depends on previous learning, even if such knowledge is experienced as immediate. Knowledge has the important characteristic that it can be retained or stored. That is to say, it does not disappear (at any rate, not altogether!) when we turn our head, or go to sleep, or do anything else to interrupt our stream of consciousness. There is thus an important sense in which we can be said to *know* something, even if it is not at the forefront of our mind at the time.

What kind of knowledge do we put in store? A straightforward view would be that we store factual information, or 'knowledge-that'. There may be many ways in which such information could be stored, which may or may not require some kind of linguistic code. We do not need to teach a pocket calculator any kind of spoken language to make it store the product of a multiplication. None the less, *if* we had a memory that relied on linguistic codes and rules, we would, on the face of it, have something very well adapted to the storage of 'knowledge-that'. We would thus be led to the view that memory stores *propositions* (e.g. leaves are green; trees have leaves) on which we may perform various operations, according to specific *rules* and criteria. Thus, we might have a propositional memory even if we do not have a propositional consciousness.

To build an alternative to such a view is not easy. Is it even desirable? One reason why it may be worth trying is the distinction introduced by Ryle (1949) between 'knowing that' and 'knowing how':

> In ordinary life . . . we are much more concerned with people's competences than with their cognitive repertoires, with the operations than with the truths that they learn. Indeed even when we are concerned with their intellectual excellences and deficiencies, we are interested less in the stocks of truths that they acquire and retain than in their capacities to find out truths for themselves and their ability to organize and exploit them, when discovered . . . (pp. 28–29)
>
> To be intelligent is not merely to satisfy criteria, but to apply them; to regulate one's actions and not merely to be well-regulated . . . Yet the general assertion that all intelligent performance requires to be prefaced by the consideration of appropriate propositions rings unplausibly, even when it is apologetically conceded that the required consideration is often very swift and may go quite unmarked

by the agent . . . when we describe a performance as intelligent, this does not entail the double operation of considering and executing . . . (pp. 29–30)

To put it quite generally, the absurd assumption made by the intellectualist legend is this, that a performance of any sort inherits all its title to intelligence from some anterior internal operation of planning what to do . . . By the original argument, therefore, our intellectual planning process must inherit its title . . . from yet another interior process of planning to plan . . . The regress is infinite, and this reduces to absurdity the theory that for an operation to be intelligent it must be steered by a prior intellectual operation. What distinguishes sensible from silly operations is not their parentage but their procedure, and this holds no less for intellectual than for practical performances. 'Intelligent' cannot be defined in terms of 'intellectual' or 'knowing how' in terms of 'knowing *that*' . . . When I do something intelligently, i.e. thinking what I am doing, I am doing one thing and not two. My performance has a special procedure or manner, not special antecedents. (p. 32)

As will be remembered from chapter 4, Ryle's main thesis is that statements about the mind do not refer to 'occult' events, separated off from the observable world of behaviour. Thus, intelligence for him is a characteristic of performance. We can discern intelligence because performance is observable. This is part of a general debunking of dualism, but it contains a more specific message too. If, despite Ryle's own prejudices, there is some purpose in the scientific study of thoughts and feelings, these phenomena must be tied in conceptually with the activities and performances of which they are a part. These activities and performances unfold in time, and involve interactions with other things and (especially) other people.

It is easy to regard thinking as something we *do* and knowledge as something we *have*. But this dichotomy may be less clear-cut than it appears. We *use* our knowledge. If we did not, it would be hard for us (or anyone else) to say we had any. When we use it, this gives our performances a 'special procedure or manner'. We can use it too, as Ryle points out, without necessarily being able to explain what it is that we know. We also can improve our knowledge, just as we can improve our performances, as we gain experience. Thinking is an activity that unfolds in time, whereas knowledge persists over time. This persistence, however, is not something static, but dynamic. If thinking can be represented as an expenditure of energy, knowledge is the trace or record or resting-place of such energy. But this resting-place is itself remoulded by the energy expended. If the perpetual flux of thought can be described as a 'stream', knowledge is the valley through which that stream flows, and which has been shaped, as it still is being shaped, by the stream itself. Just as a geography of a stream would be incomplete without a description of its valley, so a theory of 'thought' would be incomplete if it considered only the contents of immediate awareness without account of what was known or remembered. Likewise, we would not find all we needed in a theory that concentrated on knowledge-structures in long-term memory, to the neglect of consciousness and current activation. The reason for this is that knowledge and thought are part of a single system. When we think what we are doing, when we use our know-how, we are, as Ryle put it 'doing one thing and not two.'

Where, in all of this, should we place our 'knowing that'? Perhaps it enjoys a less intimate interaction with immediate awareness, perhaps it is less basic to the quality of intellectual and practical performance, but some account must be taken of it, none the less. Let us grant that we do not always 'know how' to *use* our 'knowledge-that'. We still *have* it. We still can be *tested* on it, as easily and objectively (and perhaps more so) than we can be tested on some skill. From the positivistic standpoint, 'knowing that' is no more occult or private than 'knowing how'. An important clue, I believe, lies in language: in the difficulty we have in expressing our 'knowing how' and the ease with which we can express our 'knowing that'. It seems paradoxical to suppose that 'knowing that' is a mere serendipity alongside the flow of our cognitive processes, while still assuming that language – the medium through which such knowledge is expressed – is the most distinctive feature of human cognition.

As I have argued, mental statements generally are understood because they are about things in the world and our relation to them. By the same token, statements which express our knowledge-that are intelligible because they are commenting on things in the world. They are not descriptions of mere thought processes, even though knowledge is a *product* of thought. (This distinction must be remembered, as otherwise we are committed prematurely to the view that 'knowledge-that' requires a linguistic memory-code.) They are not mere read-outs of on-going cognitive activity, even though they are certainly a behavioural *output* of such activity, and a skilled observer may be able to infer something about our cognitive activity from them. In short, knowledge-that statements lay claim to objectivity, just as surely as introspective accounts of consciousness lay claim to subjectivity.

What is the prime criterion of objectivity? The truth of a claim is independent of the identity of the claimant. Attribution theorists (e.g. Kelley, 1967) express this in terms of the criterion of *consensus* across perceivers: if everyone agrees with me that the strawberry is red, I can feel reassured that I'm not colour-blind. But consensus is merely diagnostic of objectivity, not a necessary or sufficient condition of it. If my beliefs are objective, I can expect other people to agree with me; but if other people disagree with me, that is their problem. (It can become my problem too, of course, if it leads me to doubt my beliefs; but that is a different issue. The truth or error of a belief does not depend on who agrees with me, any more than it depends on whether it is my belief or someone else's.)

Thought is an intrapersonal process, quite difficult to describe and not necessarily linguistic in its structure. From this process, however, comes a product – knowledge-that – which we bring to the market-place of interpersonal exchange. We trade it, negotiate with it, sell it, buy it, and give it to our friends. It is, in short, a *commodity*, which we can either hold in common or (more precariously) secrete in a private hoard. What contributes to the value of this commodity? It is transportable. You can take it home and make it yours without it turning to dust between your fingers. It is also durable. It might wear out with time, but it will give you many years of pleasure first. It certainly will last longer than a cherry or a strawberry, let alone the sensation of a cherry or strawberry in your mouth. We might wish to say that knowledge-that is thought, abstracted from the particularities of time and space.

Knowledge and shared reality

Knowledge possesses yet another quality of an almost magical simplicity. We can give it away, time and time again, and still keep as much of it as we had before. Economists might argue that something in such free supply should be seen as of little worth, but they are wrong in this, as in so many of their other presumptions about human behaviour. True, there are differences in novelty value, in the remoteness of the source of supply, and in the difficulty of bringing the supply to market (i.e. communicating the knowledge). Yet if we have some knowledge to give away, whatever it is about, from theories about the origins of the universe to gossip about someone we met at a party, it is almost painful to keep it to ourselves.

Communication is like some never-ending potlatch without the self-impoverishment, in which everyone gives away their prize possessions but never loses them.

We do all this, relatively easily, with language. Have we evolved this capacity because of the special value of the information or knowledge we can thus communicate? At some level, this must be so, but matters cannot be quite so simple. If adaptive behaviour at the individual level is the sole criterion, knowing how must surely be more valuable than knowing that. Communicating know-how seems to require at least as much skill as does communicating knowledge-that, but the former seems less dependent on language ('Here, let me show you' as opposed to 'Here, let me tell you'). As far as any simple notion of survival value is concerned, other species seem to do well enough with a limited repertoire of alarm calls, courtship displays, and signals related to the availability of food. Arguably, for the communication of any really important or urgent knowledge, we have other media than language available to us, and many of these media are more effective.

So what do we 'buy' with this extravagant evolutionary investment that we call language? Part of the answer, I would suggest, is a *shared reality*. Of this reality, I can say things which (I hope) are true, beyond the particularities of my own momentary experience. With language, I identify those aspects of my experience which I recognize, and expect others to recognize too. I look for patterns, for continuities, and for permanences. I talk about these aspects, these patterns, and check that you have recognized them too. When I find you have recognized them, I know, beyond all reach of scepticism, that there are other minds, that I am not alone in the universe, and that, because I can give my thoughts to you, they are also *mine* to give: *tu penses, donc je suis.*

Of what should I talk, to assure myself of this reality that you and I both share? On the face of it, almost anything which we can name will do, since any *thing* is as real as any other. If something disappeared before my eyes, or you insisted on denying that you saw something that was clearly visible to me, I should be quite as panic-struck if it was a coffee-cup as if it were a chair, or a tree or even (horrors!) my own hands (at least I imagine so; I have no experience of hallucinations). To the extent that *all* these things are real, *none* of them should just disappear. Language allows us to talk about anything under the sun. Knowledge of anything under the sun can serve as barter in the negotiation of a shared reality. As far as knowledge-that is concerned, we are omnivores. If the security of our place in the universe is at stake, we will be hungry for anything that is put in front of us.

So does this mean that we go to all the trouble of acquiring and using language merely to assure ourselves that the world exists, and we within it? Of course not, put like that. But one problem with putting it like that is the use of 'merely'. Assuring ourselves of reality and identity is nothing *mere* if it allows for the emergence of creative and coordinated *social* behaviour and relationships. This goes beyond ethological conjectures of how language first evolved and what advantage it bestowed on primitive humans or pre-humans. We are not talking just about inherited survival strategies, but of something demanded in the here-and-now, something we use all the time to achieve mutual influence over each other's thoughts, feelings and behaviour. For all manner of reasons, both trivial and profound, we need to know how far we agree about things with other people, how well they understand us and we them, and what we can expect, or should demand, of *ourselves* in the context of our social relationships.

Although we may feel threatened by the removal of any part of 'our' reality, although we can talk about anything under the sun, there may none the less be topics which assume a greater significance, where we are especially concerned with acquiring knowledge or where we most particularly wish to convince others to accept that what we believe is true. The significance of these topics will vary tremendously across historical and societal contexts, to the bemusement of any travelling Gulliver. What distinguishes them all, however, is the presence of controversy. Apart from a few physicists and philosophers, nobody considers the material existence of cherries or cats (or trees or strawberries) to be in the least bit controversial. But ask about the benefits of nuclear power, the morality of abortion or feelings of nationhood, and cracks appear in the veneer of a shared reality. It is at those fault lines that attitude theory should make its entrance.

7

Attitudes and Social Reality

The social and the individual

There is a reality, we can be conscious of it and think about it, and we can tell other people about it. These are the givens of common sense, and common sense is right. Yet reality is so vast and complex, our consciousness of it so selective, and our powers of expression so bound by convention, that common sense fails to recognize the wonder it has achieved. It also fails to recognize the dependence of this achievement on the help that others have given, in confirming the objectivity of so much that we take for granted. When we talk of seeing trees, or tasting cherries, our consciousness can seem to be a personal, private experience, which we can share with others if we feel both clever and generous, but which we owe to nobody but ourselves. In short, we take it all for granted.

This egocentrism is not just a feature of common sense, but also of much of much theorizing in both philosophy and psychology. The individual self is taken as both the starting point and the focus of analysis. Perhaps this is convenient for many of the particular questions that philosophers and psychologists attempt to answer. But when it comes to fitting the pieces together, it leaves us without a pattern or a purpose. Solitary specialisms claim as their prerogative the study of capacities and forms of thought which make sense only within a social context. Yet social psychology, as it is now, is not much better. Too often we are content with applying some 'basic' theoretical principle to something vaguely interpersonal. Too often we 'psychologize' about 'social issues' without articulating how social interaction makes psychological processes the way they are.

There are other trends, equally dangerous if carried to extremes. One is to ignore individual thinking altogether, and confine one's attention to publicly observable aspects of social interactions. Aspects which at various times have been submitted to particularly close scrutiny are eye-contact, posture, non-verbal cues and gestures, and ordinary conversations. These all reflect some kind of psychological process. Yet to attempt to build a social psychology on a mere description of such activity is as barren as the worst form of behaviourism. It would be better to acknowledge at the outset that thought comes into social behaviour, and to develop decent theories of how such thought occurs.

Another approach is to regard social behaviour as a reflection of categories imposed by society. According to more extreme versions of this dogma, individual thought is confined by the 'representations' or systems of meaning shared consensually by society as a whole, or imposed upon society by a dominant group. Such influence is commonly regarded as inexorable. Depressing though this may sound, it gives perverse comfort to those researchers reluctant to make the effort to study behaviour in its true diversity. If every member of a society is constrained by the same representations, then a single individual – *any* individual – can speak for society as a whole. Problems of sampling, of statistical inference and of individual differences, are dismissed as irrelevant by definition.

Within both these approaches, the interdependence of the individual and the social is left to go begging. The meaning of any social interaction depends on the thoughts of the participants, both in acting and in interpreting each others' actions. Of course such interpretations will be influenced by the systems of beliefs prevalent within society or within a person's immediate social group. If there is disease among the children and livestock of a village, it makes some difference if it is widely attributed to witchcraft or to radiation from a nuclear plant. It is easier to hold a belief if others share it. But holding a belief is still something which individuals do, by virtue both of their participation in social relationships and of their personal experience and capacity for choice.

Once again, common sense may contain shrewder implications than many formal theories. We take for granted the existence of objects like trees and cherries, and assume that anyone who was not intellectually or perceptually impaired would recognize such objects much as we do. But we do not take *everything* for granted in this way. There are 'matters of opinion' as well as matters that are beyond dispute. Sometimes we anticipate that others will disagree with our assessments or that we ourselves might change our minds. We experience not just a set of 'objects and events', but a reality which we allow may be imperfectly shared. In such cases, the relativity, and instability, of our own perspective comes closer to the forefront of our conscious experience. We experience reality as provisional and open to dispute. Thus, the possibility of dispute – a social thing – shapes individual experience, just as awareness of this possibility shapes the manner in which such experience is expressed. We try to take account of others' thoughts in what we think and say. We compromise our egocentrism. We acquire an attitude.

The acquisition of attitudes

Approached from the viewpoint of traditional theories of learning, the acquisition of attitudes consists of the learning of *responses*. This is a too restrictive definition to persist with for very long, but it may be a beneficial purgative for a short while, and may offer lessons that can be taken forward into a more developed account. What does this definition imply? Among other things, it implies that attitudes involve reactions to events, and that these reactions occur *in time*, with an intensity, speed of onset and duration that likewise vary *over time*. Another very important implication is that these reactions are learned in response to highly specific situations. There are severe limitations on how easy it is for learning to be 'transferred' from one situation to another. This is not simply true of non-human species. People seeking behavioural treatment for drug-abuse, alcoholism or cigarette smoking may successfully learn strategies of self-control in the shelter of the clinic which they then find much more difficult to apply when they return to their home environment and former acquaintances. Re-exposure to activities, people and places associated with drug-use in the past can all too easily trigger a relapse; in the terminology of learning theory, drug-use has become a *conditioned response* (CR) to the *conditional stimulus* (CS) of a specific situation.

This emphasis on situationality and time-dependence is quite missing from approaches that regard attitudes as somehow 'just there'. It also underlines the problematic nature of attitude consistency. Unless other pressures for consistency are introduced extrinsically, we should not expect any more consistency among the various manifestations and expressions of a person's attitude than there is similarity between the stimulus contexts in which these various responses are observed. It should be no surprise whatsoever if people appear to act and talk as though they had completely different attitudes in different situations. According to the learning theory view, we should start from the assumption that all these 'attitudinal' responses are acquired *separately* in response to separate situations. The burden of proof is on those who would claim that there *is* cross-situational consistency in attitude, not on those who claim that such responses are context-specific. There is nothing 'given' about consistency; if it is found, it needs to be explained.

A learning approach also allows us, at least under certain circumstances, to ascribe an immediacy to attitudinal experience that is much of the kind for which Zajonc (1980) argued (see chapter 1) when insisting that 'preferences need no inferences'. Granted all the inferential processing in which we *can* engage when discussing our attitudes, it is easy to overlook such immediacy. The goodness or badness of things (of some unexpected kindness, or the news of some atrocity or tragedy) can still strike us in the face as noninferentially as craving for a drug can strike an addict. Just as with the addict's craving, however, our immediate evaluative reactions depend upon a developmental history, that is, on a long schedule of previous associations and reinforcements.

The acquisition of verbal expressions of attitude

Less confidently, we might pursue a similar line regarding many verbal expressions of attitude. There is definitely a sense in which we can learn (from our friends, or teachers, or family) what kinds of things one should *say*, for instance, about Iraq, or cigarette smoking, or global warming, without necessarily having to *think* too deeply about any of these. There may well be times when verbal 'expressions of attitude' should *not* be regarded as expressive of any well-thought-out position, but rather as just what we have learnt to say within that context. Language, like anything else, can be over-interpreted. None the less, its interpretation is not without constraints. The context in which it is used (for instance, a conversation) is already more than *just* a 'conditioned stimulus'; it already involves the exchange of thoughts and meanings, and this exchange is played according to rules. If the rules of such an exchange are disregarded, the interaction becomes nonsensical, however reliable the conditioning.

The making of an attitude statement is therefore an act to which *meaning* can be imputed. It is difficult to talk sensibly of attitude statements as 'having meaning' on a purely behaviourist account. On the other hand, 'meaning' is not some private experience or thought process that just 'happens' to be associated with a particular statement or expressive act. The use of language depends on the default that people mean what they say, and say what they mean. Even non-reflective speech has meaning. Even the copying of other people's slogans implies some assertion about reality. Yet at the same time, there must be *some* room for speakers to claim that their remarks have been misunderstood. People may mean what they say, without meaning everything which others take to be implicit in what they hear. But if we are to be believed when we say 'That's not what I meant', we must be able to explain why. We must be prepared to answer the question 'What *did* you mean then?', or else concede that our thoughts are too unready to be put into words.

What is involved here is much the same problem as that addressed by Ryle when he discussed people 'exercising qualities of mind' or doing things with 'care and attention' (see chapter 4). The degree of care and attention with which people express their thoughts and attitudes is certainly very variable, and a careless expression may provide an insecure basis for predicting other behaviours. In its own terms, however, it still expresses something. If it is to be disregarded, some excuse must be offered. In the absence of a good excuse, it is vain to try and distinguish the meaning of our thoughts from the meaning of what we say. We should be very wary of defining an attitude or the meaning of a statement in terms of some antecedent state of mind by which the speech act is somehow controlled or motivated. As Ryle would put it, when we think what we say, we are doing one thing, not two: our verbal behaviour has a special quality or manner (of thoughtfulness). But there is still much that qualifies as attitudinal expression that lacks such a special quality, appearing instead as somewhat automatic and uncalculated. Behaviour of this latter kind may reflect a long history of conditioning and imitation, and cannot simply be ignored just because it lacks sophistication. Attitudes do not have to be sophisticated.

The acquisition of expectancies

So, we need to be prepared to take expressive acts as they come, without, on the one hand, jumping to over-generalized conclusions about the broader characteristics of the actor, or, on the other hand, feeling that every statement requires cross-examination before reliance can be put upon it. Such expressive acts have meaning, although such meaning is relative to their context. If we are to think of modes of expression as learned behaviours, we need a view of learning that allows some place for meaning; that is, one that offers an account of how learners *interpret* events, and adapt their behaviour accordingly. Fortunately, research on learning has already moved a long way in this direction. Even for non-human animals, it is now much more accepted to talk of learning as the *acquisition of expectancies*. Thus, a dog may salivate at the sound of a bell because it has learned to *expect* that the bell will be followed by food. A rat may turn to the left in a maze because it has learned to *expect* that food is more likely to be found in that direction. Such expectancies seem to depend very much on the kind of principles of association (resemblance, contiguity and constant succession) described by Hume.

Is all this any more than a reinterpretation of old data in a new cognitivist (and anthropomorphic) guise? Some caution is clearly needed, since it is still the same kind of behaviour we are trying to explain. We can say that an animal is behaving *as though* it expects this or that to happen, but we cannot say more than this for sure. In general, the stronger a stimulus–response connection in the old scheme, the stronger an 'expectancy' in the new. But not always. One implication of more modern theories is that responses will be learned to a stimulus if that stimulus appears to 'tell' the animal something useful about the environment. This depends on the reliability, distinctiveness and novelty of the information that a stimulus provides. It is not simply a function of the frequency of previous associations between, say, a conditional stimulus (CS) and an unconditional stimulus (US), or between a response and a reinforcement. In other words, stimulus control of behaviour depends on stimulus *informativeness*. To say that an animal has acquired an expectancy means – or should mean – just that it is this informativeness that guides behaviour.

Let us apply this logic (hypothetically) to the familiar example of Pavlov's experiments on dogs conditioned to salivate to the sound of a bell. According to the traditional interpretation, what matters is simply the number of times that food (the US) is presented immediately after the bell (the CS). According to the cognitive view the bell has 'information value' because its occurrence predicts the arrival of food. This information value would be less if there were many occurrences of the bell without food (and this would also be acknowledged in the older theory). More crucially, if the dog was constantly being given food, whether or not the bell sounded, it would be unlikely to be conditioned to the bell (i.e. salivate at its sound) even if the bell was *always* followed by food. Adding 'free' USs (or rewards in other contexts) thus undermines the value of the CS as a predictive sign (see Rescorla, 1968, for an example of this kind of manipulation). The information value of a CS can also be undermined if it is redundant to the purpose of prediction. For example, Pavlov's dog, attending to the bell and successfully predicting the occurrence of food, would be unlikely to become conditioned to a second CS, say a light flash, even though its relation to the US was just as predictable. Kamin (1969) describes this process as the 'blocking' of new learning by a previously learned association.

All this encourages a reinterpretation of the large experimental literature on (animal) learning. To learn is to adapt one's representation of the environment so as to handle new information. Put differently, it is to update one's knowledge. But what kind of knowledge? Once again we need to remember the context with which we are dealing. We can see that, as a result of learning, a rat knows *how* to find its way to food in a maze, or a trained racing pigeon knows *how* to find its way home from a distant starting point. This kind of knowledge is part of the acquired behaviour, and this behaviour seems to us to be purposive, or at least responsive to appropriate information. It seems to depend, in other words, on some form of *thinking* or information-handling.

But none of this requires us to say that the rat knows *that* there is food in the right-hand arm of the maze, or that the pigeon knows *that* a particular heading will lead it home. We do not need to assume that the knowledge they have gained from their training consists of abstract representations of 'if-then' rules or propositions; and because we do not need to assume this, we should be careful not to do so. This is where talk of 'expectancies' could lead us astray, since any *stated* expectancy is a proposition. Although pigeons and rats may act expectantly, they do not, and cannot, explicitly *state* an expectancy. But this is only a partial denigration of their cognitive capacities compared with ours. It is far from clear that we generally *use* propositional knowledge in the course of our behaviour, even though, within limits, we can *express* such knowledge if called upon to do so.

This is precisely Ryle's distinction between 'knowing how' and 'knowing that', although the conclusions I am drawing from this distinction perhaps take a different direction from his own. It *is* important to reaffirm that animal and human behaviour can be thoughtful; but to describe behaviour as thoughtful – as involving thought – need not mean that it depends on the explicit and conscious representation of factual propositions. It *is* important to reaffirm that learning, in animals as well as humans, depends on *some* kind of thinking or information-processing. We need to account for habits of thought, as well as habits. Different environmental conditions lead us not just to act differently, but to think differently too; and such thoughts, like behaviour, can persist. In the words of William James, what is important is that *'thinking of some sort goes on'* and that it goes on in time.

Attitudinal experience

Many textbooks draw an unhelpful distinction between attitudes and beliefs. The former are characterized as 'subjective' feelings, which may be more or less favourable, the latter as 'objective' reality-claims or propositions, which may be true or false. This distinction is difficult to sustain for any length of time. Possible syntactic cues are unreliable. We can preface explicit reality-claims by phrases such as 'I feel that' or 'In my opinion': for instance 'I feel that Margaret Thatcher has been good for Britain'. Conversely, we can express affective evaluations by means of particular kind of factual propositions. When Edward Heath is reported as saying 'Margaret Thatcher has a tiny mind and tells lies', it is quite clear what kind of evaluative judgement he is making. To claim that the first of these statements expresses an attitude and the the second a belief, is to stretch the syntactic distinction beyond plausibility. Clearly, both express personal feelings and both make general claims about reality – claims which might be sustained or countered by different kinds of evidence.

What is common to both these statements, and the classes of which they are examples, is more important than the phraseology that divides them. Both are claims *about* a real, objective person (Thatcher); the point of making either statement is that other people might dispute the claimed reality; and both statements may be used as part of a strategy of persuasion or of resistance to persuasion. The inclusion of phrases such as 'I feel that' and 'In my opinion' may signal that the reality-claim is made more tentatively, and/or that differences of opinion should be tolerated in this context, but it does not transform the statement into one that *only* expresses feelings. The feelings are still 'intentional', that is, about something beyond themselves. To express feelings is also to make a claim concerning what such feelings are about.

Attitude statements, then, are much the same as other kinds of statements expressing thoughts (what I have called mental statements). They are about reality and our relation to it. It is quite misleading to regard them as mere reports of private impressions. According to such a view, we would be left with just the same puzzle about how such reports could be meaningfully interpreted as was raised by treating descriptions of perceptual objects as reports of private images. In this respect, there is no essential difference, epistemologically, between making a factual statement such as 'This strawberry is red' and an attitude statement such as 'Margaret Thatcher has a tiny mind'. Both are about things in the world, viewed from our perspective. Both make reality-claims, the validity of which is to be settled by appeal to evidence and argument.

But what kinds of evidence and argument? It is here that attitudes start to appear rather more special. It is certainly easier to specify objective criteria for redness than for qualities such as 'tiny-mindedness' or 'goodness for Britain'. It is still Thatcher, rather than any commentator, to whom these latter qualities are imputed; but their imputation is likely to invite more controversy than claims about the colour of a strawberry. We can make some progress, then, by regarding attitude statements as making potentially controversial claims about reality. But perhaps this definition is too inclusive. What gives rise to this potential controversy? Claims about the existence of flying saucers would certainly invite disagreement, but it is unclear that we would want to call such disagreement attitudinal. The answer I would suggest is that all attitude statements imply an *evaluation*, and that it is mainly this evaluation that is controversial.

Evaluation and description

The evaluative aspect of attitude statements contributes to their controversiality, not because it rests on some extra private experience of which public evidence is difficult to obtain, but because of the problem of specifying exactly what criteria should be applied in judging whether anything or anybody is good or bad. Hume went further, and argued that moral statements, concerning what *ought* to be or be done, can never be derived from statements concerning what *is*. This is clearly correct if what is demanded is *absolute* proof of the goodness or badness of anything across all contexts. Apparently similar actions can be censured in some situations and praised in others. Even within the same situation, individuals can differ in their allocation of praise or censure. On the other hand, it is also clear that we typically appeal to an object's characteristics when arguing that it is good or bad *within a context*; likewise, we may insist that the context should be defined selectively in such a way that some characteristics are accepted as more relevant than others. Attitude statements are about things, and they impute characteristics to such things. However, the fairness of such imputations, and their implications for evaluative judgement, are frequently open to dispute.

This distinction between description and evaluation is both revealed and disguised by ordinary language. As I have already suggested, one of the functions of language is to describe our view of the world in such a way that others can come to share it and confirm it. Another function, closely related to this, is to express our preferences, our views of what is good and bad. The one tricky aspect to all of this is that the same words and phrases can convey *both* description *and* evaluation. This can be related back to the philosophical distinction between sense and reference (Frege, 1892). We can *refer* to the same action or person in ways that carry very different *senses* (e.g. 'dictator' vs. 'inspiring leader'). More specifically, we can talk of words or phrases *denoting*, i.e. referring to, certain attributes or characteristics, and also *connoting*, i.e. implying, certain associations and evaluations. Evaluations can be conveyed implicitly, therefore, by statements which, on the face of it, are objectively descriptive.

Language can serve both overt communicative, and covert persuasive, functions. Thus, Nowell-Smith (1956) talked of 'J-words' (after the Roman god Janus, who faced both ways) and Stevenson (1944) of 'persuasive definitions'. To describe (or denote) someone as a 'dictator' is both to make claims about that person's political style and (within our linguistic culture) to condemn that style. In fact, ordinary language is full of such words, where the evaluative aspect is covert or implicit. If broad agreement on questions of value is a major plank of the social reality we attempt to create through communication, it seems that we attempt to create it by stealth, without declaring our own values too explicitly or prematurely. In this respect, ordinary language is inherently rhetorical.

One sure sign of language's rhetorical nature is that it can be recruited to the service of contrary causes. That is, almost anything can be described in ways that make it sound good rather than bad, or bad rather than good. Abortion can be described as women exercising their right of choice, or as the murder of unborn babies. Once either description has been accepted, the argument over how abortion should be evaluated is already won or lost. We can therefore expect that supporters and opponents of particular causes will differ in their preferences for particular modes of (value-laden) description. We can expect them to differ in their selective definitions of the context in which the object or issue should be evaluated.

It is a moot point how aware people are of the selectivity, or relativity, of their own perspective and preferences. Some people may go to great trouble to anticipate their opponents' arguments, whereas others may not. However it is one thing to be aware of counter-arguments, and quite another to acknowledge their potential validity. It is one thing to be aware that some people *call* abortion 'murder', and quite another to concede that abortion could *be* 'murder'. It is difficult to see how the latter type of concession could be made without some weakening of a prior attitude (in this case, support for abortion). My own impression is that people are often somewhat aware of the arguments of the 'other side' – or at very least, of the existence of 'another side' who takes a different view to their own; however, they tend to have rather less insight into the dependence of their evaluations on their own perspective.

We tend to disentangle the evaluative and descriptive aspects of language from one another, if at all, with difficulty and reluctance. Value connotations are treated as no less 'factual' than the denoted characteristics with which they are associated. This amounts to saying that value-laden descriptions are offered as being no less 'objective' than value-neutral ones. Indeed, ostensibly value-neutral statements can serve rhetorical, and hence evaluative, functions within specific contexts. For instance, consider this imaginary exchange:

'Edward Heath says Margaret Thatcher has a tiny mind and tells lies.'
'Edward Heath is getting old.'

Here the second statement, superficially an incontrovertible assertion of fact, is used to make a controversial point: that Heath's
advanced years mean that less credence should be given to his
pronouncements. In the terminology of rhetoric, this kind of argument (indeed, like that which precedes it) is called *ad hominen*
(directed at the person). We might wish to say that the word 'old'
is being used in this context (and possibly not just in this context)
to convey connotations of negative value. Unless the tone were
sarcastic, quite different connotations would be conveyed by:

'Edward Heath is a senior statesman.'

This illustrates an important way in which evaluative language
contributes to the maintenance and advocacy of controversial positions. It can be applied not only to the object or topic itself, but also
to various positions and participants in the debate about that topic.
It can be used to claim credit for one's own side and to discredit,
or discount, the opinions of one's opponents.

Obviously, using language persuasively is a skill at which some
people are more proficient than others, and the issue itself makes
a difference to the kind of persuasive definitions which can be
brought into play. But the flexibility is already there, in the breadth
of everyday vocabulary and the diversity of everyday expressions.
A simple example of this is provided by the way in which we label
personal characteristics. Take people who spend a lot of money.
Are they 'generous' or 'extravagant'? Or take people who spend
very little. Are they 'thrifty' or 'mean'? In either case, more or less
the same behavioural characteristics can be described by words that
carry connotations of approval or disapproval.

The phrase 'more or less' is important, because it allows us still
to look for conventional objective criteria to distinguish, say, gen-
erosity from extravagance. One notion is that negatively evaluated
behaviours or characteristics tend to be descriptively more *extreme*
than positively evaluated ones. Excess or deficiency will be viewed
less favourably than moderation. This proposal dates back at least
to Aristotle, who writes (*Nicomachean Ethics*, Book II):

In agreeableness in social amusement, the man who hits the mean
is 'witty' and what characterizes him is 'wittiness'. The excess is
'buffoonery' and a man who exhibits that is a 'buffoon'. The opposite
of the buffoon is the 'boor' and his characteristic is 'boorishness'.
(tr. Thomson, 1955, p. 70)

In stressing that language serves both evaluative and descriptive functions, therefore, we are not committed to a view that preferences and attitudes are arbitrary 'feelings', split off from 'objective' descriptions of things in the world. Attitude statements make claims about what is 'objectively' the case, but these claims are typically controversial. Their controversiality does not depend on the lack of *any* objective criteria by which they may be judged. Rather, the controversy arises from imperfect consensus over *which* criteria are relevant and how they should be applied. Neither, though, are we committed to either of two alternative ethical theories. We do not have to regard the moral worth of any action as *determined*, universally and categorically, by what can be 'objectively' said about it. Nor do we have to take 'good' as meaning just whatever most people *happen* to prefer. In saying that attitude statements make 'objective' claims, I am saying just that these claims are *about* things in the world, viewed from a particular perspective. Whether these claims are *true*, either necessarily or contingently, is a quite separate question, on which analysis of the relevant psychological processes does not depend.

The relativity of attitude measurement

One area of research which clearly illustrates the importance of evaluative and descriptive aspects of language is that of attitudinal judgement. The specific question is that of how we make judgements of attitude statements, that is, of others' attitudes from the things they say. Why should such judgements be important? The answer is partly historical. In chapter 1, I mentioned the work of Thurstone (1928), which led to the development of most familiar techniques of attitude measurement. Thurstone proposed that attitudes could be measured along a continuum of unfavourability to favourability. This continuum was assumed to have the mathematical properties of a straight line, and to be divisible into intervals of equal width, much like the markings on a ruler. This conception of a linear continuum has dominated attitude research ever since and, as I shall soon argue, is overdue for replacement. For the moment, though, the issue is a more technical one. If you want to measure people's attitudes along such a continuum, how do you do it?

Thurstone's answer (in his so-called 'method of equal-appearing intervals') was as follows. Select a series of statements that express different viewpoints on a single issue, evenly distributed over the range from extremely anti to extremely pro. Then present these to the people whose attitudes you want to measure and have these people indicate which ones they agree with. If someone agrees with statements which, for instance, fall on average in the moderately pro region of the continuum, we can say that he or she has a moderately pro attitude. To make this more quantitative, what is needed is a numerical measure of where each statement falls on this hypothetical continuum of favourability. If we can obtain such a measure (termed a 'scale value') for each statement, we can feed this through to calculations of a person's attitude. Instead of just saying than someone was 'moderately pro' because she agreed with 'moderately pro' statements, we can say that she had an attitude score of 8.0 on a scale from 1 to 11, because she agreed with statements with scale values of 6.5, 6.8, 7.7, 8.0, 8.7, 8.8 and 9.5.

But what do these different scale values mean, and how are they obtained? Let us assume we are trying to measure people's attitudes to Margaret Thatcher. Obviously, the statement 'Thatcher has a tiny mind and tells lies' is anti-Thatcher, in the sense that anyone who agreed with it (or made it) could be assumed to have an anti-Thatcher attitude. But how extreme is the anti-Thatcher sentiment expressed here? Well, probably quite extreme; but we could imagine even more extremely unfavourable statements ('Thatcher was an evil dictator', 'Thatcher was a danger to life on this planet', and such like). So if we were asked to say where the 'tiny mind' statement fell on a scale from 1 to 11, where 1 represented the most extremely anti-Thatcher statement one could plausibly imagine, and 11 the most extremely pro-Thatcher statement, we might put the statement at say, 2 or 3 or 4, but maybe not at 1. Note that in doing so, we would not be (directly) saying anything about our own attitude to Thatcher; we would be saying what kind of attitude we thought this statement *expressed*. We could do the same with the statement 'Thatcher was good for Britain'. This is clearly a pro-Thatcher statement, but probably much less extremely so than, say 'Thatcher will go down in history as the greatest world leader of the twentieth century', 'Thatcher's political vision was unsurpassed', and such like. So maybe 'good for Britain' might come out around 7, 8 or 9 on the 11-point scale, but perhaps no higher.

To make this assessment of the favourability of statements less hit-and-miss, Thurstone proposed a formal procedure in which a large set of statements would be presented to groups of people ('judges') who would be asked to give judgements of the statements on the equivalent of the 11-point scale just described. For each statement in turn, the ratings of the different judges would then be averaged, and this average score would be taken as the 'scale value' or measure of expressed favourability of the statement. Note that the judges are asked to say what kind of attitude is *expressed* by each statement; they are specifically told *not* to use the scale to indicate whether they personally agreed or disagreed with the statements. This distinction is vital, since Thurstone proposed that these judgements should be *unaffected* by whether the judges were pro or anti. As Thurstone and Chave (1929, p. 92) expressed it 'If the scale is to be regarded as valid, the scale values of the statements should not be affected by the opinion of the people who helped to construct it.'

This was a strong assumption, and subsequest research has proved it to be thoroughly wrong. None the less, it took more than twenty years for the crucial evidence to be presented. Hovland and Sherif (1952) took an established scale to measure attitudes towards black people, and showed that many of the statements were rated very differently (in terms of whether they conveyed pro- or anti-black attitudes) by whites with 'average' or segregationist attitudes on the one hand, and by blacks and white supporters of black civil rights on the other. By and large, the different groups of judges agreed with each other on how the statements were to be *ranked*, that is, in terms which statements were *relatively* more pro than others. Where they disagreed was in terms of the *absolute* score, or level of proness or antiness, to be ascribed to each statement. The extent to which a statement was seen as expressing a pro or an anti attitude, therefore, was largely dependent on the perspective of the person making the judgement. Thus, the enterprise of deriving an *absolute* measure of a person's attitude, as some fixed point along a fixed continuum, must be abandonned. Attitude scales can still provide scores that are useful for a variety of purposes, but the meaning of such scores is *entirely relative*.

Evaluative language and attitude judgement

A number of studies have attempted to identify the form of this relativity and the processes that underly it (see Eiser, 1990/1991). A striking feature of the data presented by Hovland and Sherif (1952) is a tendency for black judges and whites with pro-black attitudes to rate most of the statements as expressing very anti-black attitudes. (In fact, when one looks at the actual statements used, which are now sixty years old, they certainly seem very skewed by present-day standards). This effect was described as one of judges 'contrasting' their ratings away from their own position: the more pro their own attitude, the more anti they rated most of the statements as being. Evidence from later research suggests that such 'contrast effects' are part of broader pattern: judges whose own attitudes on an issue are more extreme will *sometimes* give more extreme ratings. That is, they will tend to see more statements as either extremely pro or extremely anti, rather than as falling in the middle of the rating scale.

The emphasis on 'sometimes' is very important. In my own research, I have shown that this tendency to give more extreme ratings depends on the evaluative language in terms of which judges are asked to make their ratings. Specifically, this tendency is strongest when judges can use words with positive value connotations to describe statements of which they happen to approve, and words with negative connotations to describe statements of which they disapprove. If, on the other hand, they have a response scale where they would be forced to use a negative word to describe opinions they shared, and a positive word to decribe opinions of which they disapproved, the tendency is for judges to lump together their ratings nearer to the midpoint of the scale. A concrete example should make this clearer. In two studies (Eiser and Mower White, 1974, 1975), teenagers read ten short passages, of which five expressed opinions that were in favour of adults having a highish degree of authority over young people, and five were opposed to such authority. They then had to rate their impressions of the people who could have made each statement. These ratings were on made on a series of scales, chosen so as to be deliberately value-laden. On half the scales, one extreme was marked by a term that could be taken to denote a pro-authority attitude in a way that connoted positive value, for example 'cooperative'; the opposite, 'uncooperative', was used at the other extreme to denote an anti-authority attitude with negative value connotations. On the other half of the scales, the value connotations were in the reverse direction. Negative terms (e.g. 'unimaginative') were used to label the pro-authority end and positive terms (e.g. 'imaginative') to label the anti-authority end. We split the teenagers into different groups according to their own expressed opinions about adult authority, and compared their ratings.

In terms of how much these teenage judges 'polarized' their ratings towards the end-points of the scales, the results show a simple pattern. Those judges whose own attitudes were more pro-authority gave more extreme ratings on scales like 'uncooperative–cooperative' and less extreme ratings on scales like 'imaginative–unimaginative'. It is as though they were happy to describe opinions of which they approved (and hence to decribe themselves) as 'cooperative', but resisted calling their own side 'unimaginative'; on the other hand, they preferred to describe opinions on the other side as 'uncooperative' rather than 'imaginative'. This difference was exactly the other way round for the more anti-authority judges. These gave more extreme ratings on scales like 'imaginative–unimaginative', the implication being that they were happy to describe themselves as 'imaginative' but not as 'uncooperative'. Other features of the results fit in nicely with Aristotle's views about value and extremity. It seems that 'imaginative' was used generally to describe positions which were less excessively anti-authority than those described as 'uncooperative'; likewise 'cooperative' was seen as less excessive than 'unimaginative'.

Relativity of measurement, or judgement, is more than a simple matter of judges comparing attitude statements with their own viewpoint. It is reflected in the choice of labels in terms of which different statements and positions should be discriminated from one another. Extremity of response is generally regarded as an indication that respondents can make such discriminations more easily and confidently. What our findings show is that this ease and confidence is not just a matter of the discriminability of the statements *per se*, but of the dimensions, or language, in terms of which such discriminations have to be made. Our respondents clearly felt easier and more confident when using a response language that expressed both the descriptive and evaluative distinctions they wished to draw. They preferred descriptions that matched their own evaluations, that allowed them to commend their own side and denigrate the opinions of the other side.

The expression of attitude

This brings us back to the persuasive or rhetorical functions of evaluative language. How can we defend our own view of social reality as the 'truth', even when we are aware that some other people do not share it? The question is not so very different from asking how we might defend our belief that the earth is roughly spherical if we were ever faced with someone who insisted it was a flat disk, supported on the back of a giant elephant. Short of offering to embark on a circumnavigation, we would mention general categories of evidence, and argue that these showed our position was correct. But if all this failed, if the other person refused to yield, we would look for *explanations* of the disagreement. One such explanation, or 'attribution' (see chapter 4), would be that we are more 'rational', 'moral', 'enlightened', 'well-informed', or whatever, whereas the other person was 'irrational', 'immoral', 'bigoted', 'ill-informed', and so on. This kind of name-calling is more than just a trading of insults. It is a way of saying whose views of reality deserve greater, and whose lesser, respect.

This pattern comes out very clearly when considering how supporters and opponents of nuclear power characterize each other's positions. In the context of a debate concerning a proposed nuclear reprocessing plant, we asked nuclear supporters and opponents to choose from a list those words which they felt best described the pro-nuclear and anti-nuclear sides. Supporters described the pro side most often as 'realistic, rational and responsible', but the anti side as 'emotional, alarmist and ill-informed'; opponents, in contrast, described the pro side as 'materialistic, complacent and elitist', but the anti side as 'far-sighted, humanitarian and responsible' (Eiser and van der Pligt, 1979). Very similar preferences for evaluative labels were found among supporters and opponents of nuclear power in the aftermath of the Chernobyl accident (Eiser *et al.*, 1989).

More tentative evidence suggests that the use of such value-laden language may not simple serve to defend an existing attitude; it may shape that attitude itself, through encouraging a selective evaluative definition of the issue. For example, students who were asked to write a short essay about capital punishment (but without being told to express support or opposition) shifted their opinion in a more pro-capital punishment position when instructed to incorporate into their essays epithets that could imply a denigration of the abolitionist side (e.g. over-sentimental, starry-eyed). Conversely, if they were asked to incorporate words implying a denigration of capital punishment (e.g. callous, sadistic), they shifted towards greater support for abolition (Eiser and Ross, 1977). This may tell us something about the effects of slogans in political propaganda.

Value-laden language is thus a very important part of the way in which we describe one another's opinions, and there is evidence that such language may fulfil both persuasive and self-persuasive functions. These functions relate directly to the controversial aspect of attitudes, that is to say, to the existence of attitudinal *disagreement* as a problem with which we have to deal. Such disagreement is typically represented in terms of a difference of value. *We* are good thinkers and our thoughts deserve the most weight as definitions of reality; *they* are bad thinkers and their thoughts can be discounted where they contradict our own. However, if *all* that were involved in attitudinal disgreement was a difference in evaluative feeling, we would not need anything like so complicated a system of communication. We could frown or smile, or growl or purr, and the direction of our 'affect' would be clear enough; if others felt differently, that would be their business. The 'aboutness' of attitudes is what renders this account inadequate, and allows us to talk of disagreement and controversy. Such disagreement arises from differences in what is *thought* about the issue. These different thoughts are value-laden, and we use value-laden language to express them. The language of attitude expression is more complicated than growls and purrs because the purposes it serves are more complicated.

Language and categorization

One of the most basic functions of language, value-laden or otherwise, is to categorize. There are fewer names we can give to things than there are things we can name. By labelling different things in the same way, we are saying that they can be treated as similar or equivalent for the purposes in hand. By labelling similar things in different ways, we are stipulating that the distinctions between them are important. Categorizations therefore can be more general or more specific. The same object can be described as a tree or an oak. If the tree *is* an oak, both descriptions will be equally true. The appropriateness or usefulness of either description, however, will depend on the situation.

When considering attitudes, we find language fulfilling a similar function. We can have attitudes about either very general or very specific issues and categories of things. General attitudes and specific attitudes can be equally coherent, depending on the circumstances. Sometimes it makes sense to ask people about their attitudes to 'nuclear power' in general and sometimes it is more informative to ask them whether they would accept underground storage of nuclear waste on the outskirts of their village. Sometimes it makes sense to ask people whether they support environmental conservation and sometimes it is more useful to ask whether they feel it is worth recycling glass bottles. As mentioned in chapter 1, this relates closely to the question of how well 'attitudes' predict behaviour. There are many studies where general measures of attitudes towards, say, 'the Church', or 'black people', fail to predict specific behaviours which (according to the researchers' presumptions) *should* reflect the attitude in question. As the work of Ajzen and Fishbein (1980) especially shows, if you want to predict specific behaviours, the most effective attitude measures you can use will be measures of attitude towards the performance of just those specific behaviours. Research on learning implies that such behaviours are likely to be acquired separately, in response to context-specific cues.

If we can categorize things more inclusively, we can formulate attitudes towards *classes* of objects or issues, and these general attitudes will tend to be predictive of opinions on specific objects within a class. The main danger lies in assuming that objects form a class when, from the perspective of the individual, they may not. Can nuclear weapons be classed together with nuclear power stations or underground storage of nuclear waste to form a single attitude object called 'nuclear power'? Does saving water go along with buying 'ozone-friendly' household goods and recycling glass bottles to constitute a single concept of 'environmental conservation'? These are empirical questions, and the answers will depend on whom you ask and when.

Consistency as a social product

Categorizations can be made at different levels of generality or inclusiveness, and on the basis of different criteria. Categorizations are selective, and so too are the associations and generalizations which they permit us to make. These simple facts are of great importance in trying to make sense of one of the most widely accepted ideas in attitude research, that attitudes form *consistent* structures. I have stressed that we need to be very careful with this concept of consistency. We may, as the relevant theories claim, try to resolve inconsistencies between different thoughts and feelings, but the evidence strongly suggests that we only do so for *certain* kinds of inconsistency in *certain* circumstances. There are also

individual differences: some people are more tolerant of inconsistency than others. All this points to the conclusion that attitudinal
consistency is selective, personally defined and incomplete.

From the point of view of research on learning, however, the
acquisition of *any* form of attitudinal consistency is something that
requires a special explanation. Since learning takes place *within*
situations, consistency *across* situations must be separately learned
if it is learned at all. One possibility is that such consistency is
an accommodation to social demands or normative pressures. This
raises two questions. Firstly, what social demands might influence
us to be consistent generally? Secondly, what social demands might
influence us to be consistent in a *particular* way?

On the first point, it seems reasonable to propose that social
interaction runs more smoothly if people are able to predict one
another's wishes and actions, and that this also requires us to make
ourselves predictable. Such predictability may be achieved by the
following of simple behavioural and interpersonal rules, rules which
to some extent override the specificities of situations. We might
suppose that a good bit of socialization is directed towards the
learning of predictability, of the matching of our schedules with
those of others, and of the honouring in one context of commit-
ments entered into in another. We are rewarded for a certain amount
of dependability, whereas 'irresponsibility' can get us into trouble.

It is important not to carry this argument too far, since there are
also social demands that we should be capable of flexibility in our
behaviour, rather than responding rigidly to all situations in the
same way. The demand that we are consistent in the rules by which
we deal with one another needs to be set against the demand that
we remain open-minded and ready to examine separate cases on
their merit. Michael Billig (1987) points out that such flexibility is
a typical, and perhaps necessary, aspect of the way in which people
defend their viewpoints, even where these are strongly held. An
attitude (or prejudice) which is too rigid is one which will be less
easy to defend against counter-argument or contrary evidence. Even
so, *some* kind of consistency does seem to be required of us by
others, while extreme inconsistency is likely to earn us labels of
insanity, if not more immediate reprobation or punishment.

But what *kind* of consistency? Nothing is consistent or inconsistent with anything else absolutely. Consistency can only be defined
within a selective frame of reference, so what appears inconsistent
from one perspective may well appear consistent from another.
What might this imply for the social pressures towards consistency

just postulated? It would seem that we are reinforced, not for consistency *per se*, but for the adoption of a frame of reference that coheres with that of other people, for the adoption of a common perspective on social reality.

Other people have a stake in our consistency, but not just *any* kind of consistency. We are required to be consistent in ways they *recognize*, just as we ourselves are required to be recognizable. This will mean, in practice, that we are encouraged to select similar features of situations as the most important, that is, to adopt similar categorizations of reality. If we do not, we are affronting other people's versions of reality, and threatening or disputing their capability of distinguishing what is from what is not the case. In the case of attitudes, we are disputing their distinctions of good from bad, since these are likewise relative to the system of categories we adopt.

Self-consistency

We also have a stake in maintaining consistency, to the extent that we need to be recognizable to others. If we ceased to be a recognizable part of other people's reality, our own concept of self would be immediately threatened. James (1890, pp. 293–4) expresses this vividly:

> No more fiendish punishment could be devised, were such a thing physically possible, than that one should be turned loose in society and remain absolutely unnoticed by all the members thereof. If no one turned round when we entered, answered when we spoke, or minded what we did, but if every person we met 'cut us dead', and acted as if we were non-existing things, a kind of rage and impotent despair would ere long well up in us, from which the cruellest bodily tortures would be a relief; for those who would make us feel that, however bad might be our plight, we had not sunk to such a depth as to be unworthy of attention at all.

Just as attitudes can be held and expressed at different levels of generality, so we can adopt, and be encouraged to adopt, broader or narrower category systems in terms of which to distinguish between situations or to exhibit cross-situational consistency. Thus a single source of influence is likely to lead us to be more cross-situationally consistent in some respects, but not in others. But social influence itself is far from monolithic. Even the same people can make contrary demands of us, and there are very many different people whose expectations of us have to be considered. We may learn systems of categorizing reality from other people, but there are always many alternative systems which we can learn, or to which we can have access. There is always more than one way of looking at things. We always have a choice, although no choice may be absolutely free of conflict or ambiguity.

When we adopt an attitude, whether general or specific, we are accepting a subset of ways of defining social reality and resisting others. In so doing, we are allowing other people to regard us in certain ways (but not others) and to form certain expectations of us. We are adopting a particular social identity or personality. This process must be selective, if the resultant pattern is to be at all distinctive and recognizable. This means that different attitudes will be more central to our social identity than others, more part of how others see us, and more part of how we may define ourselves, if called upon to do so. Attitudes are not necessarily consistent across situations or different from every situation to another. It depends on the attitudes *and the individual*.

This conclusion in fact fits in well with findings in the field of personality measurement. One extreme view is that personality traits are universal human characteristics that apply relevantly to everyone, and predict behaviour across all manner of different situations (even if only partially). The trouble is, such simple cross-situational consistency is rarely if ever found, whereas situational factors tend to predominate over personality measures in the prediction of behaviour (Mischel, 1968). A compromise was suggested by Bem and Allen (1974) along the folowing lines. Some personality traits are applicable to some individuals, and other traits to other individuals. What is more, people tend to have insight into the traits which are applicable to themselves, that is, those in terms of which their behaviour can be characterized as cross-situationally consistent.

It seems plausible that we may also have insight into the different levels of consistency of our various attitudes. Do you, for instance, feel you have a consistent attitude towards the issue of environmental protection generally, or (if you prefer to think of things this way) across a range of *different* environmental issues? To the extent that you feel you can claim such consistency or generality, you will be prepared to categorize your attitude towards 'environmental conservation' in terms of a particular level of favourability. In doing so, however, you will not have found some royal road of introspection to an 'extra' motive or feeling, over and above the specific thoughts and opinions you are already likely to have expressed (say, on the topic of nuclear waste disposal, or the recycling of glass bottles). But you will have recognized a pattern, a system of categorization in those opinions. You will have identified a habit of thought which you accept as part of yourself and part of how you describe yourself to others.

8

Changing Shapes

The patterning of attitude

An attitude, I have proposed, is a habit of thought. We recognize this habit, in ourselves and others, through identifying patterns of experience over time and context. Attitudes involve an association of value with other objective properties of things: that is to say, a recognition of things as (more or less) good or bad. In so far as such goodness or badness is seen as an objective property of things (rather than a fleeting mood), attitudes take on a quality of persistence or semi-permanence. The adaptability of such patterns of association is reflected in the flexibility of evaluative language, as discussed in the last chapter. To the extent that the things themselves do not change very much, nor the contexts in which they are observed, their goodness or badness will not change very much either. If these things do change over time, moreover, such changes will often be orderly, so that we can still recognize a continuity between how they are and how they used to be. Consistency (or at least, orderly change) over time thus seems to be one criterion for saying that we have an 'attitude' towards something – that is, the kinds of thoughts that qualify for the label of 'attitude'. We can still, of course, have many other kinds of thoughts about things, including evaluative thoughts, but without the presumption of persistence or continuity, we would probably not regard these as an attitude.

Consistency over time is an important issue in attitude research, since it provides one basis for regarding any measure of attitude as reliable. The reliability of a measure, however, is often more easily established than its validity. A test is said to be valid if it measures

Figure 8.1 Attitude space as a linear continuum

what it is meant to measure. A test can give us very reliable results, but these will tell us little or nothing if we have no idea what the test is really measuring. Conventional definitions of validity rest on conventional assumptions about the nature of attitudes. These are that attitudes are not only rather persistent, but also rather *generalized* forms of thought which motivate, or predispose the person towards, many different forms of behaviour in many different situations. How justified are these assumptions? As I argued in the previous chapter, there is no absolute answer. It all depends on the levels at which we categorize things and the criteria we use for comparing things with one another. Such levels and criteria are entirely relative and so too, therefore, are the questions of consistency and validity. We can always find some way in which to link two things together and some other way to split them apart.

These concerns relate to the main themes of attitude research which I summarized in chapter 1. First of all, *attitudes can be measured*. But how? The conventional answer is to regard an individual's attitude as a kind of point on a line (see figure 8.1). This line goes from the extreme of unfavourability or opposition to some specific object or issue through to the extreme of favourability of support. According to the standard view, this line is a very well-mannered creature. It lies perfectly flat and straight. It stays where it's put without moving around. It doesn't stretch itself or curl up in a ball. It stays in one piece, without any gaps. It is unaffected by whoever uses it or looks at it. We can equate different points along it with different numerical measures (of favourability) as surely as we can equate the intervals between markings on a ruler with different physical lengths and distances. We can do a very great deal with these numerical measures, precisely because they seem to behave similarly to other numbers with which we are more accustomed – that is, they can be added together, averaged, multiplied and so on. Most importantly, we can make quantitative statements about how close or distant are the attitudes of different people, or of the same individual at different times.

What we cannot do with the conventional measurement model,

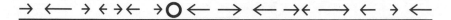

Figure 8.2   Attitude space as a linear continuum with extraneous forces

however, is make any prediction about where a person's attitude is more or less likely to lie. If we think of the point in figure 8.1 as something like a billiard ball or a ball-bearing rolling along backwards and forwards along a flat, frictionless track, then it could come to rest anywhere or nowhere: all positions on the line are equally probable and improbable, equally stable and unstable. (In fact, Thurstone assumed that attitude positions, and levels of agreement with particular statements, would be normally distributed, and hence more moderate positions would be more common than extreme ones. However, the notion of a linear attitude continuum is not modified to reflect this assumption.) We know that *attitudes can be changed*, but the model is silent on the question of what changes are more or less likely to occur. There is nothing in the model to restrain any change whatsoever, subject to the important restriction that any change would have to take the form of a *continuous* movement backwards or forwards along the line: jumps are against the rules. We know that *attitudes can be organized*, that is, form relatively consistent or stable structures, but there is nothing in the model to tell us where those structures are to be found. Organization consists of departures from equiprobability, but no such departures are represented in this simple diagram.

There is a straightforward answer to such criticisms. The model is only a technique of measurement. It does not attempt to say anything about the forces acting upon a person's attitude from within or without. If we find that attitudes are especially resistant to change in certain directions or in certain positions, or if we know that the person has been exposed to a particular kind of persuasive message, then we can expand our representation to take account of the various extraneous forces at play. For instance, we could add various arrows to the diagram to represent forces of different strengths and direction (see figure 8.2). This, however, would be a purely empirical exercise which would leave the notion of the underlying continuum of attitude favourability unchanged. Our ball on the track would be subjected to various pushes and pulls, sucks and blows, but the track itself would remain the same throughout.

Attitude space

This defence, however, rests on an assumption which, in other contexts, would be seen as indefensible (or at least outdated): that *space is unaffected by the forces acting on it and within it*. On this assumption, the kind of 'space' we are dealing with is not a literal, physical, space, but it is none the less something that can be understood by direct analogy. Objects occupy defined positions. Two objects may occupy a common position, but nothing can be in two places at once. These positions are ordered along the continuum and are separated by closer or further distances. These intervals can be added and subtracted from one another, just as journeys can be made longer or shorter by the addition or subtraction of different stages. Our measurement of an attitude boils down to a single number. Hence, our representation of the space within which different attitudes are to be found is reduced to a single dimension. The numbers we derive are interpreted in terms of an equal-interval scale. Hence our single line runs flat and straight.

If we decide to use numbers in a particular way, we imply something about the measurement space in which these numbers are ordered and separated. What is crucial to the conventional (Thurstone) approach is the notion that the numbers we call attitude scores have an absolute meaning, albeit one defined in terms of a specific attitudinal issue. Favourability–unfavourability is the same whatever we do to it or with it, and it is the same for everyone. All that changes is where we end up on this continuum. Why we end up here or there, however, is a question which has nothing to do with measurement as such. Experience is individual, but the framework within which we can measure its effects – the uni-dimensional space of favourability – is universal. In other words, the conventional model offers a thoroughly non-relativistic notion of the attitude continuum. This is its weakness as well as its strength.

Semantic space

A possible escape route from the constraints of this 'single straight-line' model of attitude space is to think of attitudes as varying along more than one dimension. This was what lay behind the early work by Osgood *et al.* (1957) on the semantic differential (see chapter 1).

From factor analysis of multiple ratings, it was possible to infer the structure of a so-called 'semantic space' describable for most purposes in terms of three dimensions: evaluation, potency and activity. This, and subsequent, techniques of multidimensional scaling can be very sensitive to differences between and within individuals in how particular concepts are judged. If we want to 'map' such judgements we have, instead of a ball-bearing on a track, a constellation of spheres floating in space (see, for instance, figures 1.1 to 1.3).

The only substantial difference from the Thurstone model, however, is in terms of the number of dimensions, not in what kinds of dimensions these are. Indeed, Osgood *et al.* explicitly equated their evaluation dimension with the continuum of unidimensional attitude measurement. The space (if restricted to the three primary dimensions) has a fixed shape. It is a cube, and differences between points on its surface or within its interior are measurable in the same way as intervals on a Thurstone attitude continuum. Osgood *et al.*, while recognizing that both adjectives and concepts can change in meaning, laid great store by the replicability of the factorial structure of this semantic space. It is, besides, a general presumption of factor analytic methods that they uncover *common* underlying dimensions, whose existence is independent of the specific objects being judged. The space is 'there', even if it is empty. By direct analogy, the continuum of attitude favourability is 'there', even if you don't have an attitude on the issue in question. The picture of 'semantic space' we are offered is that of a cube, with spheres within it, but no representation within this picture of what keeps the spheres where they are.

Phase space

Both the straight line of Thurstone's attitude space and the cube of Osgood's semantic space take on shapes that are familiar to all of us from school geometry. It is easy to assume that there is something normal or even necessary about these shapes – that the way of using numbers which they represent pictorially is the way that numbers have to be. However, this is not the case at all. Straight lines and cubes are only very special instances of ways in which we can use spatial relationships to represent particular kinds of information. They are, furthermore, only very exceptional examples of the spatial forms we come across in nature.

It is important to see diagrams, maps and even pictures and sculptures not as literal *reproductions* of any object which they depict, but as summaries of relevant *information* about that object. If the object has more or less of some feature, then it can be said to occupy a 'position' on a dimension where information about that feature is recorded. It is arbitrary whether we draw that dimension from left to right or back to front or however, just as it is arbitrary that we draw geographical maps with north to the top. Likewise we need by no means be restricted to the three dimensions of visualizable space. Physicists use the term *phase space* (or state space) to describe the state of a physical system at any point in time in terms of the 'spatial' language of positions on dimensions. (A corollary of this is that the evolution of a system over time can be described as a trajectory through that space.) Since the amount of information required to describe a system completely is immense, so is the number of dimensions.

Penrose (1989) introduces this immensity by pointing out that any single particle requires six dimensions to describe it, so that the number of dimensions required to describe a whole system will be six times the number of separate particles within it. Thus, he estimates, the number of dimensions of a phase-space description of an empty room of air molecules would be in the order of 10^{28} (ten million million million million million million million million million)! Yet this does not inhibit physicists from talking about *the entire state of the universe* as a single point in a phase space (of effectively infinite dimensionality). Even with this immense complexity, we are still offered diagrams of phase space as some kind of fuzzy cube or surface. These diagrams can still help one think about highly abstract processes, even though they cannot be regarded as reproductions of any visible object (See figure 8.3). Measurements in attitude space or semantic space are thus special and extremely simple cases of phase-space descriptions.

Implied in the use of such concepts and diagrams is a simple message. Don't be afraid of multidimensionality. However complex a state of affairs may be, we can represent it as a singular point in a conceptual space. We can handle extra complexity by adding dimensions to the space and we can allow for a multitude of dimensions beyond those we can visualize at one go. This seems to take us even beyond Thurstone, who was prepared to concede 'at the outset that an attitude is a complex affair which cannot be wholly described by any single numerical index' (see chapter 1). Thurstone perhaps should have used the word 'dimension' rather than 'index'. If physicists feel comfortable about representing the

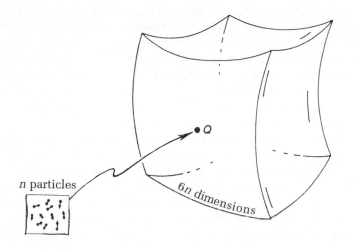

Figure 8.3 Phase space. The entire state of a physical system containing *n* particles is represented by a single point *Q* in a 6*n*-dimensional space.
Source: R. Penrose (1989) *The Emperor's New Mind*, Oxford University Press

entire state of the universe as a single point in phase space, surely we can represent an attitude by a single index, that is, as a single point, provided our attitude space has an adequate number of dimensions.

Attitudes: singular or multiple?

Attitudes are complex and multidimensional because they are about complex and multidimensional things. But they are complex in a rather different kind of way too, as I discussed in the previous chapter. They show both variability and consistency across contexts. What implications does this variability have for measurement and spatial representations of the kind I have described? The basic question is this: if you express an attitude somewhat differently on different occasions, are you expressing the *same* attitude, or different ones? This is not a question which can be settled by appeal to notions of dimensionality (although it can be *handled* by treating situational factors as dimensions of the phase space). The issue is what we take such variability to *mean*.

According to the traditional view, an attitude is some kind of relatively enduring mental state (involving evaluation of some object) that can be expressed in various ways, but especially through language. Thus, we tend to talk of the *same* attitude being expressed through different statements and actions. In the terminology of measurement theory, we can regard different expressive acts as *multiple indicators* of a single, underlying attitude or *latent variable*. No single act provides a perfect measure of this latent variable, but we can infer its presence and nature statistically from the correlations between the different acts or indicators. We interpret each separate response as partly a reflection of the variable we are trying to measure, and partly influenced by random error. The more closely the different responses parallel one another, the more confident we feel in separating a 'true' score from the random error. This 'true' score supposedly reflects the underlying latent variable common to all the multiple indicators. Such a 'true' score of attitude is a statistical abstraction, but it is an abstraction that is easily reified and treated as reflecting a singular characteristic of the person. Exactly the same happens with the identification of so-called personality 'traits' (e.g. introversion, authoritarianism), which are likewise statistical abstractions representing the tendency of certain kinds of responses to parallel each other.

In less technical terms, we often talk about having *an* attitude, in the singular, whilst allowing for the fact that this attitude can be expressed in a complex variety of ways. But why such complexity in modes of expression, if there is only one thing we are trying to express? A plausible answer might run as follows: every expressive act depends partly on the attitude itself, and partly on the situation in which the attitude is expressed. Relevant features of the situation might be the company we are with, what arguments other people have already put forward, and so on. Such situational factors need not always be seen as random, but they are still extrinsic to the attitude itself. If I want to know what your attitude *really* is, to infer your 'true' score, I need to remove this variability from the picture. (Indeed, this is precisely what Thurstone scales and subsequent techniques are designed to achieve.) This seems attractive, since otherwise we would presumably either have to posit as many distinctive attitudes as we had distinctive expressive acts, or else redefine attitude as something *inherently* variable.

Humean attitudes

But what is it that most stands in need of explanation: that our judgements and feelings can change, or that we manage to achieve any kind of consistency and continuity of attitude from one situation to another? Permit me to compose a variation on a theme.

There are some psychologists who imagine we are every moment intimately conscious of what we call our *attitude*; that we feel its existence and its continuance of existence, and are certain, beyond the evidence of a demonstration, both of its perfect identity and simplicity. Unluckily, all these positive assertions are contrary to that very experience which is pleaded for them, nor have we any consciousness of an attitude of the kind proposed. If any experience gives rise to consciousness of an attitude, that experience must continue with little variation over long periods of time, since attitudes are supposed to show that kind of stability. But there is no experience that does this. For my part, when I enter most intimately into what I call my *attitude*, I always stumble on some particular thought about something. I can never catch my *attitude* at any time without a thought, and this thought is what fills my consciousness. Instead of a singular, continued experience of an attitude, what I find is nothing but a bundle or collection of successive thoughts, flowing into one another and always changing. It is only these successive thoughts which comprise my attitude.

But this collection of successive thoughts is not entirely random or unpatterned. I think *about things*, and I think about them as existing in time and space. Just as what will be generally follows on from what used to be, my future thoughts generally follow on from what I used to think. I think about such things as happening and existing along with other things. I experience such things as contiguous with each other. In thinking, I may also focus my attention on selective properties of such things, properties which may be partly shared by other things. So my thoughts might generalize from one thing to another which resembles it. In short, I do not leave my successive thoughts in a bundle, but sort them and link them up with one another. And when these associative links become strong enough, I become conscious not just of such things in momentary isolation, but as elements within a recurring and recognizable pattern. At this point, my experience of such things starts to be something worth talking about. Talking about things and our relation to them abstracts attitudinal experience from the fleetingness of the here-and-now. Talking makes a public commodity of our experience which we trade with others in return for confirmation of social reality.

We therefore need a conception of attitude that is neither fixed nor random, neither singular nor unpatterned. As I shall soon argue, the imagery (or if you are so inclined, the mathematics) which could support such a new conception is all around us, and as familiar as anything could be. It could also allow a theory of attitude to be a theory of a physical process. But this is a dangerous course to follow. If we keep to more familiar ground, we can treat an attitude as a single underlying experience or mental state, whilst allowing it to be reflected in a multiplicity of separate expressive acts. This allows us, in turn, to ignore such multiplicity. If we stray from this position, we surely will have problems defending notions of attitudinal consistency, of stability of attitude structures, or linear measurement of attitudes along standard continua. The consequences could be most subversive. No, the standard argument implies; we have to assume that attitudes, in the absence of any external influence, are *fixed*. The alternative is chaos.

But is chaos necessarily such a bad thing? If it is the way things are, surely we should try to understand it, rather than disown it. There is plenty of evidence that attitudes (sometimes) *can* be coherent, integrated and enduring. But then we need to ask: when attitudes are this way, what makes them so? Attitudes are not something tagged on to other thoughts, any more than the self is an experience tagged on to other contents of our consciousness. Like the concept of self, the concept of attitude is a particular way of talking about our thoughts and consciousness. To define such concepts better, we need to look at what we do with them, not necessarily at something special about the thoughts in themselves. Among the many things we do with our concept of self is to assert ownership of our thoughts and memories, a continuity of identity based on the continuity of our body, and hence a continuity as an *object* of others' thoughts and perceptions. On the basis of Hume's principles of association perhaps (or other principles which would need to be just as effective), we construct such continuity by *recognizing patterns* in our experience.

It is sometimes asserted, as though it were a criticism of Hume, that the principles of association do not explain how we can achieve any particular notions of the self, or of any object with a continuing existence, since, in principle, anything can be associated with anything. And so it can, in principle. But in practice, such associations are non-random; and though there may be infinite variety in them, there are still patterns to such variety. The reason for this is that thoughts and consciousness are about things in the world, and these *things*, though highly varied, are patterned. Likewise, although we can never say that two experiences are identical (as

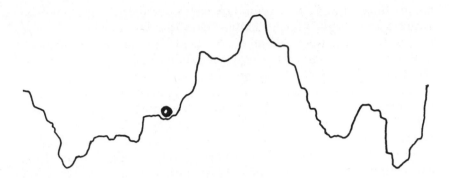

Figure 8.4   A non-linear attitude space

James stresses), we can none the less *identify* patterns and continuities that allow one experience to be connected to another.

Curves and contours

The way we identify patterns and continuities may be basic to our attitudes and self-concept (as well as other forms of thought), but conventional representations of attitude space tell us nothing about how such identification occurs. Let me ask you now, though, to try something new with your concept of space – or, to be less intimidating, something that involves thinking of space in a way that is typical of everyday life but atypical of most psychological measurement. The idea is just to see where such changes might lead us. The issue of underlying causal processes can come later. The problem I have been stressing is that conventional 'straight-line' models contain no information about the influences that keep a person's attitude or state of mind where it is; still less do they suggest the directions in which it may change. Figure 8.2 illustrates how some of these influences might operate, but it is a clumsy illustration. We have a linear attitude space, and we have some influences, but neither the space nor the set of influences depends on the other. There is no hint of relativity. The question is simply this. Can this space be changed so that the information about the influences is *contained* in the map itself? The answer is an unequivocal Yes. The illustration of it is in figure 8.4.

The marble or ball-bearing that represents a person's attitude is kept in place, not by extraneous arrows, but by the contours of the landscape. Being in a deep valley, it needs more energy to climb the hillside. If it were in one of the lesser valleys, it would need less energy to move, and if it were balanced on top of a ridge it would take very little energy at all to push it one way rather than another. What we have, in other words, is an *energy surface*, that is, a surface in which differences in potential energy are represented by the rises and falls of the landscape. The spatial representation of such energy differences, of course, relies on the fact that we interpret such bends and curves on the analogy of real hills and valleys, with a gravitational pull acting downwards. We need, in short, to interpret such contours as ordinary and familiar, and not worry about how we would write equations to define them. We know that it is less easy to push things uphill rather than down and that this is related to the height and steepness of the hill. We know that things tend to roll down to the bottoms of valleys. This is the kind of spatial knowledge that is being used to communicate a specific piece of psychological knowledge: that someone's attitude can be more stable in some positions than others, and will be easier to change in some directions than others. Through this simplest of breaks from convention, we can communicate stability and instability, departures from equiprobability, and the relative likelihood of alternative states. In short, we can illustrate a *dynamical structure* within the space itself.

Dynamics and attractors

This way of communicating dynamical structure is by now in fact quite familiar in other sciences. What has held psychology back has been the narrow view of measurement as a means of mapping *positions* rather than *processes*. Process implies movement and change over time. Position does not. If we are concerned only with positions, we can forget about time, or at least try to do so. We can forget about Hume's 'perpetual flux and movement'. We can forget about James's 'stream of consciousness'. But if we allow ourselves to forget all of this, surely, we have forgotten about thought.

The most general way of mapping a dynamical process is by combining several repeated measures of an object within a single phase-space diagram. More simply, we define the axes of our diagram in terms of the distinguishing attributes we regard as important, and mark in a dot to represent how much of each attribute the object has at time t_1. Then we move on to time t_2, and record the new characteristics of the object by another dot. And so on. If we wish, we can draw lines from one dot to another in the order in which they appear (just like in a child's 'dot-to-dot' drawing book), in which case our diagram will reveal the *trajectory* of the object through phase space over time.

There will be many cases where this trajectory is the main thing we wish to know. In other cases, what may be more revealing is the statistical distribution of positions occupied by the object in phase space over a longer period of time, regardless of their order. That is, we may be more interested in looking at clusters or clouds of dots rather than at webs of criss-crossing trajectories. Under conditions of continuous change, the distinction between these two modes of presentation boils down to a trivial question of time-sampling. With a very small time interval, successive measurements would be so close to each other in phase space as to appear joined to each other anyway.

One of the main characteristics of such maps is the presence of *attractors*. An attractor is simply any position or projection in phase space towards which the various data points appear to be pulled or 'attracted'. Thus, it could be the 'centre of gravity' of a cloud of dots, the 'best-fitting line' (though not necessarily a straight one) within a sausage-shaped scatter, or the 'plug-hole' towards which a trajectory seems to spiral. For example, if one plotted the trajectory of the tip of a simple pendulum in 'ordinary' space, it would converge over time towards a point vertically below its pivot, where it would eventually come to rest (because of the loss of energy to friction). Plotting the same trajectory in phase space, with one axis representing position and another velocity, would produce a spiral converging on a central point (see figure 8.5), representing zero velocity and the lowest vertical position. (In fact, this ignores the presence of a very weak, but non-zero, alternative attractor vertically *above* the pivot-point.)

A closely related concept is that of *basins* or *wells of attraction*. This reflects a very simple idea, namely that attractors may only be dominant over a limited field or area of phase space. Thus, the plug-hole in a bath will 'attract' the bathwater, but it will exert no 'pull' at all on the water in a flower-vase on a table in another room. Thus a well of attraction is the range, or set of limiting conditions, within which an attractor has an influence. If an event falls within the well, it will tend to converge on the attractor which defines

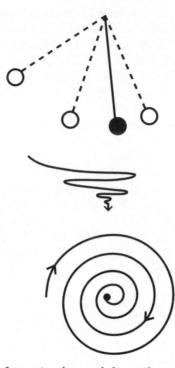

Figure 8.5 Attractor for a simple pendulum, slowed by friction. The top half of the figure illustrates the movement of the pendulum in ordinary space, the bottom half its convergence on a single point in phase space.
Source: Adapted from J. Gleick (1988) *Chaos: Making a New Science*, Sphere Books

the well's base or centre. An attractor is thus, by definition, a point of lower potential energy, or, in other words, a dip in the energy surface. If we produce a phase-space map including this information, what we have is a *contoured landscape* in which unequal conditional probabilities are represented by wells or valleys in different regions, with differences in potential energy being shown as valleys and ridges of different depth and height. The phase space therefore will include *multiple* attractors. But what is even more important than their number is the fact that the influence of each of them *depends on context*. Thus the kind of potential energy distribution we end up with is not just a departure from a state of affairs where all events are equally probable: it provides a set of *conditional* probabilities. Under these initial conditions, this attractor will dominate; under other conditions, other attractors will exert their influence. Figure 8.4 can be read as a two-dimensional map of just such conditional probabilities. The different kinds of attitudes which could be taken to correspond to the different dips in the line are attractors of different strengths (depth) and ranges of influence (width). We can therefore regard *attitudes as attractors* in a dynamical system. The same will be true of any other habit of thought or behaviour.

What applies to attitudes can apply to anything in a creature's behaviour or experience where there is some recognizable pattern of recurrence. A most persuasive presentation of this argument (and of other technical issues which I shall soon discuss) is offered by Peter Killeen, a behavioural psychologist. As he writes (Killeen, 1989, p. 56):

> Some attractors are fixed from birth, and are called reflexes. Others are acquired early in life; under special circumstances these are stabilized quickly, and the stabilization is called imprinting. Others acquired throughout life are more malleable, and are called habits. The confusion and clumsiness that attend new ways of seeing and doing act to repel innovation, even as 'habit' attracts variant behaviors toward old patterns . . . The pull of attractors may be inexorable (categorical perception), strong (persistence in a career or in personality styles) or trivial (techniques for opening a door). Each of these attractors are called fixed points, because while under the control of the attractor, the system stays at or near a fixed point in its space, locked into that pattern by negative feedback.

Stability and instability

Negative feedback, adaptation, homeostasis, assimilation and accommodation: these are the stuff of most psychological theories. We stay in control by correcting for excesses, by returning to the familiar and by becoming familiar with the new. Change occurs, but within bounds: our moods may swing, but like the swinging of a pendulum, they return to their resting place. According to much attitude theory, we strive for consistency, abhor contradiction and ambivalence, and reappraise our thoughts and behaviour to protect a stable evaluative simplicity. Psychological processes, like many in fields as diverse as physiology, evolution and metereology, appear to find their own level. Or so it seems to be for most of the time. But there is another side to the story. There is choice as well

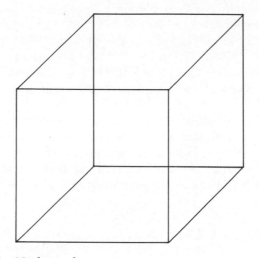

Figure 8.6   The Necker cube

as conditioning. There is the ability to imagine alternative states. There are other attractors in the field beyond the well in which we find ourselves, if somehow we can make it to the ridge. Most important of all, the pull of an attractor depends on our starting point, that is, on prevailing initial conditions or context.

Consistency and stability depend on the context in which we find ourselves and on our selective definition of it. If we look beyond the ridge, we will see a different landscape. If we resume our journey from the top of the ridge, slight changes in direction will take us into different valleys. We will be subject to the pull of multiple attractors, rather than one. A familiar example of this from research on visual perception is the figure known as the Necker Cube. This appears (particularly when illuminated against a dark background) to oscillate between a three-dimensional cube with the front below the back (as though viewed from higher up) and one with the front above (see figure 8.6). The two different perspective interpretations operate as alternative attractors.

Multiple attractors and the route to chaos

'Chaos' is the name given to a new and broad-ranging field of scientific study. It is concerned typically with what happens to a dynamical system when it is forced out of a stable state, that is, when the system is 'driven' beyond its capacity for self-correction. What happens, for instance, if a pendulum weight on a non-rigid wire, or a garden swing suspended by ropes, is pushed too high above the horizontal? We all have a pretty good general idea. The wire or rope will suddenly lose its tautness, and the weight or seat of the swing will fall inwards from the circumference of its arc. At the bottom of its fall, much of the potential energy will be dissipated in small, jerky oscillations, so that it is likely that a new push will be needed to set it swinging rhythmically again on its previous arc. Producing such events and predicting them in a rough kind of way is child's play − literally − so long as we are happy with a rather general level of description and are prepared to trust our experience in the form we receive it. But try writing a mathematical formula to predict precisely the fall of a wobbly swing on a given occasion and you will find it impossible. Not even just very difficult. Impossible.

The root of the mathematical difficulty is that the change we are being asked to predict is *non-linear*. That is to say, it is suddenly and qualitatively different from what preceded it. The mathematics we are most accustomed to − the mathematics also of Thurstone's attitude space and Osgood's semantic space − is built around using numbers as measures of continuous properties. What we are dealing with here is discontinuity. This is not just a problem for mathematics either. Most scientific techniques are geared towards the description of the 'better behaved' parts of nature, those that follow a steady and predictable course. When nature is 'badly behaved' and shows unpredictable variation, this is commonly regarded as error or 'noise' within the system − something that is a nuisance for scientific models but not something that can itself be sensibly modelled.

Much recent research, however, is contributing to a revision of this kind of outlook. Nature's 'bad behaviour' can be shown to exhibit a hidden order of remarkable generality. Some of the clearest examples of this come from taking a model of some natural control process − some negative feedback mechanism that has the function of bringing matters back to equilibrium − and changing the parameters so that that it is allowed to run out of control. For instance, you might want to predict the growth of some biological population from one year (say) to the next. A crucial factor would be the rate at which the population would grow − births minus deaths – in the absence of any environmental constraints. We then might have an equation of the form:

$$P_j = GP_i$$

where P_i represents the population in year i, P_j the population in the next year j, and G the growth rate. (For these purposes, let's define P as a proportion of some notional maximum, with possible values between 0, representing elimination, and 1, representing satiation of the environment.) It is easy to see that there is nothing in the above formula to restrict ever-accelerating growth: it even allows the population to exceed 100 per cent satiation! To prevent this evident nonsense, the formula needs to be modified to take account of various constraints on growth – such as the fact that, as the population rises, there will be increasing competition for food and nesting sites and possibly greater risk from disease and predators. These constraints produce negative feedback. That is, they make the system self-correcting so that the population is kept close to some kind of equilibrium with the environment. A standard way on representing this process mathematically is in terms of the modified formula:

$$P_j = GP_i(1 - P_i)$$

This so-called 'logistic' function fulfils its purpose admirably for moderate values of G – i.e. for values between 1 and 3. If $G < 1$, the birth rate will be less than the natural death rate, and the population will consequently decline to zero. We can express this by saying that the system possess an *attractor* A with the value of 0. If G lies between 1 and 3, P will stabilize after a greater or smaller number of iterations (i.e. 'goes'). The attractor or equilibrium point at which it stabilizes will be higher for larger values of G. Very simply:

$$A = 1 - 1/G$$

For instance, if $G = 2$, then $A = 0.5$. In other words, the population will stabilize at 50 per cent of the notional maximum.

For most natural populations, convergence on a stable equilibrium seems to be the norm. But suppose we drive the system harder by increasing the growth rate even further? Something strange starts to happen. Instead of converging on a single value, P starts to oscillate between two values that steadily diverge. In other words, the system possesses *two* attractors. For instance, at G = 3.2, the population would oscillate between approximately 0.799 and 0.513. At about G = 3.44, the system splits again, to produce *four* attractors, so that at G = 3.5, the system will stabilize to a continuous repetition of the four value sequence: 0.383, 0.827, 0.501, 0.875. This kind of effect is known as 'period doubling', and occurs ever more quickly as G rises further. That is, soon we find eight attractors, then sixteen, then thirty-two, and so on. By about G = 3.57 we have passed the so-called 'accumulation point' – the point at which any repeated pattern or 'periodicity' in the numbers is discernible. We have arrived at a state of apparent *chaos*.

But in the route to chaos – in the acceleration of ever greater complexity – there is remarkable order. In fact, not just the particular logistic function discussed above, but all others which attempt to impose a similar kind of negative feedback regime, share a common property. The pace of period-doubling is a function of a constant δ, known as *Feigenbaum's constant* after its discoverer (Feigenbaum, 1978). This is universally equal to 4.6692 . . . Specifically the rule states that the period (number of attractors) will double for the kth time when G takes the value:

$$a - c\delta^{-\kappa}$$

where c is a constant determined for the specific negative feedback function, and a is the function's accumulation point.

What happens, though, after G is increased *beyond* the accumulation point? At first, as I said, there seems to be a total absence of pattern. But after a while, new kinds of patterns appear, the first of which (around G = 3.83 for the equation I have been describing) is an oscillation between *three* different attractors. As G is driven even higher, this pattern disappears, but then others, involving many different kinds of periodicities (rhythms) take its place, to give way in turn to more phases of randomness. 'Chaos', in other words, is a state in which tiny changes in a parameter can produce either complex patterns and rhythms or unconstrained variability; it is not mere randomness, but the frontier between order and disorder.

Natural complexity

But is any of this more than a numerical curiosity? Does it have anything to do with any natural, let alone psychological, phenomena?

Although the example of population growth is certainly something natural, the manner in which it was just treated was abstract rather than empirical. A more empirical inquiry into population dynamics would reveal many examples of equilibria, some of periodic fluctuations, but few if any instances of fully-fledged disorder. There is plenty of evidence indicating that the logistic equation described makes adequate predictions of population growth under certain conditions, but if we take the equation as somehow 'real' we must accept that its parameters are constrained not just by the present environment but by evolutionary history and natural selection. There will have been strong selective pressures, in other words, against G being allowed to climb too high.

There are many other kinds of natural phenomena, however, where complexity and chaos appear much more the norm. Changes in weather patterns, for instance, can be shown to exhibit complex rhythms and periodicities. Of special use in this context is the concept of a 'strange' attractor – specifically, a state towards which the system is drawn for a while but which it never quite reaches (Lorenz, 1963). Tidal flows, likewise, can show patterns of oscillation without exact repetition. There are numerous structures, both stationary and moving, which display a kind of regular irregularity – the outline of a mountain range, the billowing of a cloud, the bubbling of sauce in a boiling saucepan, the branching of a tree and the waving of its leaves in the wind, the swirling of an eddy by a river bank, and the surf from a breaking wave. All these forms and movements exhibit a kind of turbulence, a dissipation or sharing out of energy towards smaller and smaller goals. The closer we look at them, the finer detail and differentiation we find. It is no coincidence – though the explanation is a mystery – that we can relate to all of these as things of beauty.

But let's try and ignore the aesthetics of such complexity, at least for a short while. The most important point – and one of which I shall soon try to demonstrate the psychological relevance – is that the dissipation of physical energy lays down forms in space and time which share a common property. *The closer we look at such forms, the more detail we find.* As an example of this, let's consider something of little obvious aesthetic appeal, indeed something which we can often find irritating and unpleasant: radio transmission 'noise'. As we all know and have experienced, radio signals do not always come through loud and clear. Often they are obscured, wholly or partly, by apparently random interference and crackle. Radio engineers have long been aware that such 'noise' tends to come in bursts, separated by intervals of lesser interference. The unpredictability of these bursts suggests randomness and a total lack of structure, but the facts are far more subtle. Take any time interval, say one hour, and divide it up into lesser intervals, say of one minute each. You will find that some of these lesser intervals contain bursts of noise, and others do not. This gives you a special kind of distribution of noise and silence over the one-hour period. But now take any given period of one minute in which noise occurred, divide it up into sub-intervals of one second each, and look at the distribution of noise *within* that one minute. The remarkable fact is that this second distribution will resemble the first. You can repeat the procedure, looking at how noise is distributed within each interval of one second across intervals of one-sixtieth of a second, and you will find the same distribution – the same proportion of noise to silence – repeating itself again. This kind of repetition at different scales of magnitude is conventionally termed *self-similarity*.

Fractals

The need to find a mathematical description of just this kind of naturally occurring complexity was a major impetus to the work of Bonoit Mandelbrot (1983). In looking at distributions of transmission noise, he not only discovered such self-similarity but noted one of its paradoxical consequences: however short a time interval he took, he could never find a period where the noise was strictly continuous. The distribution of noise over time was something 'between' a joined-up line and a set of disconnected points. In terms of conventional (Euclidian) geometry, a disconnected point has zero dimensions, and a joined-up line, one dimension. (Likewise, a surface has two dimensions and a solid object three. As far as numbers of dimensions are concerned, only integers, i.e. whole numbers, are allowed.) But here Mandelbrot was dealing with a sequence of points that produced almost continuous bursts, or viewed differently, apparently continuous bursts that, when inspected closely, disintegrated into a discontinuous 'dust'. Strictly speaking, the disconnectedness of the points implied that their 'topological' dimensionality was 0. However, since the distribution was almost continuous, its 'effective' dimensionality could be said to be rather greater, that is *between* 0 and 1. Mandelbrot introduced the term *fractal* to refer to any form with an 'effective' dimensionality that exceeded the number of its 'topological' dimensions, and hence could take a value which was not an integer.

This concept is difficult to grasp when taken 'cold', but it becomes less threatening on closer acquaintance. Our conventional idea of one-dimensional lines and two-dimensional surfaces, etc., is not as such *wrong*. It is merely unhelpful for describing shapes and distributions of a particular kind. A common feature of such shapes is that they are generated by the *repeated application* of some kind of rule or transformation. Examples of such shapes were known to mathematicians before Mandelbrot. For instance, the 'Cantor dust' – to which Mandelbrot saw the distribution of transmission errors to be analogous – is formed in the following way. Take a continuous line and divide it into three equal segments. Then remove the middle segment. Then do the same with each of the two continuous segments on either side, to yield four shorter lines. Then remove the middle thirds of each of these four lines, and so on *ad infinitum*. At each step, the amount of 'filled in' space is two-thirds of what it was before. According to Mandelbrot, this allows the 'effective' dimension D of the dust to be defined as $log\ 2/log\ 3$, which equals approximately 0.631.

A more easily visualized example is the 'Koch snowflake' (see figure 8.7). This is formed by the repeated adding of length to an outline. We start with an equilateral triangle. We then take each side of the triangle and mount a smaller equilateral triangle on its middle third (producing a Star of David shape). Then we carry on adding smaller triangles on the middle thirds of each side of the polygon thus produced, and so on, again and again. At each step the length of the outline is four-thirds of its previous length. Hence $D = log\ 4/log\ 3$ or approximately 1.262. (Obviously, the space within the snowflake has two 'topological' dimensions, but what we are concerned with is the outline itself, which, as a line or curve, has one 'topological' dimension.)

Thus, the fractal or effective dimensionality of a form is relatively easy to define if the form is regular and if you know in advance what tranformation rule has been used to generate it. To do the same for irregular shapes, or ones that you happen to find in the natural world, is far more difficult, but Mandelbrot is none the less adamant that the geometry of natural things is fractal – that it cannot be adequately described in Euclidian terms. As he introduces his 1983 book *The Fractal Geometry of Nature* (p. 1):

Figure 8.7 The Koch snowflake ($D = 1.262$)
Source: I. Stewart (1989) *Does God Play Dice?*, Blackwell

Why is geometry often described as 'cold' and 'dry?' One reason lies in its inability to describe the shape of a cloud, a mountain, a coastline, or a tree. Clouds are not spheres, mountains are not cones, coastlines are not circles, and bark is not smooth, nor does lightning travel in a straight line . . . Nature exhibits not simply a higher degree but an altogether different level of complexity. The number of different scales of length of natural patterns is for all practical purposes infinite.

Much of Mandelbrot's work consists of illustrations of the forms that can be generated by repetitions of different kinds of transformation rules, singly and in combination. These include simulations of more familiar shapes, such as ferns and trees, mountain ranges and lunar craters, as well as purely abstract productions. Pre-eminent in the latter category is the almost mystical *Mandelbrot set*. With the aid of a computer graphics package, this enables the generation of an infinite variety of complex and beautiful forms through the repeated application of a simple formula. The formula for the Mandelbrot set is closely related to the logistic function for population growth we met earlier in this chapter, although this time it makes use of complex numbers. (A complex number z can be defined as $x + yi$ where x and y are real – i.e. 'ordinary' – numbers and i is the imaginary number $\sqrt{-1}$.) The formula used to generate the Mandelbrot set is:

$$z_j = z_i^2 + c$$

where both z and c are complex numbers. Depending on the value chosen for c, z will either converge on a stable attractor or diverge towards 'chaos'. The set is visually represented in terms of a two-dimensional ('Argand') plane in which one axis represents x (the 'real' part of the complex number z) and the other y (the coefficient of z's 'imaginary' part). If z converges, we colour in the point on the graph, if it diverges we leave it blank (or, better still, use different hues to represent different speeds of divergence). We then choose another number for c and repeat the process. A tiny taste of the product can be seen in figure 8.8.

Infinite outlines in a finite space

It is easy to be overwhelmed by the Mandelbrot set's sheer abstract beauty. Each new scale of magnification provides new surprises of hidden detail, within which suddenly familiar forms are unexpectedly repeated. This is Art for Art's sake, if that is the way we want to see it. But what does it *tell* us? The answer depends partly on what you are looking for. If you are looking for a way of visualizing quantum uncertainty (see chapter 5), then maybe you will lay some store by the fact that both the Mandelbrot set and quantum mechanics make use of complex numbers. Is this a relevant connection? Those more expert than I am in mathematics and physics must give the answer. If you are looking for another way of visualizing chaos, then you are on stronger ground. The outline of the shaded area is

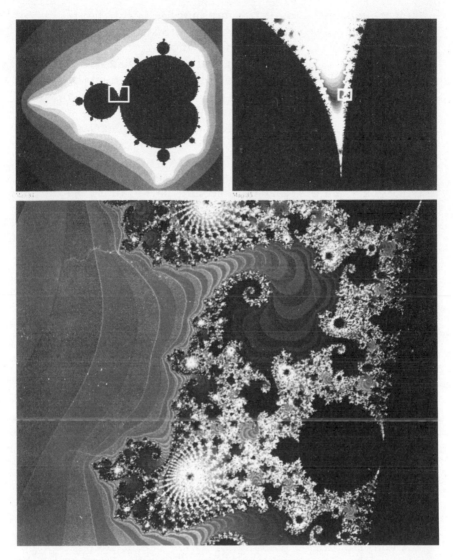

Figure 8.8 The Mandelbrot set. Details at successive magnifications.
Source: I. Stewart (1989) *Does God Play Dice?*, Blackwell

the border between convergence to a stable attractor and unstable divergence. Furthermore, the reappearance of the initial bulbous shape (for instance) at different magnifications may be likened to the 'windows' of periodic rhythms reappearing above the accumulation point of the logistic function.

But the clearest, if most prosaic, message is that the outline of the set – the border between stability and instability – is fractal. At each new scale of magnification, we discover new detail, a new spiral, or filament or indentation. Yet all this detail is the product of the repeated application of a relatively straightforward mathematical formula. A finite rule can generate infinite complexity. Unlike in the case of the Koch snowflake (see figure 8.7), no single value of D encapsulates the nature of this complexity. However, it still shares with the Koch snowflake two very important general characteristics. First, the complete set lies within a finite area, just as the Koch snowflake never goes outside a circle touched by the points of the starting triangle. Second, the length of the outline tends to infinity. This can be visually appreciated in the case of the Mandelbrot set. The formula for the Koch snowflake (multiplication of the length by $\frac{4}{3}$ for an infinite number of times) allows this to be appreciated logically. We thus have a curve or outline of *infinite length in a finite space*. (By the same token, since repeated multiplication by $\frac{2}{3}$ tends to zero, the Cantor dust can be said to tend towards infinite sparseness.)

It is this aspect that, for our purposes here, most distinguishes fractal shapes from those of Euclidian geometry and hence those of standard attitude measurement. It also is a distinguishing feature of natural shapes, for instance the coastline of an island. Take the apparently simple question: How long is the coastline of Britain? The answer is that there is no single answer: it depends on your scale of measurement.

Now this is a very strange answer. To appreciate how strange, suppose instead that we were trying to measure the circumference of a well-behaved shape such as a circle or oval. To make matters slightly more difficult, let's say that we had to do this with the aid of a rigid rod one metre in length, and that we didn't know the formula for calculating the circumference of a circle from its diameter. It is easy to see that errors could creep in, especially if we were measuring a rather small circle with a rather long rod. However, these errors could go in any direction. The smaller the unit of measurement we were able to use, the more accurate our estimate would be. (For instance, if the rod was actually a meter rule marked in centimeters and millimeters, we could place just a small section of it against the curve.) In other words, our estimate would converge onto a single value, and would depend on our unit of measurement only in the sense that smaller units would yield smaller errors.

But when it comes to measuring natural coastlines, this principle no longer applies. Take an ordinary road map, put a piece of string around the shape of the coast (or even just part of it), measure it, and multiply by the scale of the map. That will give you one answer. Do the same with a set of detailed survey maps, and you will get another answer, and it will be longer. Walk the coastal path while counting your paces, and you will get an even longer answer. Go down to the beach and walk along the water line around every headland and inlet, and it will be longer still. Now do it on your hands and knees with a meter rule, adding in each boulder or pile of seaweed. Now do the same in terms of centimenters, adding in each stone or sand ripple. Carry on this way and soon you will be counting grains of sand! Obviously, this would take for ever. Only slightly less obviously, the measured length of the coastline will tend towards infinity. The closer you look, the more you will find. Another way of putting this is that there is an *infinite interpolation of complexity*. Until we come up against something like the uncertainty principle, there is no lower limit to our measurement unit and no upper limit to the complexity (and hence extra length) that we will find. Measured length is entirely relative to our scale of measurement. This is the fundamental property of natural outlines, from the coastlines of islands to the silhouettes of trees. These are the patterns we see and know and live among.

What is true of fractal curves (i.e. shapes with values of D between 1 and 2) is also true of fractal planes or surfaces (i.e. those with values of D between 2 and 3). Simulated 'landscapes' can be generated mathematically by adding repeated indentations to a plane. The analogy with measuring the length of the British coastline is measuring Britain's surface area. But let's make the problem more contained. Let's just measure the surface area of a single field. Even if the field were a perfect rectangle, the product of its length and breadth would still offer only one estimate, one that left out any account of unevenness in the surface itself. If we go to the stage of measuring the surface area of each blade of grass, the estimate we will be making will be very, very large indeed. With natural – that is to say, fractal – surfaces, smaller units of measurement give us ever larger estimates, not converging ones. What we mean by 'surface area' is relative to how fine we want our measurements to be, so any single measurement is arbitrary, not absolute. The extra complexity revealed by finer measurement, however, may reveal important facts about the underlying physical or biological processes. Fractal shapes and surfaces are very often excellent 'solutions' to particular 'problems' – how to trap the maximum amount of sun and rain if we are talking about the surface area of blades of grass in a field and how to maximize potential processing capacity if we are talking about the convoluted surface of the human cortex, contained within the skull.

The fractal mind

Let me therefore return to the question of what kinds of maps best describe human thought and offer this proposition: when represented as an energy landscape in phase space, *the dimensionality of thought is fractal*. Thought is not a point on a straight-line continuum, on a flat surface, or within a cube or even a multidimensional hypercube. It does not even lie on a line or surface or cube which has become slightly warped or bent. It falls within a space in which we can discover infinite complexity if we make finer and finer distinctions. It falls also within boundaries, and this is no less important, about which we can make broad and simple statements if we use more inclusive levels of categorization. The level of inclusiveness or differentiation we use, moreover, is entirely relative and dependent on our own perspective.

If we now look back at the curved line of figure 8.4, we may notice that it does not do all that we need of it. It displays the presence of multiple attractors, but makes their pull appear inexorable on anything below the ridge of a given valley. To use the analogy of real hills and valleys, it is as though the hillsides are covered in sheet ice, smooth at every point, with nothing to grip onto. In the form it is drawn, the curve, though complicated, can be regarded as 'rectifiable', that is, it could be bent back to a straight line *of a definite length*. From the previous pages, it should be clear that fractal curves are non-rectifiable. If, on the other hand, we want to draw a landscape which allows people, albeit with effort, to *climb* a hillside – that is, remove themselves from an attractor – or to come to rest half-way down a slope without rolling all the way down – we need something more. We need to introduce roughness and indentation into the surface of the curve, to offer grip and friction in the same way as a real hillside. Killeen (1989, pp. 56–60) wrestles with this same problem when describing his own, very similar, spatial representation of behavioural attractors (figure 8.9):

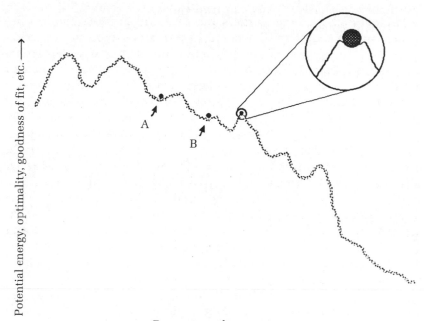

Figure 8.9 A cross-section of a contoured surface or 'hillside' to represent behavioural attractors

Source: P. R. Killeen (1989) 'Behavior as a trajectory through a field of attractors' in J. R. Brink and C. R. Haden (eds) *The Computer and the Brain*, Elsevier

A useful picture of multiple equilibria is provided by a stylized slice through a hillside . . . Each of the little gullies, or potential wells, represents a point of stable equilibrium. The potential energy of an object in the well is less than that of an object on the lip, so that activation energy is required to move the object out of the well. The tops of each of the hills are singularities: 'immeasurably small energies' applied to an object at the top will cause it to roll one way into the basin of one well, or the other way into the basin of a different well. Within a well the system is stable – the object stays in the well unless new energy is added – or the landscape is changed . . . This picture is incomplete in many ways. It does not reveal the rich complexity that may result from a more accurate higher-dimensional representation. Thus, what appears to be a lower potential well at B . . . may be a gully that runs uphill at a very shallow slope, so that it will be easier for an object to be 'walked' to a higher level on the hill by first falling back from A to B. But such retreats are difficult; once attained, local equilibria are hard to escape . . .

   Killeen thus makes a very valuable point: that the difficulty of behavioural change (or by the same token, of attitude change) depends on the cognitive dimension in terms of which the situation or problem is appraised. A cliff that is impossible to scale may be easy to walk around. Viewpoints which may seem sharply separated if one dimension is salient may seem compatible with each other if another criterion is used as the basis of judgement. Take any dip in a cross-sectional 'hillside slice' such as figure 8.4 or 8.9. The outline of the 'valley' suggests a stable attractor − a 'balanced' attitude. Such balance or consistency, however, is indicated only in terms of one dimension or frame of reference. Take a cross-sectional slice in a different direction, or replace it with a contoured surface, and we may see quite a different picture. What we took to be a region of stability might be revealed as no more than a pocket on a precariously narrow ridge. We may discover that wells of attraction have different shapes, and can be long and thin in some directions but short and fat in others, rather than simply consisting of concentric craters covering the same range in all directions.

   But Killeen's presentation still shares the same problem as my own. Even a shallow slope is impossible to walk up if it offers no friction. Even small holes are impossible to climb out of if there is nothing to grip onto. We need to assume − not just for the sake of illustrative analogy but as a fundamental theoretical requirement − that the slopes on our phase-space maps are less than completely smooth. We need to assume that, as we increase the magnification, we will find some grittiness or hairiness. We need to find extra contours and indentations, extra length and surface area, and hence a greater effective dimensionality. We need the slopes to be fractal.

Attitudes as attractors

Before considering how a phase space of this kind might come about, let us pause and consider some of the advantages of such a representation for attitude theory. First and foremost, we can infer that *attitudes involve selective information-processing*. The way things are interpreted will depend on the perspective from which they are viewed. The ease of passing from one thought to another will depend on the paths by which they are associated. This is precisely what is meant by saying that different people can regard different aspects of an issue as salient. In a multidimensional universe, the scope for individual differences in interpretation and association is, in principle, infinite.

Another advantage of this approach is that both overt actions on the one hand and verbal expressions of attitude on the other can be represented as attractors within the same space. *Attitude–behaviour consistency* will thus depend on the ease of passing from an attitudinal attractor to a behavioural attractor or *vice versa*. In other words, it will depend on the strength of association, without any requirement that such association should be unidirectional rather than reciprocal. What is important is that attitudes and behaviours *can* be distinct (to the extent that they are reached from different starting points, i.e. are activated by different sets of inputs) or closely tied to one another (to the extent that the same initial conditions can lead to both being shown together). In terms of the map, consistency will be reflected in terms of the attractors being linked by a valley, and distinctiveness by their separation by a ridge.

The same approach allows for the fact that *attitudes can be reappraised*. This is a simple consequence of the reciprocal nature of the paths of association between attitudinal and behavioural attractors. To account for standard effects of cognitive dissonance experiments, we need to assume that individuals have a range or repertoire of potential attitude positions they might endorse on any issue. These different positions can be represented by more or less shallow wells of attraction within the same general region of the space. In the absence of any special influence, an individual's expressed attitude (or preferred position) will tend to gravitate towards the deepest of these wells. However, the effect of 'forced compliance' manipulations (where people are induced to perform an act inconsistent with their previous attitude) is to 'start the ball rolling' from a different part of the space. This starting point will correspond to a new attractor representing (thoughts about) the behaviour the individual has just exhibited. The design of such experiments rests upon the intuition that it will be difficult to return from this new behavioural attractor to the original 'preferred position', but easy to reach alternative, albeit initially shallower, attitudinal attractors.

If we follow this line of argument, there are two interesting and important implications for how we may want to think about attitude change generally. The first is that the relative strength (depth) of attitudinal attractors may be modified by behavioural feedback (perhaps along the lines of 'back-propagation' within connectionist systems, see page 200). The second is that attitude change, no less than attitude expression, consists of the retrieval of positions stored in memory. In other words, our 'repertoire' of potential attitude positions may include not only those we ourselves already agree with, but also other viewpoints to which we have been exposed, and hence can recognize, even if we do not agree with them. The mere familiarity of an attitudinal position (or any other thought) may often be enough to make it 'attractive', in both the evaluative and dynamic senses of the word.

There is some experimental evidence to support this. At least under certain conditions, previously neutral or meaningless stimuli may gain in attractiveness as they become more familiar through repeated presentation (Zajonc, 1980). The Yale studies on persuasive communication (mentioned in chapter 1) contain many examples of people changing their viewpoints towards a position advocated by a communicator, even when this position was one they initially rejected. (The main limitation on this latter effect is that communications may be seen as lacking credibility if they are too discrepant from the audience's prior beliefs.) So, although there are clearly many other factors influencing attitude change, the role of mere familiarity may still be a powerful one. I am not denying that we may not all be very familiar with *some* beliefs that we strenuously reject; nor that, if we in fact conform to majority opinions, we may appear to be choosing more 'familiar' positions (since familiarity and conventionality will tend to go together). However, I *am* suggesting that the ease with which a particular attitude can be recalled or thought about will be one factor influencing the likelihood with which it can be *held*. Indeed, it may take a rather special form of cognitive activity to think about an attitude without treating it as one's own. This might perhaps involve the isolation (represented by higher ridges on the map) of that attitude from potentially associated behaviours or judgements of preference.

But these are just possible advantages. In this chapter I have argued for a more complex use of spatial concepts than is traditional within psychological theory and measurement. This extra complexity, however, is entirely in keeping both with developments in other sciences and with our everyday experience of natural objects and processes. Any use of such concepts can be described as metaphorical, but it is not *just* a metaphor that I am proposing. I am not just redescribing familiar facts in terms of new pictures. I am asserting, speculatively but not tentatively, that such new pictures help show the way towards new explanations in areas where better theories are badly needed. To defend this assertion, I will need to identify a process or set of principles that can account for how structures evolve dynamically over time. In other words, I will need to say how the phase space of thought can come to take on the complex dimensionality I have described. I will need to say, not just that attitudes could be described as attractors, but how they come to *be* so.

9

The Makings of Mind

Minds and machines

To ask how attitudes come to take on the dynamic properties of attractors is, in part, to ask the more familiar question of how they are learned. However, there are at least two reasons why the answer we will receive from traditional research on learning will be incomplete. The first is that learning research has never seriously grappled with the multidimensionality and complexity of everyday experience. For usually the best of reasons, the strategy has been to control troublesome sources of extra variability or 'noise' and to concentrate instead on the effects of a very few variables which can be manipulated independently of each other. The second is that, for all the recent developments in research on 'animal cognition', the flavour of most learning research remains behavioural. We can get a long way accounting for verbal (and other) expressions of attitude as the product of social reinforcements, if all we are interested in explaining is their situational appropriateness. The real difficulties start if we also want to say what such expressions are intended, or taken, to mean. Sooner or later, we must face up to questions of the nature of mind and the contents of consciousness. What, in other words, do we mean by 'mental processes' and what (in our case) are they like?

Behaviourism sidestepped this question by supposedly denying any interest in the mind at all, while none the less asserting that principles of behaviour are universal. Such denial is less strongly made by researchers in comparative psychology where the behavioural and cognitive capacities of different species are considered alongside one another. Of both these fields one might ask whether the evidence shows that our minds are like those of other animals, be they rats, pigeons or monkeys. However, this is not a question that will usually be easily, or even willingly, answered. Many researchers will say that they are interested in the behaviour of these other species in their own right. Others may say that they are studying animals as models for particular (e.g. physiological) reactions in human beings. All will acknowledge the importance of the environmental and biological constraints within which any behaviours are acquired. However, the question of whether human and other animal minds are similar, put just like that, has become mostly a non-issue.

In the meantime another question has moved to centre stage. Are our mental processes (or those of other animals) fundamentally different from, or essentially similar to, those of which a computer might be capable? Can computers provide a model of the human mind, and if so, what kind of model will it be? Will it deliver the patterned dynamics which characterize attitudes and other human thoughts? Recent work means that we no longer need merely to *imagine* the computational capabilities of machines. We have research to show what computers can do and what they might in principle achieve before too long.

Serial processing

Can any computer be said to have a 'mind'? As things stand, the answer must be no. But is this a logical necessity, or a limitation of present-day designs? Whatever the hopes or fears of future technological invention, conscious robots are not currently for sale in the high street. What we can find are machines with remarkable memory capacities and the ability to perform complex logical and mathematical operations reliably at great speed. In fact, present-day computers have a number of important limitations, the most crucial of which is that they are designed to perform operations singly, one step after another. This form of operation goes under the technical name of *serial processing*.

Serial processing systems are uninviting models for human thought for a number of formal reasons. An extensive discussion of these is provided in a recent book by Roger Penrose (1989). Essentially,

such systems operate deterministically, in that the immediate
future state of a given system is determined by its existing state and
any input. This is achieved through sets of 'if–then' rules or algorithms, generally referred to as *Turing machines* after the pioneering
computer scientist and war-time code-breaker Alan Turing. (These
need not be 'machines' in any ordinary nuts and bolts sense: they
are simply sets of conditional rules that could be applied automatically.) Penrose claims that a variety of mathematical problems
are insoluble by Turing machines.

One of the most general difficulties is the problem of how to
prevent such a machine simply running on for ever. As Turing
himself argued, it is impossible to devise a completely dependable
algorithm to make the system stop when it reaches a correct solution.
This is a simple enough matter if we know the answer to some
calculation in advance, or can say that the problem requires no
more that a specific number of steps. However, with more challenging tasks, such systems can get into great difficulties. A more
controversial claim is that certain mathematical statements have a
self-evidence that cannot be reduced to, or accounted for by, the
operation of any algorithmic procedure. (This involves Gödel's
theorem that any formal system of mathematical axioms must contain
some statements which can neither be proved nor disproved within
the terms of the system itself.) There are echoes here of Descartes's
notion of clear and distinct ideas. Truth may be something we
come to *recognize*, before and often without being able to provide
a formal proof. In short, Penrose argues, human beings have insight,
whereas computers (as we know them) do not.

There is a difficulty here, which is that people disagree about
many things. If they are all using their 'insight', then insight cannot
be infallible. Put differently, the clearness and distinctness of an
idea is no guarantee of its truth, and what is clear and distinct to
one person may not be so to another. The psychologically interesting
question, though, is not what truth *is*, but what it feels like – or,
more precisely, what kinds of feelings we use as criteria for deciding
on issues of truth and falsehood. In fact, most if not all everyday
judgements may depend more on *recognizing* things as belonging to
one category as distinct from another than on the use of any formal
algorithmic rule. Even though such judgements may be quite prone
to error and bias, they need not be experienced as such. We can *feel*
ourselves to be right and others to be wrong. Indeed, this feeling
and its consequences is the single most important challenge for
attitude research and should be the starting point for attitude theory.

How the brain works

If one were to caricature many non-specialists' conception of the brain, if would be as a very knobbly, half-deflated grey ball stuffed inside the skull, receiving 'messages' from sensory receptors and sending 'instructions' to muscles in different parts of the body. Slightly less crude accounts emphasize that different parts of the brain serve different functions, and this is achieved partly by their being 'wired up' in different ways. For a start, the brain consists of two 'halves' (the left and right hemispheres). Most of the connections to and from the left hemisphere are with the right side of our body and those to and from the right hemisphere with the left side of our body. The two hemispheres are connected directly to each other by a dense tube of nerve fires called the *corpus callosum*. If the corpus callosum fails to develop, is damaged by disease or injury, or is surgically severed (as part of outdated treatment for serious epilepsy), the two hemispheres seem to operate more or less independently in a number of curious ways. Philosophers have been especially fascinated by such 'split-brain' cases, since the evidence seems to point to the possibility of people's consciousness being divided. Many other subtle effects on thought and behaviour (for instance, relating to the use of language, and to different kinds of memory) can be found as a result of lesions to other specific sites in the brain. Yet it is remarkable how much of 'normal' life can often still go on, despite such damage.

A preferred technical name for the brain is the *central nervous system* (or CNS). The term *central* highlights the arbitrariness of boundaries between the 'brain proper' and more outlying or *peripheral* sets of nerves (as in the eye, or the spinal column). The term *system* stresses that we are going to learn little about the brain by regarding it as a single 'organ', but must instead consider it as performing collective and interconnected operations. In fact, the brain (as I shall still call it) consists of a vast number of nerve cells, or *neurons*. These neurons have many interesting structural properties. Typically, a neuron has a central body, containing the cell nucleus. To one 'side' of the central body emanate a number of shorter fibres called *dendrites* (from the Greek for 'branches'). In the other direction runs a longer fibre called the *axon* (the Greek for 'axle'), which ends by forking into a number of knobs (see figure 9.1). These knobs lie close to the dendrites of other neurons, the links between them being known as *synapses* ('junctions').

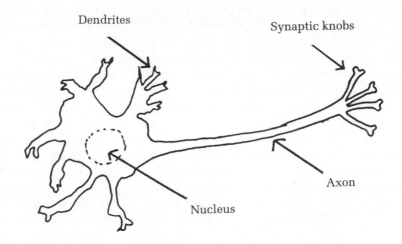

Figure 9.1   A schematic neuron

   Simply stated, the dendrites receive electrical impulses from other neurons. These then combine, and an impulse then passes along the axon to the synapses to make connections with yet other neurons. Electricity comes into it because of a high voltage gradient between the inside and outside of the neuron. Nerve fibres can be pictured as tubes containing ions of sodium, potassium and chloride. When the neuron is in a resting state, the sodium ions are in a minority inside, which means that it has a negative electric charge. Surrounding the outside of the axon, sodium ions predominate over potassium, producing a positive charge. The 'firing' of a neuron consists of a local reversal of this voltage gradient (by transfer of sodium and potassium ions through the wall of the nerve fibre) leading to a positive charge which travels along the fibre. One can picture such activity as a wave or sequence of 'spikes' with a particular amplitude and frequency. Connections at the synapses are dependent on the presence of *neurotransmitter substances*. The study of these substances has many important and subtle applications (with regard to the understanding of drug action, for example). For the present discussion, however, it is sufficient to regard neurotransmitters as controlling whether the firing of one neuron increases or decreases the likelihood that another neuron (whose dendrites lie at the far side of the synapse) will fire in turn. Whether the second neuron will fire depends on the combined total of such excitatory or inhibitory impulses received by its dendrites.

At this point, many philosophers (and others) despair. This seems to reduce the brain to a set of switches. If we are prepared to attribute powers of thought to neurochemical switches, why should we not do so to a silicon chip or printed circuit? It is a fair question, but it rather underrates how special the brain's electrical circuitry really is. The number of neurons in the human brain is estimated at some ten billion, but this is almost the least remarkable aspect of the brain's structure. Even more significant is the immense *interconnectedness* of the different neurons with each other. Any single neuron can have synaptic connections with possibly ten thousand others (estimates vary). Activity in any one part of the brain, or stimulation of any one receptor, can fan out to produce activity in many other parts *at the same time*. Likewise, whether any one part is active may depend on the joint activity of many other parts. With such a structure, it is quite implausible that the brain operates as a serial processing system. Rather, it appears to have all the necessary qualities to be a *parallel processor*.

Parallel processing

In contrast with serial systems which are constrained to perform one step at a time, parallel systems depend on large numbers of interconnected units dealing with information simultaneously. Because many units are handling the same information at the same time, pieces of 'knowledge' are not stored in any single unit, but are 'distributed' throughout the system. Parallel distributed processing (PDP) simulations of visual pattern recognition, for instance, assume that different units react differentially to the presence of particular features, and that recognition depends on how these different units combine with one another. For instance, the recognition of an object as being (say) a cat, depends on combined input from units responsive to different features (aspects of size and shape). These same units, however could combine differently with other units to yield a quite different representation (as say a dog, or tiger, or marmoset). Or, if we are talking about recognition of printed words, the words *cat* and *hat* share features in common but are distinguished by their first letter. (Letters in turn can depend on lower-order features.) But although *c* distinguishes *cat* from *hat*, it does not define it. The word needs the last two letters too; but these *same* two letters are also part of *hat* and of numerous other words as well. *Distributed* representations are those where several units combine to yield a single concept, and any single unit contributes to several concepts.

Because several units are being activated simultaneously in a parallel system, it is more difficult, and beyond a certain level impossible, to define the entire state of the system at a fixed point in time. This is not to say that we cannot *suppose* the entire system to be in one state rather than another, but simply that we cannot determine it to be so, at any rate until after the event. This disallows the rigid determinism of Turing machines. (Remember that these require definition of the pre-existing state of the system, any input, and a rule by which to calculate the new state into which the system must move.) Short of 'freezing' all the separate units or processors, so that they all stop operating together and are then restarted after read-outs have been attained, we simply cannot take in all that is happening while it is happening. We are faced with a system which depends on the levels of *activity* of its various sub-units, and on the manner in which the activity levels of some sub-units affect one another. If we try to 'fix' all this activity by trying to define the entire state of the system at one time, say immediately preceding the presentation of a stimulus, we immediately lose appreciation of the evolution of these activity levels over time. Conversely, if it is the activity levels in which we are interested, we need to look for patterns *over* time. As with Heisenberg's uncertainty principle (see chapter 5), some kinds of indeterminacy can only removed by accepting others.

It is not just the simultaneity of parallel processing that produces advantages over serial processing, but the fact that the activity levels of different sub-units can influence one another. This property of interconnectedness opens up many exciting possibilities. It has also given rise to a number of excited speculations about the physical basis of thought. A popular notion is that the brain's capacity for parallel processing depends on quantum mechanics. Roger Penrose (1989) and Michael Lockwood (1989) both put forward the notion that the brain may be a 'quantum computer'. I am content to remain agnostic on this question. As things stand, no such thing as a quantum computer has actually been manufactured. (Even more modestly, budgetary constraints mean that most present-day computer science research on PDP systems consists of simulations using serial processing computers, with computations that should be performed simultaneously being carried out sequentially. A good deal of extrapolation is therefore required to conceive of how a fully-fledged piece of PDP hardware would actually work.)

It may be that aspects of parallel processing exploit a 'quantumness' in the physical properties of the brain. Even so, the argument seems rather stronger the other way round, that is to say, that various quantum processes (superposition of alternative states, aspects of 'spin') exhibit qualities of parallelism. Where I think this leaves us is that people with a good understanding of quantum theory may be able to use some of its concepts to represent the interconnectedness of brain activity. Whether such a 'quantum' representation is to be interpreted literally or metaphorically is not something which I feel can be determined on the evidence we now have available. As things stand, what is most important is that we need a concept of interconnectedness to understand the nature of brain activity, not that we may need quantum theory to understand or account for such interconnectedness. In fact, such interconnectedness can be represented reasonably simply without any explicit reference to quantum processes. The essence of this representation is the notion of 'neural nets'.

Neural nets

Neural nets are computing systems constructed as deliberate analogues of the structure of the human brain. Such analogues are extremely over-simplified, but this hardly counts as a criticism when set against the unimaginability of the brain's complexity. But model-building has to start somewhere, and it starts with an idealized picture of connections shown in figure 9.2. This illustrates a set of neurons simultaneously responding to multiple inputs received through its different dendrites. The multiple inputs are drawn in parallel (as are the outputs), but this 'parallelism' is obviously a geometrical fiction. 'Parallel' processing in a real brain just means processing that goes on in different locations simultaneously. The same picture can be redrawn schematically as in figure 9.3. Here the crucial elements are a set of input units (along the top), a set of output units (along the right-hand side) and a set of connections between them, that is, the nodes where the vertical and horizontal lines join.

Now, despite the complexity of the problem, some relatively simple working assumptions begin to pay dividends. First, the various units (neurons) are assumed to be essentially similar to one another but to function differently because of the particular inputs to which

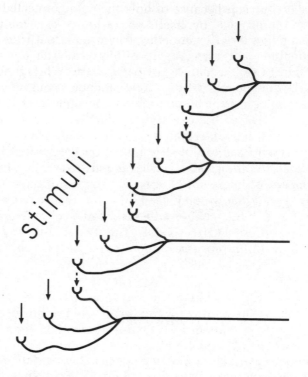

Figure 9.2   A schematic assembly of neurons capable of parallel processing

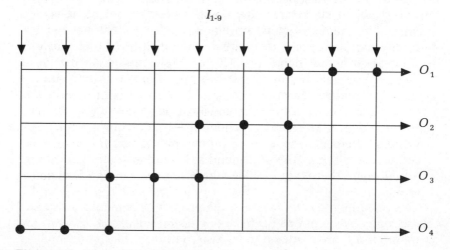

Figure 9.3   A neural net represented as a matrix

they are sensitive and because of how they are connected up with other units. Each unit, by itself, performs an extremely simple operation – either it fires, or it doesn't. For most purposes, then, it can be thought of as a binary 'on–off' switch. The power of the system derives from a simple principle determining *whether* a given unit fires or not: if the total activation received by an output unit exceeds a threshold value, it will fire, otherwise it will not. Total activation is defined simply as the sum of the 'messages' received from all the input units, weighted (i.e. multiplied) by the weights of the (synaptic) connections at each node. (The mathematical representation of such a system is relatively simple too. In terms of matrix algebra, the sets of inputs and outputs can be defined as vectors, and the set of connection weights as a matrix.)

Multiple layers and hidden units

Much research has concerned the potential of different forms of connectionist 'architechture' for solving different kinds of cognitive tasks. An important refinement is the inclusion of one or more extra layers of units between the input and output units. Typically, these 'hidden units' collate information from the input units (or another layer of hidden units closer to the input layer) and feed the representation forward for further processing. There are a number of problems which nets appear unable to handle without the help of such hidden units. One of the most widely studied concerns the logical relationship XOR or 'exclusive OR' (i.e. 'A or B but not both'). Although superficially simple, there is no obvious way of representing this relationship in terms of a single layer net (i.e. a net with just one layer of units preceding the output).

Assume we have two input units I_1 and I_2. I_1 returns a value of 1 (fires) if stimulus A occurs, otherwise 0. Conversely, I_2 returns 1 if stimulus B occurs, others 0. If there is a single output unit O, this can be made to fire (return a value of 1 or 'TRUE') if the summed activation from I_1 and I_2 is *at least* 1 – i.e. if either A or B are present ('inclusive OR') – but O cannot be made, at the same time, *not* to fire if *both* are present, i.e. if the summed activation from I_1 and I_2 is *more than* 1. This is because, if we say the summed activation must attain a threshold of 1 for O to fire, we must allow it to fire if both A and B are present and the activation is 2.

This problem can be solved by adding a layer of two 'hidden

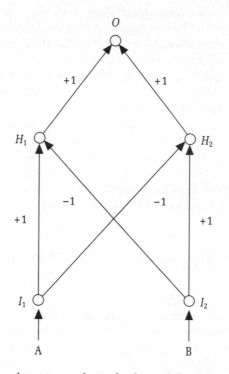

Figure 9.4 A neural net to perform the logical function XOR ('exclusive OR'). The output unit O will fire if either stimulus A or stimulus B is present, but not both.

units' H_1 and H_2. In the expanded net, we introduce a weight of +1 for the connection between I_1 and H_1, and a weight of −1 for the connection from I_1 to H_2. In other words, the presence of A will stimulate H_1 to fire but inhibit H_2. Conversely, the connection from I_2 to H_1 carries a weight of −1 and that from I_2 to H_2 carries one of +1. The weights from H_1 and H_2 to O are both +1, which means simply that their activation is summed. Once again, we set a threshold value of 1 for this summed activation to cause O to return a value of TRUE. However, in this new net, the summed activation received by O can only equal 1 or 0, never 2. If only A is present, H_1 but not H_2 will fire; if only B is present, the reverse will happen. However, if *both* A and B are present, *neither* H_1 nor H_2 will fire (see figure 9.4).

This example illustrates the capacity of multi-layer nets for solving logical problems. But what of more psychological questions?

How about making inductions from uncertain information, and adjusting decisions in the light of feedback and experience? How about the kind of more flexible intelligence of which human beings seem to have so much and traditional computers so little (if any)? Connectionist systems claim to be 'neurally plausible', but is it plausible that the human brain is a connectionist net? In general terms, the brain clearly *can* perform operations in parallel and is extremely interconnected. However, direct neurophysiological evidence for the existence of any specific kind of net or connectionist architechture in the brain is difficult to obtain. For the most part, the arguments in favour of connectionism depend on simulations of increasingly complex cognitive capacities. If a net can be made to produce intelligent output, maybe intelligence can be interpreted in network terms.

Rules and recognition

In a traditional computer program, if it has been properly written, there is no uncertainty. The programmer defines the mathematical and logical operations to be performed on a specified set of inputs, and these inputs are transformed into outputs in an entirely deterministic way. We may ask a computer, for instance, to generate a list of all the prime numbers between 1 and 1000. We do not know the answers in advance (although we might have access to a separate list), but with a little thought we could define an algorithm which could be applied to any number to determine whether or not it was prime (e.g. by consecutively dividing any integer x by all integers above 1, up to and including $0.5x$ – or more economically by all previously identified prime numbers within this range – and rejecting x as non-prime if the outcome of any of these divisions was an integer). In other words, traditional programs are invaluable when we do not know the answer, but do know how to calculate it, given sufficient time and concentration. But suppose we are presented with a different kind of problem, where we can, within broad limits, *recognize* whether a particular answer is correct or satisfactory, after we find it or after it is offered to us, but where we cannot *define* in advance what rules should be followed to generate all correct solutions without allowing any errors to intrude.

To return to the example of prime numbers, I have no idea, off the top of my head, whether 3574213 is a prime number, although I can say it stands at least a small chance of being so in that it is not divisible by 2, 3 (since the sum of the digits is not divisible by 3) or 5. Thereafter, my powers of mental arithmetic abandon me – but I can say that I *know* that I could determine whether 3574213 was prime by applying the algorithm outlined above, had I the patience and curiosity to do so. My knowing that the algorithm would provide me with a correct answer one way or the other, however, is not something which appears to depend on some other algorithm; it depends instead on a kind of *recognition*, involving a representation of what it means for a number to be prime. Another way of putting this is that I could not write a program to determine if my algorithm was valid without some separate rule against which to compare it, or alternatively a 'look-up list' of known prime numbers; and to build in such a prior rule or list would beg the question of how I could tell whether *that* rule or list was correct.

Let us pursue the notion of recognition more literally. Think of recognizing one of your friends. You *know* that the person you are looking at is your friend, is called Jim or Jenny or whatever, but you cannot say *exactly* how you know, how much weight you have put on this feature rather than that. This does not mean at all that the separate features are unimportant – quite the contrary. It just means that you could not define how you processed information of such features in terms of 'if–then' algorithms. Another way of putting this is that we could not write a traditional program of 'if–then' rules to identify someone as Jim or Jenny on the basis of a particular feature set – at any rate, not in such a way that would allow us to recognize Jim even after a hair-cut, or to guess that someone we hadn't met before might be Jenny's sister. The surest way to make a traditional program produce an error is to redefine the problem half-way through without specifying how.

Possibly the most impressive general characteristic of connectionist nets is their capacity for 'recognizing' the categories to which particular inputs belong *without* needing to be programmed with any rules which specify the features defining such categories. For instance, a net could be trained to tell the difference between Jim and Jenny without the use of any explicit rule such as 'Jenny has curly hair'. Instead, nets can develop their *own* representations – for instance of the distinction between male and female faces. These representations do not depend simply on specific features in isolation and can generalize reliably to new male and female faces of which the net has no experience. It is like – maybe it is the same as – our being able to say that *we* can tell the difference between (most) male and female faces, including ones we have never seen, but cannot say exactly how we do so. As far as our own cognitive capacities are concerned, we need to be able to interpret *new* information all the time. We do not and cannot know in advance everything that we are likely to encounter in the world. Yet the 'world' of input to a traditional computer program *is* something that must be specified in advance and in precise detail, otherwise the program will produce errors or simply fail to run. The radical innovation achieved by connectionist nets is that they are *not* constrained by any such advance specification. On the contrary, they can adapt themselves to new inputs while continuing to make use of existing memories. They can, in effect, reprogram themselves if their output from their existing program in unsatisfactory. In living creatures, we would call this 'learning'. How, then, do networks 'learn'?

Nets that can be trained

Donald Hebb (1949) speculated that learning may be achieved by the nervous system through a strengthening of the connections between two neurons whenever they fire at the same time. Building on this idea, connectionism views learning as consisting simply of modifying connection weights so as to produce satisfactory output. Training a net, likewise, consists of providing it with feedback in such a way that the weights will be appropriately modified. Take the simple case of a single-layer net, with a set of input units, a set of connections, and a set of output units. Suppose that the purpose of this net is something fairly elementary, like discriminating between printed alphabetic characters. The standard procedure is broadly as follows:

1 Identify particular input units as responsive to different features (e.g. a vertical line in a particular position) and particular output units as representative of different characters (M, N, T etc.).
2 Define an initial set of connection weights at random.
3 Present the net with different input patterns, and see what outputs it produces (by multiplying the input activations by the connection weights).
4 Compare the outputs with the correct answers, express errors in

terms of difference scores between achieved and required output activation levels (for a given input pattern).

5 Calculate corrections based on these difference scores and add these to the previous matrix of connection weights.

6 Then re-run the procedure. After a little while the weights will converge on a set which will provide a correct set of outputs (i.e. on a set where the relevant output activations are above threshold).

Elaborations of this basic procedure have been developed to deal with more complex problems. For instance, in multi-layer nets (those involving hidden units) an incorrect output needs to be interpreted in terms of what happens both at the connections from input to hidden units, and at the connections from hidden to output units. (Part of the complication arises from the fact that one cannot calculate errors in the activations of the hidden units by comparing them with correct solutions, since these activations are not, in themselves, outputs or solutions. Currently, the preferred approach to this problem is to take a measure of the output error and feed it back to the hidden units as though it was a kind of input activation. This is an example of what is known as *back-propagation*.)

Another very important area is that of designing nets that take account of *context*. This is typically handled by adding a set of units, similar to input units, which store and respond to information about the context in which the input is presented. Where this context remains constant over the course of training, it might as well be regarded simply as part of the input. However, there are many cases where the context will change. This applies, for example, to sequential activities, like reading or interpreting words in a sentence. The previous words in a sentence define (part of) the context in which a particular word is interpreted, but as each word is processed and the reader moves on, the context also changes. So-called *recursive nets* can be designed to update the stored contextual information on the basis of particular kinds of feedback (e.g. from hidden units). A closely related concept is that of *interactive nets*, in which connections between units can be two-way.

All this happens without the researcher needing to specify or even know in advance the kinds of weights or hidden unit activations required to produce correct output. What is more, we do not even have to insist on there being just a single unique solution (in terms of weights, etc.) to any given task. Suppose we train a net until it satisfies a criterion of producing correct answers (i.e. until the required outputs are above threshold levels) and then start all over again with a new set of random connection weights and retrain it on the same problem. The second solution will almost certainly show some departures from the first, even though the answers it provides are equally correct.

Content-addressable memory

Once a net has been trained, the patterns of connection weights record the information gained by such training. That is, they define the system's memory. Such a memory will exhibit a very important property; it will be *content-addressable*. This means simply that it can be cued by mentioning a particular input variable or attribute, without prior restrictions on what that attribute might be. The advantages of such a system become clear if one considers the standard alternative – a register of (non-distributed) representations each occupying a single location. Imagine looking up someone's telephone number in a directory. There will only be one location where it can be found, but finding it is usually quite easy if one remembers the person's surname, together with one or two other disambiguating details. This ease of search depends on an arbitrary rule – alphabetical order – which determines the serial position of a particular name in the directory. This rule happens to be a very familiar one. Even so, it is very brittle – that is, very likely to break down if faced with an unanticipated problem. An obvious example is that you cannot use the directory at all if you don't know the person's surname. Another problem is where you look for entries that have some unusual feature, so that the rule has to be adapted arbitrarily to include the exceptions. For instance, current British telephone directories put abbreviations above non-abbreviated names under each alphabetic heading, so that you would fail to find 'VW Services' (in our local directory), where you might reasonably expect it, between 'Vulcan Garage' and 'Vye E.A.'. Instead, you have to turn back seven pages to the beginning of the 'Vs' where it appears below 'V & R Jewellers Ltd', immediately above 'V52' (whatever that might be!) and two above 'Vacher P.' Doubtless there is a rule being followed here, but without knowledge of the rule, you can easily get lost. This kind of difficulty is shared by any system that stores information serially without reference to its content. If you don't know exactly what you are looking for, and you don't know exactly how to find it, the system will be no use to you at all.

Content-addressable memory works quite differently. There is no rigid filing system or serial list of addresses. It enables us to recall ideas or locate concepts by thinking of *any* cue that can identify the concept or object in question. There is no possibility of finding a name or number in a telephone directory all you knew was that the person was twenty-four years old and had red hair! The information is simply not stored or 'addressable' in that form. Yet if I were to ask you to name a person you know who has red hair, you could probably do it very quickly. You could then proceed to tell me, quite probably, what happened when you last met, and what you expect this person is doing now. This is because human memory is very flexible in terms of its routes of access (and indeed of egress). Choose more or less any attribute, and one can identify objects to which this attribute belongs. Patterns can be retrieved from memory (i.e. re-activated) by thinking of (i.e. activating) even quite small parts of their *content*. Retrieve a pattern, and further associations will come to mind, leading to the activation of yet further patterns.

Nets that find things out

The procedures so far described all require the person training the net to know whether a given output is correct or not. These procedures are referred to as instances of *supervised learning*. This requirement might seem to undermine the claim that a machine can be 'intelligent', since the 'real' intelligence resides with the machine's controller. None the less, we should not underestimate the implications of such work for many kinds of learning. The kind of 'supervision' required is essentially just the provision of feedback regarding correct or incorrect responses. This feedback can be seen as directly analogous to reinforcement in operant conditioning, where again reinforcement schedules, contingent on behavioural *output*, are specified in advance. In terms of extrapolation to learning in naturalistic situations, all that needs to be assumed is that the environment itself contains reinforcement contingencies – that some courses of action produce desirable outcomes and other courses of action produce outcomes that are discrepant from some desired goal. This assumption is much the same as that involved in extrapolating to the real world from experimental studies of operant conditioning. Implicit in it, though, is a cognitive interpretation of operant conditioning – reinforcements work because of the information and feedback they provide. When appropriate feedback is provided, nets, like animals, can be trained to discriminate between different stimuli and to generalize their discriminations to new situations.

There is yet another form of learning of which nets are capable, which is potentially of even greater significance for some of the broader issues I have been considering. *Unsupervised learning* does not require feedback based on the discrepancy between achieved and desired output. Thus it does not require a trainer to define what answers are correct or incorrect. The basis of this form of learning is the ability to detect covariation between the activation levels of different units, i.e. whether some units tend to come on and go off together, or whether some only tend to come on while others are off. More simply, nets can recognize patterns.

Presented with information containing non-random associations, nets can be designed to detect such associations (without being told specifically which associations to look for). The basic idea is to have output or hidden units (let us call these, unconventionally, 'pattern units') which are each responsive to activation in a range of input units. When the activation received by a given pattern unit exceeds threshold (so that the pattern unit 'fires'), this is assumed to strengthen the positive connection weights to it from the input units active at the time, while weakening – or making more negative – the weights from any inactive units. Next time around, the pattern unit will be more likely to fire if more of the previously active input units are active again, and less likely to fire following activation of a new input unit which was not part of the previous pattern.

This is essentially Hebb's principle of simultaneous activation leading to strengthened connections. It may also be interpreted as analogous to classical or Pavlovian conditioning. But its importance for psychological theory does not stop there. It provides a plausible neural analogue for the process of *categorization*. The presence or absence of a category can be represented by the activation of a pattern unit. Furthermore, just as categories can be organized hierarchically within one another – just as smaller patterns can combine to form larger ones – so the activations of pattern units at one level in a multi-layer net can feed-forward to yet more pattern units at a higher level. Interactive connections with other patterns at the same level may also be possible. Thus we could have the kind of system that can make broader generalizations and finer differentiations at the same time.

Nets, therefore, can learn to do more than recognize distinctions imposed by the experimenter. Such learning tasks are merely special cases that are relatively easy to study. Any non-randomness in the input can define a pattern to which a network can make its output approximate by systematically revising its matrix of connection weights. Memory for such a pattern, moreover, will be content-addressable, whether or not it has been acquired through specific feedback. In supervised learning, this non-randomness derives from the 'answers' defined by the experimenter. In unsupervised learning, it derives from the patterns recognizable within the stimulus environment itself.

With suitable elaboration, this principle is invaluable for any organism that needs to find its way around in a non-random universe. If the universe was random, the principles of connectionism – like Hume's principles of association with which they are so compatible – would give no guarantee of sanity or even of survival. Anything could be randomly associated with anything. This is precisely the starting position for connectionist nets *before* any learning takes place – all connection weights are set at random. If reality itself was random, this is precisely how everything would stay. One random pattern of weights would replace another without convergence on any stable solution. But if the universe *is* patterned, we – no less than artificial minds – can come to recognize at least small parts of that pattern. We can do so without knowing what it is we are looking for or how to explain what it is we find. Yet when we find such a pattern, we know there is something we have found which exists beyond ourselves.

Patterns and dynamics

If thought consists of our internalizing the patterns to be found in the world outside, what kind of organization is thereby produced? To approach this question, it must be appreciated that we are looking for patterning and coordination within a system of *activity*. We need to understand the nature of patterning within a dynamic process, not just within a static arrangement. We are looking for coordination in vectors and forces, in the direction of energy flow. To understand what is meant by organization within a dynamic process, one starting point is to consider the opposite state: disorganization or, as physicists refer to it, *entropy*. In the context of thermodynamics, it is a state of complete equilibrium in which everywhere is at the same temperature. That is, there is no flow of heat in any one direction rather than another. There are no coordinated temperature gradients within the system and hence there is zero potential energy. There is no reliable possibility of differentiation or even of generalization across time or space or context, beyond the generalization associated with universal indistinguishability. This nightmare is no hypothetical abstraction. Other things being equal, it is the ultimate destiny of all physical systems, including ourselves. More precisely, all systems considered individually in isolation from the rest of the universe tend towards maximum entropy. Only the consumption of energy from outside and its transformation into more ordered structures (e.g. proteins) keeps us from dropping into the abyss of disintegration – and that only for a while.

Contrasted with the lack of coordinated energy flow which defines maximum entropy, any organized dynamic system, whether physical or psychological, will display a directional character. Any organization will facilitate some changes and inhibit others. Any organization will depend on patterns of constraints, of inequalities between the probabilities of different states. If we represent these probabilities as a surface of phase space, their inequalities will be reflected in its contours, with wells of attraction defining more probable end-states of low potential energy, exactly as described in chapter 8. Neural networks specify a set of processes whereby an initially random configuration can transform itself into just such a pattern of attractors and constraints.

Attractors and neural networks

Let us remind ourselves of the job we expect any model of a cognitive system to do. What we need is a representation of deviations from equiprobability, something that allows us to say which cognitive events are more or less likely to occur. Connectionism addresses precisely this question. It provides an explicit account of how a particular pattern of input can lead to particular forms of output (attitudes, behaviours, judgements, etc.). As an account of learning, it also describes the evolution of the system over time. Such evolution consists of modifications to initial patterns of connection weights, so that the probability of a preferred 'solution', given a specific stimulus input, is increased at the expense of non-preferred alternatives or 'errors'.

This kind of process is equivalent to the introduction of one or more attractors into the system's phase space. The greater the difference in connection weights leading to alternative cognitive outputs, the greater will be the difference in strength between attractors and/or between any single attractor and its surrounding field. Add the by now familiar representation of attractors in terms of vertical depth, and learning can be regarded as the carving of wells and valleys from an initial energy surface or landscape. This initial surface can be allowed to reflect constraints of previous learning and instinct, but will otherwise be random (and will typically be so in most network learning simulations). It is the transformation of disorder into organized pattern.

The link between connectionist learning processes and physical concepts of entropy and attractors was first noticed by John Hopfield (1982). Hopfield, himself a physicist, remarks that, in physical systems, stable attractors, such as orientations in a magnetic field or vortex patterns in a fluid flow, can emerge from the collective interactions of elementary components. He then poses the question:

> Do analogous collective phenomena in a system of simple interacting neurons have useful 'computational' correlates? For example, are the stability of memories, the construction of categories of generalization, or time-sequential memory also emergent properties and collective in origin? (Hopfield, 1982, p. 2554)

His answer, of course, is Yes. But there was no 'of course' about it at the time. These were early days in the history of connectionist research, and many of the computational capacities of neural networks had yet to be demonstrated convincingly. Hopfield's argument was based, not on a large body of successful simulations of cognitive performance, but on an analysis of what connectionist principles implied in terms of physical dynamics.

For example, consider the question of content-addressable memory, where input relating to some partial characteristic of an object allows one to recall the object as a whole. Hopfield likens this to a physical system where there is a flow in phase space 'toward locally stable points from anywhere within regions around those points'. In other words, having one's full store of information about an object 'triggered' by some partial cue is like moving towards an attractor from anywhere on the perimeter of a well. A useful memory system, however, requires that different items are recalled as a consequence of different inputs. The system must respond discriminatively. Hence, one needs multiple attractors which are each dominant over smaller regions (input configurations). As Hopfield puts it (p. 2554):

> Any physical system whose dynamics in phase space is dominated by a substantial number of locally stable states to which it is attracted can therefore be regarded as a general content-addressable memory.

The process of recall can thus be seen as a flow through a phase space pock-marked by numerous smaller and larger wells of attraction. The bottoms of these wells represent points of local minima as far as the potential energy of the system is concerned. Thus, flow towards an attractor results in lower potential energy. When the attractor is reached (as when some output is produced), there is less available potential energy to move the system into a different state.

Hopfield devised a set of connectionist learning models involving an algorithm whereby units within the network 'update' or reset their activation levels to 0 ('off') or 1 ('fully on'). This updating takes place at random time intervals and on an individual unit-by-unit basis, without any demand for synchronization. The algorithm requires simply that any resetting of an individual unit should reduce the *overall* mismatch between the system's output and the set of correct solutions − for instance, a set of memories needing to be retrieved. Hopfield's algorithm incorporates a measure E, which represents the overall 'goodness of fit' of output with a solution. The basic idea is that a unit's activation level will be reset if this increases E but otherwise will remain unchanged. Hopfield actually presents E as a measure of the system's *entropy*. Thus, his algorithm for moving the system closer to a stable solution (by increasing E at each step) involves a reduction of the potential energy for change in the system as a whole. Thus, a discrepancy between the initial state of the system and its final output can be regarded as a source of potential energy, subsequently dissipated through cognitive activities such as recall, recognition and decision-making. Maximum entropy, within this context, is said to be achieved when there is a perfect 'fit' between the system's output and a specified set of 'correct' solutions.

The need for chaos

A problem with Hopfield's algorithm is that it can lead the system to get stuck in 'local minima' or sub-optimal solutions. Because the resetting of individual units must increase E at *each* step, there is no provision for breaking up an output pattern approximating imperfectly to the required solution if this requires a short-term worsening of the overall goodness of fit. This difficulty is similar to that experienced when trying to solve puzzles such as Rubik's Cube (a cube made up of rotatable smaller cubes with different colours on each side). The aim of this puzzle is to make each face of the cube show squares of a single colour – literally, a maximum 'goodness of fit' between colour and position. To achieve this, it is often necessary to break up sub-optimal patterns, that is, to spin the smaller cubes so as, in the short term, to *increase* the mix of colours on each face, thus reducing goodness of fit. This problem of 'local minima' or sub-optimal solutions is easily visualized in terms of wells of attraction. The local minima are equivalent to small dips or pockets halfway down the hillside of a larger well (as Killeen likewise pictures them, see figure 8.9). If phase-space flow can never decrease entropy (if our ball can never roll uphill), then a system that falls into such a pocket must stay there.

The fact that 'Hopfield nets' can produce errors of this kind is actually quite appealing if what we are trying to do is model human decision-making. Many maladaptive responses, from addictive behaviours to mutually destructive conflicts and environmental degradation, can be understood in terms of reinforcement 'traps', where the short-term costs of changing a habit may obstruct the route to long-term benefits. Even so, later research has attempted to devise procedures to deal with this problem. The favoured solution is to introduce random variation into the activation levels of the separate units. Pictorially, this is like 'bouncing' the ball-bearing out of the pocket through causing a convenient earthquake (or by using an inflatable beach-ball that is less likely to come to rest in the first place).

This is referred to as raising the 'temperature' of the system, on the analogy of certain physical phenomena (formation of crystals, polarization of ferromagnetics) where adding 'temperature' introduces random or chaotic variation in the orientation of 'spin' of the constituent particles. Depending how literally one wishes to interpret this analogy, there is possibly a very significant opportunity here for quantum physics (see chapter 5) to contribute to an understanding of psychological processes. More generally, adding temperature can be compared directly to driving a system normally characterized by negative feedback into a temporary state of instability or chaos. Another example is the logistic equation for population growth described in chapter 8: adding temperature is like increasing the growth factor beyond the accumulation point.

Thus, although the processes decribed by connectionist models tend towards stability, they can show more chaotic features. Chaos may need to be introduced so as to provide an escape route from the dominance of a set of immediate constraints. It can also be the outcome of the operation of the system itself, granted certain conditions. When testing his model with different starting para-meters, Hopfield found that outputs might oscillate between alter-native solutions, depending on the size of the net and the relative closeness of different attractors to one another, in a manner remi-niscent of near-chaotic systems. As he puts it:

> The flow is not entirely deterministic, and *the system responds to an ambiguous starting state by a statistical choice* between the memory states it most resembles. (Hopfield, 1982, p. 2557; emphasis in original)

Non-linearity in neural networks

Although I have concentrated on Hopfield's work in these last few pages, the main conclusions I wish to draw are not specific to his formulations. Decision-making, discrimination and recall are dynamic processes which may be represented as flows through a particular kind of phase space. One of the most important charac-teristics of such flows is that they are *non-linear*. This is not just a consequence of treating hypothetical neural units as binary ('on–off') switches (which may anyway prove an oversimplification). An even more important feature is the stipulation that the firing of a hidden or output unit will depend on the (weighted) activations of *all* the units in the preceding layer which are connected to it. If too few of these preceding units are activated, so that their total activation is too low, then the hidden or output unit will not fire. Any randomness or noise in the distribution of activation levels of individual units within a given layer can lead to a dissipation of energy, again in a non-linear fashion. And then there is the control mechanism of the matrix of connection weights themselves. The lower their value, the more 'resistance' is introduced into the net-work. In other words, there is no one-to-one relationship between a change in input and a change in output, as a model of linear flow would demand. The relationship depends on the interactions defined by the matrix of connections.

Underlying this non-linearity of flow is the dimensionality of the energy landscape itself. My claim that it is *fractal* (see chapter 8) rests on the proposal that it displays an infinite interpolation of complexity. Attractors emerge as the collective effect of the activations of separate units. More detailed information about these separate units and their individual interconnections is still there to be discovered, however. It constrains but is not itself completely constrained by more global descriptions of the configuration of the network as a whole. (As I mentioned earlier, a net trained on the same problem on two separate occasions – that is, with its weights reset randomly in between – is very unlikely to generate *exactly* the same weight matrix the second time around.)

The minimum level of analysis in a neural network is the single neuron or synaptic connection. This is not *infinitely* small, strictly speaking, but relative to the size of a human brain it might as well be. But even this limit of detail is a matter of convention. If it is a real brain we are considering, it would be quite legitimate to re-define the state of any neuron, say, in terms of the states of its constituent sodium and potassium and chloride ions; and so onwards and inwards to the limits of indeterminacy. With natural objects as distinct from purely abstract formulations such as the Mandelbrot set, the Heisenberg principle must eventually call a halt to such delving, but this is a very distant limit for most purposes. If we allow 'infinite' to stand in this context for 'as far as can in principle be determined', then the interpolation of complexity within a neural network, or the phase space which describes it, can reasonably be said to be 'infinite'. Thus the mind is at least as fractal as any other natural object.

Carving the landscape

The challenge that remains is to show that connectionism can do more than help us design machines to solve a few problems – that it can be extended to account for the shape of mind – its *fractal* shape. Critical to this attempt is the notion of attractors and the part they play in neural networks. In discussing this issue, I have relied so far on examples from research on 'supervised' learning. In this type of learning, the 'correct' solutions – the memories to be recalled or the categories to which objects belong – are specified in advance. In other words, contours are imposed on the phase space, and the net is set the task of finding a way through them. In the human or animal context, this corresponds broadly to reinforcement learning. But if we are trying to model the human mind, we need to say how such attractors are *acquired*. More generally, we need to be able to model how memories, categories and attitudes are built up through more spontaneous forms of reality-testing. We need to be able to say that we think the way we do because it makes sense in terms of our own experience. This is not the same as saying that we think the way we do because others have told us what to think.

Within the language of connectionism, this takes us back to the issue of 'unsupervised' learning. It is easy enough to see what end result we are after. We want unsupervised learning to lay down attractors in the phase space, to sink wells and valleys and scour surfaces. We want to be able to look at a smooth surface and say that it reflects little experience or differentiation, but see the evidence of learning and knowledge in roughness of a more complex landscape. How can we carve such landscapes?

The answer is by now quite simple. We are looking at yet another example of a dissipative dynamic process. Stand at the head of any real valley in a natural landscape and ask yourself how it was formed. Half the answer you will know without even looking, that the earth's crust buckled as it cooled and that rivers and streams then did their work. But then *look* at how the rivers and streams have done their work, and you will see something more complex than this bland account suggests. Looked at in detail, the branching of the streams, and the curve of the riverbank follow a course which is never perfectly straight, and approximately so only where engineers have tried to bring it under artifical control. Beyond a shadow of a doubt, the shape is fractal. There is an infinite interpolation of complexity. Yet we can easily tell where a river is likely to be, or the route it followed centuries ago, even without seeing the water, simply from the lie of the land. The lie of the land shows us where the river has flowed, gradually eroding the land on its way. And where the river has flowed in the past, there it is likely to flow again. Despite all its turns and wriggles, the river course is confined within the boundaries of the valley which it has itself carved through the hillside over many centuries or millenia.

This is an example – and one which we can visualize – of how a dynamic process is shaped by its own past and how its lays down attractors which direct its own future behaviour. Thought is also a dynamic process, shaped by and shaping its own history. All that is needed to interpret cognitive dynamics as analogous to the erosion of a river valley is an elaboration of two extremely simple and widely accepted principles. The first that, other things being equal, *previous responses will tend to recur* under repeated stimulus conditions. If we return to the image of a ball-bearing rolling around on a surface (within a cognitive phase space), we can represent this principle by assuming that the ball-bearing cuts or burns a groove in the surface wherever it passes or comes to rest, thus laying down both a track of previous cognitive events and attractors for future events.

In terms of a similar but earlier empiricist metaphor, the mind at birth could be seen as a wax tablet, scraped smooth (a *tabula rasa*). Experience then inscribes, or carves, itself into this tablet. This image was used as part of the argument against 'innate ideas'. We can afford to take a less extreme position. Inherited predispositions can send us into the world with a cognitive space that is already contoured to some extent – i.e. has some pre-experiential organization, which can direct, but may also be overlaid by, subsequent learning. Returning to the analogy of the river valley, part of the shape will be due to the folding of the earth's crust, part to the erosion by the river itself.

The second principle is that proposed by Hebb, that *when two cognitive units are activated together, the connection between them is strengthened*. What happens with a strengthened connection? Future cognitive activity will be likely to travel along that same connection, making it even stronger, and widening its field of attraction to cover yet more units that are simultaneously active. There is a drive towards the strengthening, the overlearning, of associations that are already formed. Initially rather weak, or shallow, attractors become stronger and deeper through being repeatedly approached, and the connecting routes (associative links) through which they are approached become deeper and wider too, that is, more likely to be activated across a range of input configurations. One can picture this process as a ball-bearing rolling backwards and forwards over a pass between two basins on a contoured surface. As it does so, it wears the pass into a gully, which then, over a period, broadens to link the two basins together to form a single valley.

The phase-space map of any thought process is therefore shaped and carved by past thought and experience. This is as inexorable as the fall of a mountain stream towards the valley floor, cutting an ever-deeper course for itself as it passes. Any past thought produces a pocket, any past association carves a gully. Yet the edges and slopes of such pockets and gullies – like the banks of any mountain stream – will show chaotic variation (or fractal detail), which will be the consequence of the many chaotic cognitive events which a connectionist model of mind permits and even requires. Every thought, however trivial, leaves its trace, however small. Every simultaneity of activation, however passing, may add weight to the connection between the activated units. For a trace to become a valley and for a weak connection to become a firm association, what is needed is that the local minima they represent grow in strength through repetition, and come to function as attractors for more collective and distributed activity.

Connectionism thus provides a framework for the mapping of thought processes with many advantages over more traditional 'Euclidian' measurement frameworks. It incorporates sensitivity to context, and to differences as a function of broader or more fine-grained levels of categorization. It gives due prominence to notions of habit and stability, with previous experience and memories providing stable equilibria to which the system is likely to be attracted, whilst allowing for the occurrence of sub-optimal responding and unreliable discrimination. With rather more extended extrapolation from established findings, it suggests how decisions may be reappraised through cognitive restructuring, that is, by re-orientating the dimensions of the space and following the path of new associations. But above all, it proposes a *dynamic* view of mind. It affirms the continuity of experience while acknowledging, as James insisted, that *thought is in constant change*.

10

The Emergent Self

Social connections

If thought is an emergent property of the collective activity of vast numbers of separate neurons, how absolute is the distinction between the individual and the social? Within connectionist systems, representations are distributed over several different units, and any single unit typically can influence many different kinds of decisions and judgements. Even if we allow for 'modules' or specialized subsystems, we still need these modules to be interconnected with each other. Thought, in other words, is a property of the whole, but not of any of its parts treated in isolation – or at any rate not of any of the parts remaining after more than a few stages of division. We do not want to say that a single neuron is conscious or has a sense of self, but we do want to say just that about the collectivity of neurons that constitutes a human brain.

But what are the boundaries of this collectivity? A single brain is itself arguably a social system, depending on some division of labour but primarily on its capacity for coordination through connections strengthened through learning and experience. This metaphor should not be pressed to far, or it is too easy to see the brain as comprising, not special processors, but loads of 'little people' (or *homunculi*, as philosophers once called them), each with 'minds' of their own. We are then left with describing the minds of these 'little people', and will quickly find them even more inscrutable than that of an undivided human being. Yet if we resist treating modules as full minds in their own right, we can usefully regard the brain not just as a physical object, but as an object engaged in a physical activity. This activity consists of communication of information and mutual influence through electrochemical discharges. It is because of this communicative activity that we can say things about the collectivity of the brain that we cannot say about isolated neurons.

But communication is not just something that occurs *within* brains. The whole point of applying the social metaphor to the brain is that communication is something different people do with each other. Furthermore, it is because different people communicate and influence one another that it makes sense to talk about social collectivities, of groups of friends, of families, of cultures, of societies and social movements, of nation states and international communities. Such collective terms mean something in so far as they help account for social behaviour and relationships, and the reciprocal influence of individuals and collectivities on each other. Just as thought and behaviour at the individual level does not have to be uniformly consistent, social behaviour need not be conformist and social beliefs need not be consensual. For the word 'social' to add anything meaningful, what is required is simply that the activities and thoughts are *interconnected*.

This suggests that the basic notions of connectionism can be adapted to describe the operation of social systems – that is to say, networks of people – and need not be restricted to networks of simple neurons. Obviously, the concept of a social system has to be presented in a very simplified form to allow such an analysis to get started, but this is no worse than saying that one needs to start with a very simplified model of the brain. In fact, a few significant steps have already been taken in simulating social processes, treating individual members of a social group as though they were units in a connectionist net.

Simulating social impact

Nowak *et al.* (1990) present a simulation of attitude change within a group of forty individuals, all of whom could potentially influence each other. Such a matrix of reciprocal influences, though easily conceived of in principle, is a far more complex structure than any that can practicably be studied in social psychological experiments with real subjects. Most theories designed around such experiments deal with questions such as whether one person would change his or her opinion in response to influence from, say, three or more others, or whether a confident minority group of three people could sway the opinions of a less committed majority of nine. It is far less clear what such theories would predict about the processes of social influence within a set of 1560 two-way relationships. Hence, a simulation can help us see what could happen within a more complex set of relationships, if a theory developed from simpler data was in fact correct.

The theory which Nowak and his collaborators put to this kind of test was Latané's (1981) Social Impact Theory. This theory attempts to predict the amount of impact or social influence there will be on a person to change or maintain his or her opinion as a (multiplicative) function of three factors relating to the sources of such influence (e.g. other people). These factors are: the *number* of sources advocating a particular position, their *immediacy* (closeness in space and time) to the individual subject, and their *strength* (authority or persuasiveness). This formulation readily translates into approximate connectionist terms, with sources corresponding to inputs (so that their number defines the size of the input vector), strength corresponding to input activation levels, and immediacy to the connection weights. The outputs, of course, are the subsequent opinions of the individual group members. For simplicity, these opinions can be considered in simple binary terms (i.e agree–disagree). Since no 'correct solution' (defined pattern of final opinions) is imposed, this constitutes an example of 'unsupervised learning' (or 'auto-association').

The Nowak simulations confirm the intuitive prediction of the theory that majority opinions within a group tend to become more dominant, i.e. win converts, over time. However, the most striking feature of the data is that uniformity of opinion is rarely achieved. On the contrary, pockets of minority opinion, though they may lose a few members at the margin, can prove quite resilient in the face of an opposed majority. This seems to come about because (a) individuals are unevenly influenced by other people, as a function of their 'immediacy', so that, if more immediate sources of influence share the same minority position, that position will be locally stable; and (b) since every individual is both a source and a recipient of influence, there can be *mutual* support of minority, as well as majority, opinions. In other words, you are more likely to be influenced by your friends than by distant acquaintances, and you will support your friends' opinions when they agree with you and so they will remain a source of support for *your* opinions in return.

'Together we stand, divided we fall' seems a very fair description of what Social Impact Theory predicts can happen to holders of minority opinions.

Although still in its early stages, this approach has some exciting implications. The links with more 'mainstream' connectionist models could be elaborated further, though the resemblance to Hopfield nets and their sequels is already fairly close. For instance, a 'temperature' parameter can be incorporated to control the likelihood of individuals changing their opinion at random. However, the practical benefits – or even conceptual equivalence – of incorporating multiple layers has yet to be seriously explored. For instance, one could develop a multi-layer representation of the intra-group processes leading to the emergence of a majority norm, which was then taken forward by representatives of the group into an inter-group context.

Another possibility suggested by Nowak and his colleagues is to incorporate two or more attitude issues at the same time. Here an important stage might be the emergence of an accepted definition of the agenda – essentially, what issues are most salient or important – before the group engages itself in reaching a majority position on the issues chosen as priorities. However, from work I mentioned previously (in chapter 7), we should not underestimate the extent to which attitudes and perceptions of salience sustain each other. Once the agenda has been defined one way rather than another, certain opinions may be less easy to argue for than others.

A more general conclusion from such research is that recognizable social phenomena, such as the survival of coherent minorities and subgroups, can emerge from what happens at an individual level, without any superordinate guiding force. The only organizing principle necessary is that individuals are *non-randomly* influenced by other people, being responsive instead to how strongly others' opinions are held and being most susceptible to influence from those nearer at hand. This non-randomness of connectivity is enough to produce a patterning of output into differentiated social clusters without any need to propose any motivation on the part of the individuals concerned to seek a distinctive social identity. Many groups and subgroups, in other words, may just 'happen' because of chance factors such as proximity of residence. (For a classic study of the emergence of social groups among residents of a new housing estate, see Festinger *et al.*, 1950). This, however, is not to say that groups, once defined, are defended any less loyally on account of their accidental origins. Nor is it to say that *all* group divisions originate accidentally, even though many may do so.

Personal boundaries

If models designed to tell us something about the workings of a single brain (or even much simpler devices) can throw light on collective phenomena, what does this do to our distinction between groups and individuals? One of the unhappier concepts within the earliest writings in social psychology is that of the 'group mind'. According to Gustav Le Bon (1895), once ordinary people become submerged in a larger group or crowd, they regress to a more 'primitive' level and *lose* their capacity for individual, rational thought. This notion was embraced by the political establishment of the time as a justification for the suppression of popular demonstrations. It could not be more different from what is here proposed. Rather than making people less thoughtful as individuals, the processes and phenomena that emerge at a supra-individual or collective level demand analysis in their own right. The ability to describe things at the level of a group or society does not deny differentiation at the level of the person.

Forests consist of trees, but the individual trees in the forest can still be very different from one another. One can look at a forest, and go into it, and find ever more detail the closer one looks. To find such interpolated complexity does not make it any less a forest. (Indeed, the more 'natural' the forest, the more complexity we will find.) The collectivities that emerge naturally from the coordination of their constituent parts do not abolish such complexity or impose mere uniformity – indeed they require the constituents to retain their individual characteristics. Take a leaf on a tree in a forest. In its own right, the leaf is as complex (as a leaf) as the tree is (as a tree) or the forest is (as a forest). Complexity and consistency are not absolute concepts, but depend on the context and level of categorization. Social groups are also naturally occurring things. They are not something *other than* the people within them (any more than forests are something *other than* trees), but neither are they merely haphazard sets of individuals who have nothing to do with one another. 'Groupness' emerges not from the fact that more than one individual is involved, but that they are involved *together*. This 'togetherness' does not require sameness, but it does demand interconnectedness.

But still the question of identity comes back in a less extreme form. Let's draw a 'super-net' to represent, on the one hand, the kinds of connections that account for the interrelationships between different individuals in a group, and, on the other hand, the interrelationships between the different units of the individual schematized 'minds'. Let us even suppose the impossible – that we can include nodes for all the neurons in the brains of all the individual members of the social group, and join up the effective connection paths between them. Granted that we will find connections between as well as within different people, will we be able to say with any confidence where one person 'starts' and another one 'ends'?

In fact, if our 'super-net' is that complete, it should be very easy indeed to make that kind of discrimination. Just think what it would look like if we put a dot for each unit and a line for each effective connection. From close to, obviously it would be an uninterpretable mass of criss-crossing lines, but from further away we would see these lines clustering, so that they were extremely dense in some areas and relatively sparse in others. There would then be no prizes for guessing that the densest clusters corresponded to separate individuals. Having identified separate individuals, we could then infer a good deal about their relationships with each other (along the lines of sociometric or social network analyses in sociology): friends would be more 'inter-connected' with each other than strangers. Yet however well two people communicate with one another, interpersonal connections can never be plausibly supposed to approach intrapersonal connections in either strength or number.

Even so, although defining personal boundaries on the basis of patterns of connectivity may be easier than it sounds, the use of such a criterion implies an important concession. Such personal boundaries are statistical rather than absolute. Although there are immensely more intrapersonal than interpersonal connections, there are still plenty of the latter within any well-formed social group. If we define thought and mental life in terms of the processing and transmission of information, we must allow for some of that information to be transmitted inter-personally and not just intrapersonally. It could sometimes be appealing intuitively to talk of people with very close bonds to each other as being 'almost the same person' or sharing the 'same consciousness'. However, the bonds would have to be exceptionally close, and the context extremely circumscribed, for such figures of speech to be anything but dangerously misleading. If we are not very careful, we may find that we have let Cartesian dualism return through the back door, while ignoring the physical basis of the processes we are describing.

Transmitting thoughts

But why should we bother about the physical basis? Surely what lies behind some of mankind's greatest achievements is the fact that information can be transformed from one physical medium to another, pretty well at will. The codes used – from brush strokes on papyrus to radio signals – need to conform to rules, but these rules can be anything we choose that others will accept. Returning to our 'super-net', we need to accept that interpersonal connections (except in a computer simulation) exploit different physical mechanisms than do intrapersonal connections (for instance, they can depend on sound waves rather than neurochemistry). But so what? There is nothing intrinsically more 'mental' about a potassium ion, say, than about a vibrating air molecule.

It is indisputable that we share information with one another, although what *kinds* of information are most easily shared is another problem. (As I argued in chapter 6, language is better suited to the communication of propositional thoughts or 'knowledge that'.) It is also indisputable that we can *influence* one another's feelings, although whether this means that our feelings are the same is not a question we can answer without first accepting common criteria for making such a comparison. What is more contentious is what such mutual influence and communication does to our concept of identity, of self and of consciousness. Essentially, the problem is this – if mental activity (and hence, presumably, consciousness) is to be defined in terms of information, and if information is freely exchangeable and separable from its physical code, may not consciousness be also something that can be passed from one mind to another, irrespective of the physical systems by which such minds are supported?

Let us consider some examples which might seem at first to point in different directions. First, what is a computer? I might answer: This grey box-thing on the desk in front of me. Well and good, but where does one computer start and another one end? This seems a strange question. What could be more self-contained than a grey box? The answer is: A grey box with no wires coming out of the back. With a few key-strokes, I could transform the function of my computer from a word-processor to a terminal for another (main-frame) machine to which many other people have access for tasks such as statistical analysis. With a few more key-strokes, I can send messages to friends on different continents over the electronic mail network. I can then switch over and inspect the contents of a library catalogue. Not bad for a little grey box! But the point is that many of these achievements are not attributable to the grey box by itself, but to the extent of its linkages with other grey boxes. What is important is the *system*. In other words, a concept of a computer as a self-contained machine does not explain everything I can do through and with my 'box'. However, a concept of a computing *network* takes us at least part of the way.

Could this be a model for the kind of 'super-net' which I was using earlier to describe group structures? Perhaps, but there are some very important differences. We know that ordinary interpersonal communication is a chancy business; the advantages of computer communication are its speed, capacity and reliability. Furthermore, with a computer network, there is no such thing as privileged access to particular kinds of information from particular starting points (still less particular machines) unless constraints are deliberately imposed (e.g. through the use of passwords). So it really makes very little sense to define the 'personal' boundaries of 'my' computer in terms of the grey box that contains its internal circuitry.

Mental action at a distance

But now consider this. I open a book, look at some black ink markings on the page, and make a clumsy attempt to play a passage from a Beethoven sonata. Despite my lack of skill, it is still incontrovertibly the case that Beethoven's mental activity has affected my own, over a great distance of time and space. The arbitrary physical code of the musical score provides a channel through which his thoughts have influenced mine. Yet it would be the vainest of conceits for me to say that I thereby *have* Beethoven's thoughts, or that Beethoven's consciousness somehow 'comes alive again' through my performance. Beethoven is dead and isn't thinking anything, and no performance – not even one a million times more proficient than my own – can make the slightest bit of difference to that. Maybe we want to say that his *music* lives, but then we are using language loosely to mean simply that it can still move us. We do not even have to say that the criterion of a great performance is that it should recreate what Beethoven would have wanted – that would probably be a recipe for stereotypy rather than creativity. Yet even so, even through the missed beats and smudged notes of my own performance, I fancy – although it can be no more than that – that *something* has got through. The output of his consciousness has provided input to my own, and it is a recognizably different kind of input from, say, a piece by Chopin. There is a pattern in my musical memory that I can recognize as what *I* call Beethoven. Even if this not a pattern he himself would own to or recognize, it is still a pattern for which his own compositions are in very large part responsible.

But not wholly responsible. My experience of his music is very patchy and selective. With most of it, I have only a passing acquaintance and am capable myself of playing only a tiny portion. To appreciate the rest, I must listen to recordings on which different performers have put their interpretations. But even more importantly, I cannot possibly experience Beethoven's music now exactly as I would have done if I had been present at its first performance. It is not just its familiarity that makes the difference. I do not just hear it, but hear it in relation to *other* kinds of music I have heard. There is nothing particularly clever about this. It is how we react to *all* kinds of stimuli: we compare them with other things we know. The musical idioms that are familiar to anyone who has ever switched on a car radio are quite different from those available to an audience of some two hundred years ago. We cannot help but make different associations and distinctions, and it is these, and not just the sounds of the instruments themselves, that are likely to colour our experience of any single composition. Against this it may well be argued that truly great music has the power to absorb our attention – to 'transport' us so that listening to it becomes an experience within itself. What is at issue, however, is not the absorbingness of this experience, but its distinctive character. And distinctiveness, with or without any process of conscious comparison, is relative.

It can therefore be simultaneously true that the influence of another mind or consciousness on our own is real and powerful, and that it can be remote and indirect. A consciousness does not need to be shared or reincarnated in order to have an influence on another. It needs only to produce – or leave behind – an expressive or communicative act which others can then interpret in terms of their *own* experience. But for this to happen, this act must take the form of a physical event or leave a physical record that can serve

as an input in its own right. The fact that information is transform-
able and separable from its physical code *does* mean that it can be
communicated from one mind to another, but for this very reason
we cannot presume that anything *other than* information is directly
transmitted.

What are the implications of this for a 'super-net' conception of
social processes? One is that connections can depend on different
forms of activity at different levels. Although all may involve
transmission of information, there will be differences in the kinds
of information transmitted and the means of transmission, depending
on whether we are considering intrapersonal or interpersonal
connections. These differences will matter. But at the same time we
can legitimately consider social phenomena as emergent products
or properties of the collective activity of separate individuals. We
do not need to be mystical about such social phenomena, or try to
redescribe them on the model of a single consciousness. The
members of an orchestra do not have to all 'become' Beethoven in
order to perform a Beethoven symphony. They merely need to
coordinate their individual performances with each other, and the
minimal requirements for this are prosaic enough: they need to
each play their parts according to the score in front of them and
keep time as dictated by the conductor. It also helps if they listen
the sounds made by the other players and regulate their own in-
tonation, rhythm and dynamics accordingly. Yet if such coordination
works, what emerges is a creative product beyond the range of any
single instrument, celebrating rather than suppressing the variations
between them. Unison is not the only harmony, nor conformity the
only social structure.

Patterns of experience

We can therefore treat collective social phenomena as important in
their own right, without embracing the mythology of a 'group mind'
or the passing of subjective experience directly from one mind to
another (or to many others). Although common principles may apply
at different levels, this does not mean that the different levels are
indistinguishable. Our concept of a person must allow for distinctions between people as well as for interactions between them.
These distinctions will be reflected in the ways in which separate
mental events are connected to each other. Within a single person,

they will be extremely interconnected, between people, far less so. Thus the relationship between personal identity and the patterning of experience is a close and dynamic one. The patterning of our previous experience constitutes our present identity and it also shapes our present and future experience. We interpret new events, as far as possible, in terms of pre-existing concepts and knowledge. This knowledge, however, like ourselves and our thoughts, is in constant change. How are we to represent this interaction in terms of what we now can say about the underlying cognitive processes?

From the discussion in chapter 8, defining a person's experience or state of mind at any point in time is to offer a particular kind of phase-space description. The contours of the landscape within this space will define the departures from equiprobability – in other words, the *organization* – which specify the person's dispositions to think or behave in some ways rather than others. Regarding the valleys of this landscape as *attractors* allows us to interpret this organization in dynamic rather than static terms. These attractors are not simply 'habits' in the sense of patterns which are frequently repeated; they are regions of relative stability towards which thoughts and actions are *drawn* from within a range of situations (or input configurations). From chapter 9, we can see that connectionist processes can define and produce organization at a cognitive level in a way that reflects past experience and shapes future thought and behaviour. If we put these two lines of argument together, we arrive at the contoured maps of cognitive space, described in chapter 8 and then revisited in chapter 9 as the outcome of unsupervised learning. Connectionist principles, therefore, offer us a representation of experience which is also a representation of identity.

This approach can also allow identity to be complex and to vary with the situation. As different units acquire more specific connections in specific contexts, attractors will be laid down that depend on detailed pre-conditions and hence have a limited range of influence. Such pre-conditions are assumed in almost every explanatory account of behaviour, but this assumption is all too rarely made explicit. Small differences in initial conditions can lead to the emergence of radically different attractors dominating the dynamic process. We find a similar sensitivity in physical systems and take it as the starting point for the science of chaos. In psychological systems, we have the prospect of a science of choice and individual adaptability. What we may sometimes need is not simply a phase-space map, but a book of maps, each page summarizing what we know of a particular local context. More precisely, our experience within a specific situation will generate a matrix of connection weights specific to that situation. If we shift to another situation, this matrix will change. The matrix, or system of attractors, operative at any one time will depend on our own personal and selective categorization of the situation which confronts us. Yet alternative matrices must be simultaneously available in our memory, superposed on one another.

An attractor can be any relatively stable or recurrent state of the system. It can be an attitude, a way of thinking about yourself, a memory for a telephone number or an itch in your left nostril. The concept is an extremely general one, perhaps so general that it may be difficult to see always what mental phenomena it specifically explains. If this is a difficulty you are experiencing, let me offer this reassurance: it is not intended generally to undermine existing explanations of specific phenomena, but rather to offer a representation of how apparently disparate phenomena can be thought about – indeed explained – in similar terms. The laying down of attractors can be represented spatially in terms of valleys on a contoured map, and the carving of such valleys can be seen as the representation of the strengthening of connections within a neural network. This much, I hope, is easily enough understood from this metaphor. It should also be clear enough by now that variables familiar by other names, such as the stability and resistance to change of a thought or behaviour pattern, or its generalization to different stimulus inputs, could be represented respectively by the depth and breadth of any valley. But still, such maps contain two major ambiguities: what are the coordinates of the surface; and secondly what does the point (or ball-bearing) stand for?

Which dimensions?

These questions are less daunting than they might appear, once it is realized that there can never be just one right answer to either of them. As for the coordinates, let us remember that we are not dealing with a plane, or with a geographic surface varying in altitude, but with a *hyper-plane*, that is to say, with a multidimensional space with many more 'hidden' dimensions than those we can represent diagrammatically on our map. In fact such spaces are quite familiar in many areas of psychological measurement, for instance personality research, where factor analysis is used to identify numerous supposedly stable and distinct dimensions of individual differences. There is nothing mysterious about an object being multidimensional. Once your personal details such as age, gender, income, educational level, parental occupation, marital status and home address are entered into some data file, *you* are a multidimensional object from the point of view of the information that has been recorded. What is difficult is *picturing* such multidimensionality in spatial terms. Reliance on a visual metaphor thus has its limitations as well as its advantages, and I would have no quarrel with anyone who found it easier to think of attractors and phase space, say, more algebraically.

Even so, in practice one may be able to represent important distinctions within a small number of dimensions. For much of the time, Thurstone managed quite well with just one and Osgood very well with just three. My difference from them is not so much in pressing for a huge number of extra dimensions to be considered, but rather in arguing that those dimensions which *are* used should be relevant and sensitive to the specific context or frame of reference. There simply is no need – conceptually or empirically – to demand that the important dimensions of similarity and differences between people, or between objects of thought, should be universal. The more general we make the task of judgement, the more general will be the dimensions in terms of which these judgements will be distinguished. However, the more specific the judgements, the more specific will be the dimensions which carry the main weight of discrimination.

We therefore *cannot* say, in general, what characteristics or attributes will correspond to the coordinates of any specific cognitive map. On the one hand, there is no absolute reason for choosing one set of coordinates rather than any other. On the other hand, it is an empirical question which dimension will be most salient or discriminatory within a given context. This is where the broader literature on attitudes is especially instructive since, more than in any other area of psychology, we can see how the salience of dimensions varies both with the person and with the topic or context. Within more familiar research paradigms, we can consider salience in relation to self-ratings of commitment to particular attitude positions, judgements of the relevance of particular aspects of an issue, and preferences for different kinds of value-laden language.

But can we look at a cognitive map drawn in terms of a specific set of dimensions and decide whether these dimensions are the 'right' ones for the mapping we have attempted? Can we be sure that these dimensions are the salient ones? If we take this to mean 'Can we be sure that we couldn't draw an even *better* map?' then the answer is No – though for reasons that have nothing especially to do with this problem. This merely reflects the fact that the set of possible solutions (maps) is unrestricted, and we can never prove a negative statement of the form 'No better solution exists'. But, leaving such absolutism to one side, can we look at two maps and say which of them is better in *relative* terms? The answer is definitely Yes, for reasons which are quite simple if we remember what it is we expect such maps to do. We need them to summarize the organization of the system, that is to say, to identify the presence of relatively powerful attractors which account for deviations from equiprobability in the system's dynamics. A *useful* map – one that enables us to predict the dynamics of the system – will be one that displays such attractors, in other words, one that is more sharply contoured. On a flat plane, all points are equiprobable, which is to say that no useful predictions can be made. We can therefore say that a more contoured map will be one that displays the more salient dimensions of discrimination for the individual's point of view. And we can say even more than this. Since the contours are laid down through personal experience, a more contoured map will not only afford better predictions for the future but contain a fuller record of the individual's learning history. The carving of the landscape is also the construction of personal salience. Viewed either way, the process reflects familiarity and the strength of previous associations.

Points on the map

So then, we have our map and we mark it with a point (like putting a ball-bearing on a contoured surface). What does this point mean? The general answer is that it summarizes the state of the system at a given time, by specifying where the system is in terms of the dimensions or coordinates used to define the phase space. So, to return to the example of a file of survey data, if the dimensions are defined in terms of age, gender, income, etc., then *you* could be a single point in this multidimensional space. Although you are 'reduced' to just a point, this point still conveys all the information that has been recorded about you and which is borne by the multidimensionality of the space. This is the shift in perspective that allows theoretical physicists to talk about the entire state of the universe as a single point in phase space. To add complexity to our comprehension of the universe, we add complexity to the dimensionality of the phase space; but since this anyway has infinite dimensionality, adding a few more million dimensions makes no real difference to the picture. At this level of high abstraction, one point could represent every thought of every person in the world (just as a start!).

But would a map that represented the entire state of the universe as a single point be any *use* to anyone? The answer is Yes, *if* what you are interested *is* change in the entire state of the universe over time – for instance, if you are asking how the universe started and if it will continue to expand. But if our interests are more mundane, the kinds of maps we will find more useful are those that highlight changes and differences along those dimensions relevant to our local and personal interests. We need to zoom in on the tiny corner of our own concerns. Now suppose that our concern right now is a survey of residents of your home town. We could still represent the 'entire state' of your town as a single point in a multidimensional phase space. Another thing we could do, however, would be to represent every separate individual by a separate point. This would yield a much more familiar picture – a multidimensional scatterplot. We could the use this picture to discern such information as the similarity of two individuals to each other, the presence of separate clusters, or subcategories, of people within the larger group, and such like.

Now, in a sense, nothing has been strictly gained by any of this. No more information has been provided by the scatter of points than the single one. All we have done is taken one dimension ('individuals') out of the space and exploded the point with it. Another way of putting it is that we have subdivided the phase space into as many separate spaces as we have individuals, and then projected these spaces onto each other to produce the scatterplot. The same data file accounts equally for both presentations. Even so, there could be arguments for reducing the dimensionality of the space to the level that the points, though there would be more of them, refer to things that are more easy to comprehend. As with the issue of choice of dimensions, however, there is no absolute answer to the level we should choose. It is a matter of practical utility in relation to the specific questions that interest us.

Remembering this, let us consider just the state of mind of one individual at one time. From all that I have said so far, the preferred mode of representation should surely be that of a single point on a contoured map – a single ball-bearing resting at the bottom of a well or rolling towards it. But is this necessarily so? Suppose that we wanted to say, not just that the person's state of mind had many dimensions, but that it had multiple *content*. Again, these statements could be regarded as equivalent mathematically, but they might none the less commend different kinds of representations. Suppose your state of mind involves you thinking of more than one thing at the same time – the words on this page *and* the itch in your left nostril *and* your telephone number *and* your attitude towards the outcome of the last election. Impossible? Well try the opposite – try thinking about anything you want *except* the itch in your left nostril. If my guess is right, the itch you never knew you had may by now be almost impossible to ignore! The point of this exercise is to show that our states of mind are never strictly singular, but have multiple objects which can each command varying levels of our attention. Again, there is no firm answer to how many points we should include, but *if* we want to represent the multiplicity of the objects of which we are aware, we may sometimes do better with a multiplicity of points – with a bagful of ball-bearings scattered over different attractors or activated units.

Synchrony

But what would be the consequences of picturing a person's state of mind in terms of a scatter of ball-bearings finding their ways towards separate attractors? To use Hume's words again, there would be 'properly no simplicity in it at one time, nor identity in different, whatever natural propension we may have to imagine that simplicity and identity'. But worse, if there was only a random scatter, there would be nothing our 'natural propension' could work on to produce a sense of pattern and unity. Hume was at pains to show that such simplicity and identity is *constructed* subjectively rather than objectively given. However, for us the more important issue is *how* identity is constructed. Hume's own principles of association take us a remarkably long way, but they cannot take us anywhere at all if both the initial input and the feedback we receive is completely random. Objective patterning is vital because it allows subjective associations to be formed.

The question is therefore not whether it is 'better' to display a

person's state of mind as a single point in a multidimensional phase
space or as multiple points in a phase space of slightly reduced
dimensionality. What matters is the kind of multiplicity any single
point subsumes. Does it break down into a chaotic agglomeration
of haphazard and unconnected mental events? Or can we find new
patterns and covariation among and within these mental events?
The designation of the mind as a fractal object points us in the
latter direction, but where does this lead us? To ask whether the
patterning of mental events makes a difference is very close to
asking: When do mental events constitute a mind?

What would we want to say about a state of mind constituted
entirely of *uncoordinated* mental events? At a logical level, it would
be unclear what would be gained by regarding these events as
constituting a 'mind' at all. Nothing we could say about one event
would have any implications for anything we could say about any
other event. The events would, by definition, be independent of
each other and so no sensible statement could be made about them
as a collectivity. In the terminology of connectionism, all we would
have would be a list of units and their activations (e.g. $unit_1$ is on,
$unit_2$ is on, $unit_3$ is off, etc.), but we would have no connections
between the units and hence no network. This would also mean
that we could not use connectionist principles to account for the
laying down of attractors in the first place.

But even without these fatal difficulties, what would an uncoordinated mental event *feel* like? What we need to do is to force
ourselves to break down an experience into its smallest imaginable
parts. Let's borrow Berkeley's example once more:

> I see this *cherry*, I feel it, I taste it: and I am sure *nothing* cannot be
> seen, or felt, or tasted: it is therefore *real*. Take away the sensations
> of softness, moisture, redness, tartness, and you take away the *cherry*.

But how do we know that the sensations of softness, etc., belong to
a cherry? If we conceive of sensations that are not *about* anything,
we lose any sense of a reality beyond ourselves. But let's ask an
even more basic question. How do we know that the softness,
moistness, etc. actually belong *together*? Why don't we experience
an isolated sensation of softness, another sensation of moistness,
etc.?

This question relates closely to contemporary research on the
neurophysiology of perception, where it is referred to as the 'binding

problem'. A great deal is already known about the sensitivity of different centres in the brain to different kinds of perceptual input. For instance, some cells may respond differentially to lights of different colours, others to particular angles and edges, others to directional movement. But how does the sensory information received by these separate cells 'bind' together to form a *single* percept of, say, a red square moving from left to right? Some striking recent evidence (e.g. Gray *et al.*, 1989) gives a clue. Assemblies of neurons specializing in the reception of different kinds of sensory input, will come to *oscillate in synchrony* if activated simultaneously by the same visual object. Covariation of stimulus information thus produces a remarkably fine-tuned covariation of neural activity.

The coordination of awareness

What extrapolations is it reasonable to draw from such findings? Clearly they point to the importance of the interconnectedness of the brain. (Actually, the evidence so far is from cats' reactions to visual stimuli, but the generalization to human brain function is a relatively easy one to make in this context.) Whatever the conceivable involvement of quantum mechanical processes in achieving such synchrony, observable neuroanatomical structures are vital to these effects. The synchrony of oscillation is destroyed by surgical section of the corpus callosum (Engel *et al.*, 1991). We therefore can plausibly argue that brains have evolved with particular neuroanatomical structures suitable to the detection and use of patterned stimulus information.

How important might synchrony be for allowing a brain to behave in a way that we would recognize to be a 'mind'? This is one of those questions that invites a host of 'It depends what you mean by . . .' responses. One criterion for being a 'mind' might be to have the capacity for responding 'thoughtfully' rather than 'automatically' to stimulus inputs. Although this distinction can be ambiguous in its turn, one view might be that 'thoughtful' information-processing involves a more coordinated focusing of attention. According to Koch and Crick (1991, p. 684), synchronous neural activity may help explain, not just binding, but coordinated or 'focal' attention generally:

One needs to distinguish at least three types of binding:

1 A simple cell in visual cortex has its preferred orientation always perpendicular to its preferred direction of motion. Thus, orientation and motion are combined. Neurons throughout cortexseem to compound a number of variables in this manner.

2 A second type of binding is probably acquired by overlearning. Thus, ecologically important and frequently viewed stimuli, such as grandmothers or letters or words, may be represented by the firing of small groups of neurons.

3 Because the capacity of both types of binding is limited, however, we need to postulate a third, very rapid and transient type of binding mechanism with essentially infinite capacity. It is likely that focal attention instantiates this type of binding mechanism.

> Specifically . . . we suggest that this binding is achieved by all neurons that are associated with the perceived object firing in synchrony. Thus, phase-locked oscillations *are* the cellular expression of attention . . . Furthermore, such a theory would also explain why certain processes can be carried out in parallel, without requiring awareness. We simply assume that repeated synchronous activation of groups of neurons responding to a particular stimulus (e.g. a letter or face) cause individual neurons or small groups of neurons to become directly activated in response to this stimulus, on the basis of some Hebbian rule. Such a learning mechanism would eventually bypass the need for a focal attentive mechanism for the perception of such frequently viewed stimuli (i.e. transforming a type 3 binding problem into a type 2).

The reference to a 'Hebbian rule' underlines the link with connectionist principles and their capacity to explain how we may come to give special treatment to important and/or familiar patterns. Special treatment, however, is not necessarily the same as special attention. Indeed, what Koch and Crick are suggesting is that achievement of 'type 2' binding allows the person (or system) to respond *without* awareness, or at least, without a deliberate focusing of attention. Their remarks, in fact, are part of a commentary on a longer paper by Velmans (1991), who reviews evidence that much stimulus information (particularly if it is simple and familiar) is processed at a 'preconscious' or 'pre-attentive' level – that is to say, 'automatically'. To say that processing of simple, familiar stimuli can be accomplished automatically, is to say that it could be accomplished by an automaton – that is, by a computer. Connectionism explains how such automaticity can be achieved, certainly in a computer and possibly in the human brain. But can we use this approach to explain consciousness? Should we even try?

This is a difficult question, particularly because it leaves unresolved the question of whether 'consciousness' refers to some kind of process, or to the *contents* of thought and experience. I shall shortly argue that it must be partly both, but for the moment let's start by considering what this might mean for 'conscious processing'. If Koch and Crick are right in their speculation, the synchronous oscillation of large numbers of neurons associated with a single perceived object is something that *precedes* the 'automatic' recognition of a familiar pattern. In other words, the pattern is still being learned and no stable output has yet been achieved. Speculatively, we may be observing the auto-association of input units without a stable representation of the pattern in terms of a hidden or 'pattern' unit at the next layer (what Koch and Crick describe as type 2 binding). In terms of Hopfield nets, the system would not yet have achieved maximum entropy. It would still be in a state of dynamic change.

This is obviously only a very minimal criterion for saying that a system was 'thinking', but it's a start. We would need much more to say that a system was thinking *consciously*, but again, synchrony may be especially important in that the binding problem it illuminates is intuitively very much a problem of *conscious* experience. If we can identify what we are looking at as a particular kind of object, we have already achieved a representation of its global properties. That is to say, we have achieved (at least type 3) binding of its separate attributes. The point is that, if we didn't have to be *aware* that the separate attributes belonged together, we wouldn't have a binding problem to 'solve'. There are still major difficulties here concerning both the upper limits of machine 'intelligence' and the lower limits of human 'consciousness'.

In keeping with this, it can be shown that, with people who have suffered certain kinds of brain damage, so that their brains no longer can entirely function as a single whole, some very strange things can happen to their consciousness and awareness. For instance, in so-called 'split-brain' patients with lesions of the corpus callosum, information of which one cerebral hemisphere is aware is not directly accessible to the other hemisphere. This must surely be related to synchrony. Logically, if two neurons are synchronized, the information carried by one is necessarily available to the other. Moreover, as indicated by the Engel *et al.* findings, synchrony between the firings of neurons in different hemispheres is absent when the pathways connecting them are severed. The 'divided consciousness' of split-brain patients would be reflected in a divided pattern of interconnectedness, with most interconnections (and, one would surmise, synchrony) being evident within rather than across hemispheres. Mapping such a divided consciousness would require a division of the phase space. In extreme cases, a separate 'map' would be needed for each hemisphere; alternatively, if one map was used, there would need to be two 'ball-bearings' (or clusters of ball-bearings) to represent the separate activation patterns of the two hemispheres. Similarly divided representations could be used for other forms of disassociated functioning, possibly including personality disorders of the kind described by Osgood and Luria (1954; see chapter 1).

I can see no objection in principle to synchrony being effectively simulated within a neural network – indeed, something very near to this can already be done by 'clamping' units together with strong connection weights. Whether it can be done on the same scale and with the flexibility observed within the cortex of a living brain, on the other hand, is quite another matter. It is quite reasonable to maintain, on the one hand, that we are observing, in human and animal consciousness, an emergent property of coordinated activations of separate neurons; and, on the other hand, that the scale and complexity of such coordination is so vast that we cannot adequately simulate it within any artificial system we can yet imagine. This comes down to saying that, although we can simulate aspects of neural activity, we are still a long way from simulating the brain as a whole, and hence the properties that apply to it *as* a whole. Even so, one implication of this approach is clear: if a cognitive system achieves consciousness it is by virtue of the coordinated activity of its constituent parts. There is nothing extra that sits on top of this activity but is separate from it. If we search for something extra *inside* the system, we will never find it.

Fictitious identity

But is this the whole story? To be a person, to have a sense of self, still seems something special. Cats may have some fuzzy concept of self. Computers surely have no such idea. We, however, are supe-rior beings, and we have no doubt at all who we are. We therefore cer-tainly are conscious in a way no computer and most probably not even the cleverest cat can be. At least, that is an intuition to which many people lay claim. But is this intuition justified? Let us revisit once again Hume's disturbing insight:

> The identity, which we ascribe to the mind of man, is only a fictitious one, and of a like kind with that which we ascribe to vegetable and animal bodies. It cannot, therefore, have a different origin, but must proceed from a like operation of the imagination upon like objects.

Our concepts of self, of mind and of identity are not 'given' to us before experience, but proceed or emerge *from our experience* of *objects*, that is, of physical things and events. Hume's thesis was in the first place a negative one: such concepts *cannot* be had except through experience. However, it contained also a more positive element: the 'operation of the imagination' can be defined in terms of specific principles, namely, his 'principles of association'. Al-though he defines these principles at a very general level, they are easily related to those of modern cognitive psychology, in particular those hypothesized by connectionism. For 'operation of the im-agination' read 'cognitive process' and for 'association' read 'con-nection' and neither party need feel embarrassed by the liaison.

But if our 'imagination' operates along the lines of a neural net-work, what kind of identity could it allow us to ascribe, either to other people or ourselves? Hume already gives us part of the answer: it will be like the identity we ascribe to 'vegetable and animal bodies', which share with people the interesting property that they can change qualitatively while remaining numerically the 'same'. Another way of putting this is that we recognize a pattern or continuity over time, and this is extremely important, since pattern recognition is one of the things neural networks do very well indeed.

Hume does not seem to be insisting here on any special distinction between the identity we ascribe to ourselves and that which we ascribe to other people. The latter, up to a point, presents no spe-cial difficulties, in that other people are observable physical bodies and their actions are observable physical events. A concept of identity could therefore be built up through recognition of patterning and continuity in such events and 'like objects'. Recognizing other people is something a net could definitely learn to do. When it comes to identifying ourselves, however, it is less clear exactly what kind of pattern it is that we need to recognize. Personal memories must play some part in this, but how?

When trying to deal with the difficulty that we may not always recall our past actions and feelings, Hume says that 'memory does not so much *produce* as *discover* personal identity'. This helps us in thinking about remembering as a process of reconstruction. However, it leaves out how we might have come to have a (discoverable) identity in the first place. I am suggesting, quite simply, that the having of a discoverable identity depends on a recognizable patterning in one's experience over time and context. A *discovered* identity is what constitutes a sense of self. This is compatible with Hume's stipulation that the self is not something we can 'catch' independently of our other thoughts and feelings. However, a sense of self can be acquired or constructed through principles of association *provided there are associations there to be found*. Another way of putting this is that, if our experience lacked patterning, continuity or covariation, we could have no sense of self. By the same token, if for any reason (brain damage, loss of memory, personality disorder) our capacity for recognizing patterns across time and context was compromised, so too would be the coherence of our self-concept. Our sense of self depends *both* on our capacity to form associations *and* on the actual associations themselves.

Self-reflection

Of our capacity to form associations, I have said a great deal. But what of the experience from which such associations are drawn? It is here, I suggest, in the *content* of experience rather than in an exclusive analysis of process, that an understanding of human consciousness is to be found. Let us apply this to the question of machine intelligence. Penrose (1989) insists that a computer could not, in principle, have the kind of consciousness that involved a sense of self. Much of his argument depends on the kinds of operations of which computers are capable, particularly those that process information serially rather than in parallel. It is less clear to me whether he would object so strongly to a parallel distributive processing (PDP) system. On the one hand, *any* system that evolves through the application of an algorithmic rule would seem at first sight to incorporate a determinism quite different from the 'quantum-like' indeterminacy which Penrose sees as intrinsic to mental life (though even algorithms can lead us into chaos). On the other hand, a possible advantage of thinking of the brain in quantum terms is that it allows for parallelism on a massive scale. If parallelism holds the key to consciousness, though, can this not be simulated on computers? And if it can, then where is the objection, in principle, to computers being capable of self-reflection?

The error lies in trying to settle the matter by identifying the classes of information-processing operations of which human beings and computers are each capable, whilst ignoring the classes of information with which human and artificial systems actually have to deal. If we say there is something special about how we process information, we may well be right, for now. But as soon as we reach the point of being able to define the ways in which our cognitive processes are special, we are committed to saying how, in the abstract, they might be simulated. Otherwise we are left insisting that the distinctive attributes of human thought processes must *in principle* remain undefinable and hence undiscoverable. Such a dogma is not only indefensible but unfalsifiable. If we cannot find distinctive attributes, a simpler reason is that perhaps there are none – not, that is, at the level of information-processing operations.

If there *is* something distinctive about human consciousness, where should we look for it? The old talk about 'hardware' and 'software' is no longer helpful. The difference in hardware between a brain and a computer is undeniable but possibly inconsequential. The software, i.e. the processing system, exploited by the brain may be no different in principle from any which could be simulated on a computer. But this does not mean that the software is applied to the same input or *data* in the different cases. I have been happy enough to claim that the states of mind of different individuals can be represented in terms of different phase-space maps, with attractors laid down by past experience. Such differences can be represented even though it is assumed that the *processes* employed by the different people are the same. What differs is the *content* of their state of mind, the particular attractors which dominate it, the contours reflecting different patterns of association, and such like. These attractors and contours, according to the principles I have outlined, are the record of each individual's *experience* and learning history. Why should the same not apply to differences between species, or between animate and artificial minds? Most obviously, but most importantly, the sensory input we experience will be very different from that experienced even by a cat and certainly by a computer.

Thus we can try and specify the pre-conditions of consciousness, in terms of massive parallelism, complexity and coordination at the level of process. We can suppose that such coordination serves a vital function in enabling organisms to interpret novel stimuli and plan adaptive behaviours. We can further suppose that organisms that show greater flexibility and capacity to learn are more likely to have *some* kind of consciousness. We could not have the thoughts we have without the capacity to form associations, to relate new experience to old, to categorize and to differentiatiate at many different levels of detail. The human brain possesses this capacity in inconceivable abundance, yet even so, human consciousness is not an all-or-nothing affair. We react to many stimuli of which we are barely aware, if at all. Many bodily processes are regulated by our brains without the need for conscious control. There is no longer support for the old notion of an 'absolute threshold' in perceptual research: the boundary between stimuli that are strong enough or too weak to detect is variable and uncertain. Similarly, when considering the capacities for consciousness of other species, we are on shifting sand if we try to draw a hard-and-fast line. The dangers of 'anthropomorphic' sentimentality – of pretending that animals have just the same feelings as we do – are balanced by the dangers of denying that they have any mental life at all. The processing capacity of the human brain is vastly more powerful than that of a cat, and cats are pretty clever creatures compared with most other species. If we are concerned with what can emerge from the interactions of simple units, processing capacity *matters*, since this is what sets the upper limit to the complexity of such interactions. Questions about the possibility of machine consciousness are more troublesome, because the limitations on the processing capacities of computers are rapidly upwardly mobile (in a way that the capacities of cat brains are not).

But none of this, neither the ability to plan, nor even the immensely interactive parallelism, *constitutes* consciousness in its full sense. Consciousness, as a state of mind, is not just a capacity but the exercise of such capacity. Consciousness is indescribable other than in terms of its contents, that is, the contents of our thoughts. Even if we could build a machine with this full capacity of a human brain we would still be reluctant to attribute to it the *kind* of consciousness, the sense of self, to which we ourselves lay claim. But is this reluctance justified? A quick reading of Hume might suggest that our own sense of self is an illusion, so that there is nothing real to which we can lay claim which computers could not also have. But Hume is not just saying that the sense of self is an illusion. He is saying that, like other concepts of identity, it emerges from the association of ideas, that is, from connections between the objects of our experience, particularly connections over time.

To ask what is special about human consciousness, therefore, is not just a question about process. It is to ask what is special about our experience of the world, the experience we have by virtue of physical presence *in* the world. This relates to other issues discussed in earlier chapters of this book. Mind–body dualism – the idea of a mind that, in Descartes's words, 'has need of no place' – is objectionable precisely because it severs mental from physical experience. The most continuous feature of our experience is our own body. Not only when thinking about other people, but also when thinking about ourselves, personal identity depends on physical identity. We feel our body and we feel the world *through* it. It provides the anchor and viewpoint from which we experience other things. It provides a continuous patterned stream of input in itself, and (simply from the fact that we cannot be in two places at once) imposes constraints on the information received by the brain from the world outside. Closely related to this is the issue of 'aboutness'. Our thoughts and experiences are *about* things in the world, and there *is* an objective, physical world for our thoughts to be about. This physical world is itself patterned and continuous, rather than random and interrupted. Our experience is patterned because we experience patterned things. These patterned things, moreover, can be part of *other* people's experiences too, so that we can come to talk about them together.

We acquire a sense of self, and the capacity for self-reflection, not just through the power of parallel processing, but from the patterning of the information which we process. This information changes dynamically over time and place, but such change is patterned and constrained by our own physical instantiation in time and place. We are physical things, in a world of other physical things. Our physical existence structures both our own behaviour and that of other people towards us. Others' behaviour carries information about the ways in which we are distinctive and thus can influence the salient dimensions of our self-concept. Every second of our waking life we are bombarded with a mass of complex input. If this input was random, we would have no sense of self or consciousness, but it is not. There is redundancy, covariation and recurrence, and these provide the basis for the differentiated strengthening of connections. Such connections lay down a pattern of attractors which we experience as habits and memories. This pattern will be highly complex, but the principles which generate it are, for the most part, surprisingly simple.

These principles can be simulated on computers. At the present state of the art, this is somewhere between a demonstrated fact and a prediction, but this seems clearly to be the direction in which current research is leading us. But is it leading towards machines that will think like we do, and will have propensities for feelings and self-reflection? Like Penrose, I doubt it, but on different and possibly weaker grounds. What would it take for a computer to have a human, or humanoid, mind? A vastly interactive parallel processing system, perhaps even using quantum mechanical technology? Well, maybe at great expense that could be arranged. But even then, what would we have? A machine which could handle *any* kind of input that was thrown at it, from *any* set of data to which it was given access. It would be a machine without prejudice, without preferences, without personal boundaries. It would have memories – no doubt vastly more extensive and reliable than our own – but these could be deleted, installed, or modified by a few key-strokes. On a small scale, we have these machines already. What extra would be needed for a fully-fledged robot, a computer with a mind like ours?

Invent a machine that acquired the same experience as a human being, through birth and childhood, that received not just the same visual and auditory information, but also the same experiences of its own body, of movement, of physical growth and pain and tiredness, of hormonal fluctuations, of hunger and sexual desire. Ensure that it was treated by (other) people as though it were alive, and was conscious of *us* as conscious and bodily beings. If *all* of that could be simulated in such a way as to recreate the quality of human *experience*, then I would have no objection to calling the *consciousness* that comprised it a recreation of a human consciousness. But then we would have a robot which, by definition, thought, lived, loved, was born and grew and died like a human, and passed *and was accepted* as a human throughout its life. Under such impossible circumstances, the term 'robot' would cease to have any applicability, beyond the level of some irrelevant label of ancestry.

If both the machine's processing operations *and* the information it processed were indistinguishable from those of a human being, so also would be its mind and consciousness. It is the second of these two conditions, rather than the first, which strikes me as the major stumbling block. This may seem strange, in that putting information into a computer is generally an easy thing to do. But we are not dealing with just a few data files to be read in and stored. We are dealing with information in a constant process of flux and change. And quite apart from all of this, why would we want to invent such a machine in the first place? To impose a human consciousness on it would be to impose the very kinds of physical vulnerability and cognitive fallibility from whose consequences we were trying to free ourselves.

Could computers none the less be conscious, but in a different way from us? The issue is not whether computers can react to stimuli (they can, but so can we, and without awareness). Nor is it whether computers can form associations between stimuli (again, they can, but so can we, and without awareness). Consciousness is an emergent property of immensely interactive information-processing operations, but it is not these operations *per se*. Consciousness also reflects the content of our thoughts, and particularly *habits* of thought, many of which will be self-referring. These self-referring habits of thoughts, memories, attractors – call them what you will – depend on constraints and continuities within our experience, in the information with which we have to deal. Furthermore, it is not just our *own* experience we need to consider. We learn that there are other minds, that we can influence what other people think and feel. Without this awareness of others as *thinking* beings, we would not merely have no *need* for a distinct concept of ourselves, we would simply have no basis for one.

The whole point of a computer is that there *are* no necessary constraints or continuities in the information with which it is presented. Any constraints are arbitrary, externally imposed, and modifiable at the user's whim. The patterning of input, let alone social experience, necessary for the acquisition of a sense of self simply is not there. No personal boundaries could be distinguished and no continuity of temporal and spatial perspective could be recognized. The identity of a human mind may be 'fictitious', but it is discoverable through the associations we can form within the real patterns of our experience. Computer consciousness – in the sense of self-awareness – is merely science fiction.

Attitudes: a final word

And what of attitudes in all of this? I started this book with a review of how attitudes have been studied by social psychologists.

This was an arbitrary starting point, perhaps, reflecting my own special interests. Yet it remains a useful one for many of the broader issues I have since discussed. One does not have to delve very deeply into attitude theory and research to discover a number of general and fundamental questions – of the relationship of experience to reality, of the communicability of such experience, of its acquisition and its evolution over time. Addressing these questions takes one beyond the conventional borders of the discipline of social psychology, towards philosophy, cognitive science, and the study of dynamical systems. Too often social psychologists have stayed within their own borders speaking a language which, like that of many other specialisms, shows an increasing divergence from that used in the world outside.

It does not need to be this way. The search for universal – or at least unifying – principles is still one that can be undertaken with good hope. Unifying principles do not mean uniform products. Attitudes vary – that is one of their most important features. We can just describe such variation as we find it, or we can try and account for it in terms of general principles. Above a specific level of detail, there is no need to posit one set of cognitive processes to account for how we recognize our friends, another for how we play chess, and another for how we form attitudes. Obviously there are important differences between the demands of these different cognitive tasks, but it is the differences in demands which are important, not the differences in process.

None the less, the intellectual traffic does not have to all be one-way. We can learn a great deal about processes by looking at the tasks and problems to which they can be applied. Attitudes are a particular kind of habit of thought or memory. To claim, as I have done, that they can be seen as attractors within the phase space of a neural network *is* to treat them like other memories or habits of thought. But an attitude is not 'just another' thought or memory. It is a kind of thought which is distinctively human and distinctively social.

These are not empty epithets, although they can all too easily be used that way. Attitudes are human in that they reflect the distinctive attributes of human consciousness – an awareness of the self as well as of objects beyond the self. They are social in that they reflect an awareness of other minds, whose thoughts can both influence and be influenced by one's own. They have a further property quite missing from any artificial intelligence – they are evaluative. They involve, not just comparisons, but preferences; not just calculations, but feelings and emotions. If, as I believe, such sophisticated states of mind can eventually be shown to be emergent properties of the interactive parallelism of the human brain, then connectionism will have satisfied a stringent test of its generality. It is a test that cognitive science, no less than social psychology, needs to face.

If this enterprise is successful, what might social psychology gain in return? For most of this century, the primary concerns of attitude theory have been simplicity, stability and consistency. Attitudes *can* be simple, stable and consistent, but they are not necessarily or easily so. Attitudes are not absolutes. They are relative to the situation, to the selective perspective of the individual and to the communicative context in which they are expressed. They allow for broad generalizations on the one hand and infinitely complex differentiations on the other. We have been concerned too much with steady states, too little with dynamics, too much with the resting places of the human mind, too little with its rhythms.

Along with this, we can hope for an end to the isolation of what *is* an important and useful discipline from the mainstream of scientific thought, from what was once called, and could again be, 'natural philosophy'. Let us ask again without fear such naive and fundamental questions as what it is to think, to know ourselves and to understand what others say; why we like some things and dislike other things and why not everyone shares our point of view. In short, let us ask why things are as they are and what they might become, and we will we find ourselves on the same journey as those from many separate intellectual starting-points. We are not just spectators, but active participants in the natural world, and our attitudes arise from that participation. Our attitudes have the patterned complexity of all natural things, yet the principles which generate their patterns are comparatively simple and familiar. This is not a reductionist philosophy, but one in which human individuality and identity emerge from interaction with the physical environment. In the complexity of attitudes lies our freedom; in their patterning, our dignity.

References

Ajzen, I. (1991). The theory of planned behavior. *Organizational Behavior and Decision Processes, 50,* 1–33.

Ajzen, I. and Fishbein, M. (1977). Attitude-behavior relations: A theoretical analysis and a review of empirical research. *Psychological Bulletin, 84,* 888–918.

Ajzen, I. and Fishbein, M. (1980). *Understanding attitudes and predicting social behavior.* Englewood Cliffs, N.J: Prentice-Hall.

Allport, G. W. (1935). Attitudes. In C. Murchison (ed.) *Handbook of social psychology,* vol. 2. Worcester, MA: Clark University Press.

Aristotle (translated by J. A. K. Thomson, 1955). *The Ethics of Aristotle.* Harmondsworth: Penguin.

Aronson, E. (1972). *The social animal.* San Francisco, CA: Freeman.

Bem, D. J. (1967). Self-perception: An alternative interpretation of cognitive dissonance phenomena. *Psychological Review, 74,* 183–200.

Bem, D. J. and Allen, A. (1974). On predicting some of the people some of the time: The search for cross-situational consistencies in behavior. *Psychological Review, 81,* 506–520.

Bentler, P. M. and Speckart, G. (1979). Models of attitude-behavior relations. *Psychological Review, 86,* 452–464.

Berkeley, G. (1709/1910). *An Essay towards a New Theory of Vision.* London: Dent.

Berkeley, G. (1713/1910). *Three Dialogues between Hylas and Philonous in opposition to sceptics and atheists.* London: Dent.

Billig, M. (1987). *Arguing and thinking: A rhetorical approach to social psychology.* Cambridge: Cambridge University Press.

Bower, G. H. (1981). Mood and memory. *American Psychologist, 36,* 129–148.

Brentano, F. (1874) (translated by A. C. Pancurello *et al.* 1973). *Psychology from an empirical standpoint.* New York: Humanities Press.

Cialdini, R. B., Petty, R. E. and Cacioppo, J. T. (1981). Attitude and attitude change. *Annual Review of Psychology, 32,* 357–404.

Cooper, J., Zanna, M. P. and Taves, P. A. (1978). Arousal as a necessary condition for attitude change following compliance. *Journal of Personality and Social Psychology, 36,* 1101–1106.

Cooper, J. and Fazio, R. H. (1984). A new look at dissonance theory. In L. Berkowitz (ed.) *Advances in Experimental Social Psychology, 17,* 229–266. New York: Academic Press.

Dennett, D. C. (1986). *Brainstorms: Philosophical essays on mind and psychology.* Brighton: Harvester.

Descartes, R. (1637) (translated by J. Veitch, 1912). *A discourse on method.* London: Dent.

Eagly, A. H. and Chaiken, S. (1993). *The psychology of attitudes.* Orlando: Harcourt Brace Jovanovich.

Eiser, J. R. (1990). *Social judgment.* Buckingham: Open University Press. U.S. edition (1991), Pacific Grove, CA: Brooks/Cole.

Eiser, J. R., van der Pligt, J., Raw, M. and Sutton, S. R. (1985). Trying to stop smoking: Effects of perceived addiction, attributions for failure and expectancy of success. *Journal of Behavioral Medicine, 8,* 321–341.

Eiser, J. R. and Mower White, C. J. (1974). Evaluative consistency and social judgment. *Journal of Personality and Social Psychology, 30,* 349–359.

Eiser, J. R. and Mower White, C. J. (1975). Categorization and congruity in attitudinal judgment. *Journal of Personality and Social Psychology, 31,* 769–775.

Eiser, J. R. and Ross, M. (1977). Partisan language, immediacy, and attitude change. *European Journal of Social Psychology, 7,* 477–489.

Eiser, J. R., Spears, R. and Webley, P. (1989). Nuclear attitudes before and after Chernobyl. *Journal of Applied Social Psychology, 19,* 689–700.

Eiser, J. R. and Sutton, S. R. (1977). Smoking as a subjectively rational choice. *Addictive Behaviors, 2,* 129–134.

Eiser, J. R. and van der Pligt, J. (1979). Beliefs and values in the nuclear debate. *Journal of Applied Social Psychology, 9,* 524–536.

Engel, A. K., König, P., Kreiter, A. K. and Singer, W. (1991). Interhemispheric synchronization of oscillatory neuronal responses in cat visual cortex. *Science, 252,* 1177–1179.

Fazio, R. H. (1986). How do attitudes guide behavior? In R. M. Sorrentino and E. T. Higgins (eds), *Handbook of motivation and cognition: Foundations of social behavior.* New York: Guilford Press.

Feigenbaum, M. J. (1978). Quantitative universality for a class of nonlinear transformations. *Journal of Statistical Physics, 19,* 25–52.

Festinger, L. (1957). *A theory of cognitive dissonance.* Evanston, IL: Row, Peterson.

Festinger, L., Schachter, S. and Back, K. (1950). *Social pressures in informal groups.* Stanford, CA: Stanford University Press.

Fishbein, M. and Ajzen, I. (1975). *Belief, attitude, intention and behavior: An introduction to theory and research.* Reading, MA: Addison-Wesley.

Fodor, J. A. (1975). *The language of thought.* New York: Cromwell.

Frege, G. (1892). Ueber Sinn und Bedeutung. *Zeitschrift für Philosophie und philosophische Kritik, 100,* 25–50.

Freud, S. (1922). *Introductory lectures on psychoanalysis.* London: George Allen and Unwin.

Gray, C. M., König, P., Engel, A. K., and Singer, W. (1989). Oscillatory responses in cat visual cortex exhibit inter-columnar synchronization which reflects global stimulus properties. *Nature, 338,* 334–337.

Hawking, S. W. (1988). *A Brief History of Time: From the Big Bang to Black Holes.* New York: Bantam Books.

Hebb, D. O. (1949). *The organization of behavior.* New York: Wiley.

Heider, F. (1958). *The psychology of interpersonal relations.* New York: Wiley.

Hewstone, M. (1989). *Causal attribution: From cognitive processes to collective beliefs.* Oxford: Blackwell.

Hopfield, J. J. (1982). Neural networks and physical systems with emergent collective computational abilities. *Proceedings of the National Academy of Sciences, USA, 79,* 2554–2558.

Hovland, C. I., and Sherif, M. (1952). Judgmental phenomena and scales of attitude measurement: Item displacement in Thurstone scales. *Journal of Abnormal and Social Psychology, 47,* 822–832.

Hovland, C. I., Janis, I. L. and Kelley, H. H. (1953). *Communication and persuasion: Psychological studies of opinion change.* New Haven, CT: Yale University Press.

Hume, D. (1748/1962). *Enquiry Concerning the Human Understanding.* Oxford: Clarendon Press.

Hume, D. (1740/1911). *A Treatise of Human Nature.* London: Dent.

James, W. (1890) *Principles of Psychology.* New York: Henry Holt.

Janis, I. L. and Feshbach, S. (1953). Effects of fear-arousing communications. *Journal of Abnormal and Social Psychology, 48,* 78–92.

Kamin, L. J. (1969). Predictability, surprise, attention and conditioning. In B. A. Campbell and R. A. Church (eds) *Punishment and aversive behavior.* New York: Appleton-Century-Crofts.

Kelley, H. H. (1967). Attribution theory in social psychology. In D. Levine (ed.) *Nebraska Symposium on Motivation, 15,* 192–238.

Killeen, P. R. (1989). Behavior as a trajectory through a field of attractors. In J. R. Brink and C. R. Haden (eds) *The computer and the brain: Perspectives on artificial intelligence.* New York: Elsevier (North-Holland).

Koch, C. and Crick, F. (1991). Understanding awareness at the neuronal level. *Behavioral and Brain Sciences, 14,* 683–685.

Latané, B. (1981). The Psychology of Social Impact. *American Psychologist, 36,* 343–365.

Le Bon, G. (1895) (translated 1947). *The crowd: A study of the popular mind.* London: Ernest Benn.

Linder, D. E., Cooper, J. and Jones, E. E. (1967). Decision freedom as a determinant of the role of incentive magnitude in attitude change. *Journal of Personality and Social Psychology, 6,* 245–254.

Locke, J. (1690/1964) *An Essay Concerning Human Understanding.* London: Collins.

Lockwood, M. J. (1989). *Mind, brain and the quantum: The compound 'I'.* Oxford: Blackwell.

Lorenz, E. N. (1963). Deterministic nonperiodic flow. *Journal of Atmospheric Science, 20,* 130–141.

Mandelbrot, B. B. (1983). *The fractal geometry of nature.* New York: Freeman.

Mischel, W. (1968). *Personality and assessment.* New York: Wiley.

Nagel, T. (1979). *Mortal questions.* Cambridge: Cambridge University Press.

Newcomb, T. M. (1981). Heiderian balance as a group phenomenon. *Journal of Personality and Social Psychology, 40,* 862–867.

Nowak, A., Szamrej, J. and Latané, B. (1990). From private attitude to public opinion: A dynamic theory of social impact. *Psychological Review, 97,* 363–376.

Nowell-Smith, P. H. (1956). *Ethics.* Harmondsworth: Penguin.

Osgood, C. E. and Luria, Z. (1954). A blind analysis of a case of multiple personality using the semantic differential. *Journal of Abnormal and Social Psychology, 49,* 579–591.

Osgood, C. E., Suci, G. J. and Tannenbaum, P. H. (1957). *The measurement of meaning.* Urbana, IL: University of Illinois Press.

Penrose, R. (1989). *The Emperor's New Mind: Concerning computers, minds, and the laws of physics.* Oxford: Oxford University Press.

Petty, R. E. and Cacioppo, J. T. (1986). The elaboration likelihood model of persuasion. In L. Berkowitz (ed.), *Advances in Experimental Social Psychology,* vol. 19. New York: Academic Press.

Pratkanis, A. R. and Greenwald, A. G. (1989). A sociocognitive model of attitude structure and function. In L. Berkowitz (ed.) *Advances in Experimental Social Psychology, 22,* 245–285. New York: Academic Press.

Rescorla, R. S. (1968). Probability of shock in the presence and absence of CS in fear conditioning. *Journal of Comparative and Physiological Psychology, 66,* 1–5.

Rosenberg, M. J. and Hovland, C. I. (1960). Cognitive, affective, and behavioral components of attitudes. In C. I. Hovland and M. J. Rosenberg (eds), *Attitude organization and change: An analysis of consistency among attitude components.* New Haven, CN: Yale University Press.

Ryle, G. (1949). *The concept of mind.* London: Hutchinson.

Schwarz, N., Strack, F., Kommer, D. and Wagner, D. (1987). Soccer, rooms, and the quality of your life: Mood effects on judgments of satisfaction with life in general and with specific domains. *European Journal of Social Psychology, 17,* 69–80.

Stevens, S. S. (1975). *Psychophysics: Introduction to its perceptual, neural and social prospects.* New York: Wiley.

Stevenson, C. L. (1944). *Ethics and language.* New Haven, CT: Yale University Press.

— Sutton, S. R (1982). Fear-arousing communications: A critical examination of theory and research. In J. R. Eiser (ed.) *Social psychology and behavioral medicine.* Chichester: Wiley.

Thigpen, C. H. and Cleckley, H. (1954). A case of multiple personality. *Journal of Abnormal and Social Psychology, 49,* 135–151.

— Thurstone, L. L. (1928). Attitudes can be measured. *American Journal of Sociology, 33,* 529–554.

Thurstone, L. L. and Chave, E. J. (1929). *The measurement of attitude.* Chicago: University of Chicago Press.

Tversky, A. and Kahneman, D. (1974). Judgment under uncertainty: Heuristics and biases. *Science, 185,* 1124–1131.

Velmans, M. (1991). Is human information processing conscious? *Behavioral and Brain Sciences, 14,* 651–669, 702–726.

Weiner, B. (1985). An attributional theory of achievement motivation and emotion. *Psychological Review, 92,* 548–573.

— Wicker, A. W. (1969). Attitudes versus actions: The relationship of overt and behavioral responses to attitude objects. *Journal of Social Issues, 25,* 41–78.

Wittgenstein, L. (1953). *Philosophical investigations.* Oxford: Blackwell.

Zajonc, R. B. (1980). Feeling and thinking: Preferences need no inferences. *American Psychologist, 35,* 151–175.

Subject Index

Author Index